WHEN HOPE FINDS A HOME:

*The Influence of Caring Adults in the Lives of Urban,
African American Youth*

WHEN HOPE FINDS A HOME:

*The Influence of Caring Adults in the Lives of Urban,
African American Youth*

MARCUS L. ARRINGTON

XULON PRESS

Xulon Press
2301 Lucien Way #415
Maitland, FL 32751
407.339.4217
www.xulonpress.com

Printed in the United States of America.

ISBN-13: 978-1-5456-7881-7

DEDICATION

To all the unheard youths of color in the United States and abroad; to the unsung heroes and heroines in their lives who've inspired them; to the thousands of educators who make a difference every day. I salute you.

TABLE OF CONTENTS

Introduction. ix

Chapter One: Making the Case for Hope 1

Chapter Two: Reaching Youths on the Margins 39

Chapter Three: Clarifying Hope 63

Chapter Four: The People (Part One) 77

Chapter Five: The People (Part Two) 101

Chapter Six: The Places 125

Chapter Seven: Education the Woodson-Newton Way
(Part One) 167

Chapter Eight: Education the Woodson-Newton Way
(Part Two) 187

Chapter Nine: Everybody's a Leader 213

Chapter Ten: Answering Hope's Call 245

References. 259

Appendix A: Conscious Reflection Rubric: Characteristics
of High-Hope Individuals 274

Appendix B: Summary of Dominant Themes and Subthemes
Related to the Characteristics of Students Who
Experience Hope. 275

Appendix C: Summary of the Aspects of WNHS that
Students Attributed to their Experience with Hope 277

Appendix D: Final Themes Related to WNHS Students and
their Experience with Hope 278

Appendix E: Elements of Hope 279

Notes 280

INTRODUCTION

"Hope, it is the only thing stronger than fear. A little hope is effective. A lot of hope is dangerous."
-President Snow, *Hunger Games*

The world needs more hope. Nations are beset by myriad social problems. Despite the uniqueness of countries and the particularities of the people groups that inhabit them, issues of great magnitude bring disparate locales together in a type of global jigsaw puzzle. This transcontinental picture is troubling to say the least. On one hand, poverty dominates the details of this pictorial landscape. No matter where one travels its effects can be seen. Economic disparities prolong the nefarious and disheartening history of "haves" and "have nots". Environmental concerns are broached as human knowledge and technological savvy increase. Violence abounds. Civil wars threaten to decimate nations. The threat of nuclear warfare lingers.

On the other hand, urban centers are growing at exponential rates of speed. Towers of great height and complexity are being erected every year. Cities such as Dubai and Shanghai boast two of the worlds most sophisticated skylines. Communicative abilities have expanded. High-speed internet is available in Accra, Ghana and in Saigon, Vietnam. International corporate relations continue to develop drawing more and more citizens out of their home nations and into foreign lands for life, business, and travel. Americans, in particular, globetrot like never before. Both urbanites and folks with rural backgrounds bravely apply for international work assignments, not because they have to, but because they can.

Certainly, these seemingly positive developments may appear to balance out the notion of this worldwide picture, but they do so at great expense. Amid the economic improvement of many nations, the phenomenon of individualism is spiraling out of control. The more connected the world has become; the more people esteem self over community. Hence, social stratification realities remain the same. Inequity yet lives. In spite of our physical and technological ability to come together, ideologies of old resurrect and breathe life into harmful prejudices that undoubtedly keep us apart. And, where does that leave us? Better yet, where does that take us? What are our prospects for the future? Drawing upon the words of Charles Dickens, it's the best of times and the worst of times. Human progress cannot be disputed, but human devastation is equally incontrovertible. And, *this* is the global image that our children are forced to view and to accept. We [adults] can't disguise it. It's hidden in plain sight. Thus, if for no other reason, our world needs hope so that our children don't grow up riddled with pessimism and fatalism.

People need to know that humanitarian virtue is accessible in a world rife with contradiction and irony. We need to hear narratives of goodwill and generous service. Tales that describe the best of human potentiality should be trumpeted so that our progeny can evade the lure of despair and nihilism and draw upon their creative genius to produce ideas that will turn this world around.

The Journey

Ask 30 different people to define hope and you'll surely receive 30 different answers. Nevertheless, I believe hope, though universal in its reach and need, is more rigid in its substance. I believe that hope is dynamic in its expression while at the same time defined by specific parameters. Still further, I argue that hope is both "a thing" and "an act", a noun and a verb. I'm convinced that hope is something that can be engendered and reproduced. I'm concerned that without hope, the trajectory of the world is uncertain. Yet, I'm convinced that with hope we can affect change in our immediate environments.

My journey to explore hope began while I served marginalized African American high school students in a small, urban alternative school named Woodson-Newton High School — WNHS (A quick sidebar: I argue that marginalized African American youths are also oppressed. Borrowing from the viewpoint of Duncan-Andrade (2010), I consider oppressed youths to be children who hail from disadvantaged communities (e.g., African American, Hispanic/Latino, and Native American). Many of these youths suffer from material and structural injustice. They are children who lack critical resources to change their immediate situation; children who are deprived of an education that adequately prepares them for college and career possibilities. They suffer from a miseducation that devalues their identity and culture and at the same time consequently demonstrates asocial behavior and a disposition that results in adjudication, expulsion, proclivities for deviance, and chronic truancy). Many of the youths at WNHS overcame tremendous challenges. Through fire and pain they not only lived to tell their stories, but they obtained goals in the process. As I reflected on these youths, I couldn't help but wonder how they made it.

Or, better yet, I tried to ascertain what was at work behind the scenes, in their innards, that manifested in the perseverance that I observed on a daily basis. For days and months, I failed to trace the source of their desire, so I made the a priori assumption that the youths at WNHS possessed *hope*.

Initially, I embraced the viewpoint that hope was a feeling or the belief that good will somehow overtake evil. With additional contemplation, I realized that that perspective was an oversimplification. In other words, I believed that hope had to be more sophisticated and deep. Eventually, my quest for insight turned into my dissertation entitled; *Never giving up: A phenomenological study of hope in urban African American youths in a small urban pubic high school.* At the conclusion of my research project, I learned that my original thoughts about hope were not only narrow, but also erroneous. Hope is so much more complex than I could have ever imagined. It possesses a quality of beauty and swagger akin to the likes of male peacocks when they display their feathers to attract the attention of a female peacock that they've set their desires upon. In regard to the peacock reference, some would presume that I'm referring to a sense of cocksureness and perhaps a disdainful overestimation of self. However, the peacock, as it concerns hope, is emblematic not only of supreme confidence in self, but also the staunch defiance of anything else in the immediate environment that could or would contest its beauty and ability to obtain its goal of female attraction. You see, hope has an edge, a brazenness that indicates an unwillingness to be moved or impeded. Hope says, "I want what I want, and I want it now!" Hope also says, "I'm not leaving until I get what I came for." Pompous? Maybe. Egostical? Quite possibly. But, the revelations about hope among the youths that I observed suggested that with the heft of the personal and socio-ecological issues they faced, a strong sense of self-assuredness was critical to their survival and subsequent goal attainment.

Equally important to the experiences of the students that I observed was the influence of the school and the people that worked in the school. Therefore, the title of this book is, *When hope finds a home: The influence of caring adults in the lives of urban, African American youths*. It was written for two reasons. First of all, I address the possibilities of human strength and provide insight into the nature of hope. Second of all, I provide a platform for student voice. Third of all, I argue that hope needs a locus for introduction, cultivation, and promotion. The basis for this locus is human conversation. Very plainly, hope needs a home. Interestingly, I contend that the term "home" is not only indicative of a physical space, but it's also indicative of a place within the human heart. People are carriers of hope. And, when a group of people in the same locale possess and demonstrate hope, then that space morphs into a place of hope. When this occurs, success is inevitable.

The Research Process

So many marginalized youths are suffering, especially those from historically disadvantaged urban communities. For years I've listened to pundits and community activists alike mention that everyone needs to contribute to efforts that help to enhance the conditions of neighborhoods and communities, which would eventuate in better life satisfaction opportunities for youths. For some this rhetoric gets spewed ad nauseam and with little effect, but I was compelled to discover my lane, my in-roads to becoming part of the solution. Since I worked with urban African American youths and had done so for several years, I thought that I had a degree of expertise on the subject matter. I thought that through my vocation, I was doing enough to help affect change. Some would argue that I was doing enough. Being an educator in the inner-city is no easy task. But, I wasn't satisfied. I wanted to contribute in a different way.

The year was 2011. I was in my second year of graduate school and at a point of bewilderment in my matriculation. I was stuck. I was in an accelerated doctoral program, and I had to devise my research question or risk falling behind. I knew I wanted to address issues facing inner city African American youths, but so much had already been written that I simply couldn't find an entry point that seemed satisfactory. One day I had a conversation with a colleague and the topic of hope was broached. My colleague suggested that I consider hope for my exploration. Now granted, I was already interested in hope. I'd previously enjoyed the work of Dr. Jeff Duncan-Andrade (2010) whose articulation of "critical hope" is absolutely brilliant. So, I decided to take my colleagues' advice and I began to explore Hope Theory. Before long, I was convinced that my research question had to somehow include hope.

As I stated previously, I was aware that numerous authors (Hilton-Pitre, 2009; Kafele, 2010; Kunjufu, 2002; 2005; Ladson-Billings, 1994; Pitre, Ray, & Stubblefield, 2009; Watson & Smitherman, 1996) had discussed issues facing urban African American youths. Some of these observers recommended implementation of programs, strategies, and approaches that can mitigate the damage incurred from constant encounters with harsh realities in their environments and address the concomitant academic and psycho-emotional needs of African American youths. But, the articulations of Jean Anyon (1997) in her book, "Ghetto Schooling: A political economy of urban educational reform, confirmed that my anticipated research path was appropriate. With the amelioration of marginalized youths in mind, Anyon (1997) pushed for discussions about education and funding to shift to include matters of human capacity and strength, namely hope.

> *"Considerable amounts of money have already been spent on schools in America's inner cities, often with disappointing results. I do not believe that the reasons for the failure lie in the inability of urban children to learn or even in the inability of urban teachers to teach. I believe, rather, that both students and teachers are failing at least in part because they have lost hope. They have lost hope that hard work will produce results." (p. 181)*

Anyon's (1997) argument helped to shape the direction of my inquiry. As a result, my primary research objective was to examine hope and its influence among marginalized youths. Secondary research objectives included developing a more accurate understanding of the characteristics of students who possessed hope and determining if student enrollment at a school that focuses on addressing the academic and socio-emotional needs of marginalized youths somehow contributed to the way in which they experienced hope. Specifically, my research question was: In what ways do students who attend Woodson-Newton High School (WNHS) experience hope? Three sub-questions supported the investigation:

1. What are the characteristics of students who experience hope?
2. How do students at WNHS describe their experience as it relates to hope?

3. What aspects of WNHS do the students attribute to their experience with hope?

To be sure, theory and literature related to marginalized youths and hope exists, yet few studies reported the experiences with hope from the perspective of students. My purpose was to examine the influence of hope in the lives of several urban African American high school students who attended an urban public high school that served predominantly marginalized urban African American youths. I wanted to contribute relevant information to the existing body of literature by amplifying youth voices.

Phenomenological Approach

Since I aimed to apprehend the way in which WNHS students experienced hope, I opted to utilize qualitative design for my research project. I've always preferred words over numbers. Reflexivity was my lane, unlike positivism which Taylor and Bogdan (1998) argued places emphasis on "facts or causes of social phenomena apart from the subjective states of individuals" (p. 3). Further, these authors contended that qualitative research provided a way for investigators to break away from the restrictive approaches of positivism and "go to the people" (p. 3) to discover the true meaning of phenomena.

Quite interestingly, Taylor and Bogdan (1998) also argued that qualitative methodology is theoretically rooted in the phenomenological tradition of inquiry. Phenomenology is an approach to research that is generally considered the brainchild of German mathematician Edmund Husserl (1859-1938). Several contend that Husserl's contemplations were expanded upon by other research giants such as Husserl's pupil Martin Heidegger and philosopher Hans-Georg Gadamer. According to Briedis (2009) Husserl pushed for deconstruction of traditional philosophy to redefine the essence of human existence and how it is examined. For Husserl, this meant removing the distance associated with typical empiricism and espying the social world "from the first person perspective" (p. 72). Laverty (2003) argued that Husserl favored a new scientific approach that would accord researchers a new way of "reaching true meaning through penetrating deeper and deeper into reality" instead of the stodgy routine of examination of external realities (p. 5). Husserl's ideas were risky and quite revolutionary for his time. The first person perspective that Husserl sought to apprehend required an in-depth look into one's consciousness and its structures to grasp the meaning of phenomena. Husserl aimed to obtain meaning of phenomena that was significantly beyond the surface. He wanted an intimate understanding. Hence, Husserl suggested that a process that he called "intentionality", whereby the researcher directed his/her mind towards objects of inquiry (in one's consciousness), could assist the researcher in obtaining insightful descriptions and accounts of social reality, i.e., essences.

Indeed "essence" was Husserl's "holy grail". In order to arrive at the essence of phenomena, Husserl declared that the researcher must engage in phenomenological reduction or a process known as *epoche*. Epoche is the intentional bracketing (suspension) of personal biases, assumptions, and/or judgments so that the subject's account of their lived experience may emerge rather than the researcher's interpretation. It's the attempt to understand phenomena strictly from the perspective of the individual by "transcending" one's own prejudgments. Husserl specifically referred to this approach as transcendental phenomenology.

In sum, phenomenology is a commitment to ferret out the meaning of social realities and existing phenomena based on the knowledge and meaning constructed by the one who experiences it. Stoller (2009) described phenomenology as "a philosophy of experience" (p. 707). I was in pursuit of student experiences with hope. Thus, phenomenology became my preferred line of inquiry.

Data Collection

In order to gather participants for my study I employed "purposeful sampling" as recommended by Creswell and Plano-Clark (2011). With purposeful sampling, the researcher "identifies and recruits a small number that will provide in-depth information about the central phenomenon or concept being explored in the study" (p. 174). My goal was to recruit 10-15 current WNHS students between the ages of 14-20 to participate in individual interviews. To this end, I attempted to identify WNHS students who attested to the influence of hope in their lives.

Initially, I utilized one of the school's warm-up activities referred to as "Conscious Reflections". "Conscious Reflections" are questions, statements, news stories, short stories, or axioms presented to students to spur critical thinking. WNHS staff wanted to help students develop and deploy critical analyses of relevant issues, problems, or community scenarios. Generally, students were required to read "Conscious Reflections" and respond to any questions prior to accessing their actual coursework. In fact, students were not allowed to proceed to coursework until they read and responded to the prompt. In a typical day, nearly 90 students responded to "Conscious Reflections".

I asked for and received permission from the WNHS Principal Malik Stokes to write a "Conscious Reflection" about hope that students could respond to. Each response was submitted to a "cyber-station" managed by the school's technology coordinator. Incidentally, submissions were not anonymous. Therefore, the technology coordinator was able to see the names of students who participated. The ability to see who actually participated (followed directions) supported the school staff's efforts to hold students accountable for completing this required exercise. Through this feature I was also able to read student responses.

I received and examined over 70 responses. Twenty responses were culled for reexamination. The point of a second review was to more accurately discern which students among the respondents had exhibited and could articulate hope according to the operationalized definition and characteristics offered by Snyder (2002). To remain consistent with Snyder's (2002) identified characteristics of hope, I created an informal rubric (Appendix A) with 15 characteristics of high-hope individuals as articulated by Snyder (2002). Assessment of students' knowledge, understanding, and experience with hope was determined by the evidence of high–hope characteristics. The following descriptive scale was utilized: present; absent; or unsure. I sought to reexamine the remarks of students whose responses revealed the presence of eight or more characteristics. After concluding the reexamination of 15-20 student writing responses, I identified and targeted 10-15 students for recruitment into the research project.

Once the students were identified, I invited them to have a conversation about their responses so they could learn the rationale of the project and so that I could gain additional insight into their understanding of and experience with hope. I successfully recruited eight enrolled students to participate in the project. I also decided to interview at least two former students (recent graduates) who would be able to provide a post-graduate perspective of their experience with hope. All study participants were African American. I interviewed five males and five females.

Organization of the Text

Although my research project provided impetus for this book, the subsequent chapters will entail discussion of several of the study findings and the revelations that I obtained. In **Chapter One**, I consider and challenge America's commitment to the well-being of children. I turn my attention to policy changes and examine government support for mothers and families. America's government subsidies for childcare and financial support for parents who decide to stay home and raise their children pale in comparison to Scandinavian nations in particular. I make the case that the limited amount of support for children at the onset of their lives puts American children at risk. Youths from historically disadvantaged communities suffer the most. Gaps of support generate the need for hope. These gaps give hope its entry point. I point out some of the historical roots of our present issues and mention that even during the epic era of former United States President Barak Obama, youths from communities of color had it the worst, despite his emphasis on advancing hope. I close Chapter One by comparing the conditions under which many youths of color live to the intense and frightful conditions experienced by youths in the motion picture, *Hunger games*. This analogy provides the springboard for my discussion about hope and the ways that caring adults engender it.

The primary focus of **Chapter Two** is establishing the context in which my research project was conducted. I reflect on my time as an administrator at WNHS (WNHS is named for the imminent Black scholar Carter G. Woodson and the intrepid black revolutionary and Black Panther Party co-founder, Huey P. Newton.). I briefly share examples of interactions that I'd had with a couple students. Through these examples I aim to provide insight into the rationale that informed our work at WNHS. More specifically, I highlight Woodson-Newton's principal, Raheem Stokes, and reveal the underpinning values and philosophy that he introduced and promoted. Drawing upon Principal Stokes' articulations, I share my interpretations of these guiding values and principles as well as my current understanding of the 21st century youth.

In **Chapter Three** I provide an explanation of Hope Theory, largely referencing the work of the late C.R. Snyder. I explain that hope is more than a feeling; that it is in fact a bi-dimensional phenomenon that actually entails action. I'm careful to distinguish hope from optimism. Optimism is simply the belief that good will overtake evil or that despite numerous failures, a favorable outcome will emerge. Hope on the other hand involves setting goals, determining strategies or pathways to reach those goals, and consistent belief that the devised strategies will work (Snyder, 2002). To further elucidate the depth of hope, I briefly mention three different kinds of hope: global (trait) hope, domain-specific hope, and goal-specific hope. The type of hope that is discussed in the research study is global or trait hope. This is hope in its basic expression. The other two types of hope are more contextual. Since the milieu of my research project was in a social setting (a small alternative high school), I share perspectives on the relevance of hope amid social groups and contexts. Specifically, I point out what the literature reveals about the impact of hope in schools. I echo arguments from the literature (Snyder et al. 2003; Post, 2006) that hope can be introduced and promoted among children. In other words, educators can grow hope.

Chapters Four and Five highlight the findings from my research project. After briefly recapping the way I went about gathering my findings, I identify and expound upon themes that emerged as students discussed their experience with hope. The emergent themes were: "Disposition"; "People and Places Matter"; "The Power of Reflection"; and "Elements of WNHS". Most striking among the four themes was the discussion related to the theme, "People and Places Matter". This theme became the foundation for this work because the students that I interviewed made it abundantly clear that a key individual in their lives was associated with their experience with hope. Chapter Four reveals the influence of parents. Chapter Five highlights the importance of extended family members, peers, and educators. I include student quotes to help convey the significance of the theme. Many of the quotes are followed by my interpretations and discussion.

While Chapters Four and Five emphasize people, **Chapter Six** continues the discussion of the theme "People and Places Matter" by shedding light on the way students experienced hope in certain places. In particular, students comment on the importance of colleges and universities, church, community centers, and a non-profit organization. Similar to Chapters Four and Five, in Chapter Six I share student quotes that clarify the significance of these institutions. I also share interpretations and discussion.

In **Chapters Seven and Eight** I take a closer look at WNHS. Specifically, I turn my attention to the fourth theme that emerged in the research project, "Elements of WNHS". The study participants revealed details about their participation in online classes and their interaction with various WNHS staff members. The interaction with WNHS staff contributed to the students' experience with hope. Interestingly, students referenced the care exhibited by WNHS staff members and the willingness of WNHS staff members to listen. In several instances, conversations with WNHS staff members stirred students to make personal adjustments in an effort to improve the probability of their goal obtainment. Thus, relationships with WNHS educators contributed to their experience with hope.

Chapter Nine explores the link between leadership and hope. Drawing upon Wheatley's (2010) notion that leadership is predicated on one's willingness to take steps to change a situation, I argue that anyone can possess and promote hope. Since hope has to do with one's obtainment of a goal while being confronted with an obstacle, those who have the gumption to provide assistance become leaders. Care, compassion, and creativity are core elements when leading and in essence spreading hope. WNHS staff assisted students with goal obtainment through their physical presence, accessibility, and expertise. They guided WNHS youths through strategic thinking. They led problem-solving efforts. When necessary, they provided feedback and listening ears. By standing with WNHS youths and developing healthy relationships with them, the staff members demonstrated leadership and distributed hope.

I conclude the book in **Chapter Ten** with a review of the *Hunger Games* analogy. I make connections between the relationships with key individuals mentioned by the study participants and the relationship between Haymitch and Katniss, two main characters in the story. I focus on the critical nature of service and how service is a wide-open field. I emphasize the virtue in caring for children and assert that by attending to the urgent needs of children, we engender hope. The relationship between a caring adult and a student in need is itself the seedbed for hope. It's where hope actually finds itself at home.

Note: The name Malik Stokes is a pseudonym used in place of the actual name of the school principal at the time of research project. In fact, most names of people and places utilized are pseudonyms in order to protect the privacy of the associated students, staff members, and schools. WNHS is also a pseudonym used to protect the identity of the actual high school which is still in operation. The only exceptions are the YMCA and Public Allies. The description and manner in which each is used is safe and non-injurious to either entity. Incidentally, I use the terms African American and black interchangeably. While some consider the term "black" derogatory or somehow demeaning, I choose to embrace it and affirm the richness of the heritage of black people in America and beyond.

Chapter 1

MAKING THE CASE FOR HOPE

"We must accept finite disappointment, but we must never lose infinite hope."

-Dr. Martin Luther King, Jr.

In 1985, songstress Whitney Houston popularized a song entitled, *The Greatest Love of All, written by songwriters Michael Masser and Linda Creed.* Although it was originally recorded by jazz legend George Benson, Houston's smooth, soulful vocals made the song an instant American musical hit. Many revere the song as a pop culture classic. Some educators love this ballad because of its initial line:

"I believe the children are our future
Teach them well and let them lead the way..."

Surely, this song contained other respectable lyrics, but that inaugural line endeared children to adults in the realm of education with intoxicating effect. And while Whitney Houston never practiced education, her opening declaration clarified the "why" of the work of education for many. I can imagine that some current practitioners were inspired to enter the ranks of teaching after contemplating those words. I must admit, "I

1

believe the children are our future," is a lyric that pulls at my heartstrings. But, after reflecting on the current state of children in America, particularly children of color in America, I get the disturbing sense that our society no longer believes what Whitney so smoothly articulated. When I consider the amount of harmful images, harmful conversations, harmful practices, and harmful policies that are affecting children in the United States; I'm extremely concerned about their future.

Perhaps Whitney's lyric was a bit misleading. Now, for any Whitney fans, I don't mean to insult your vocal heroine, and in no way am I impugning her integrity. But, I wonder if that lyric actually had the indirect effect of swaying public sentiment and vision to a time of nothingness. In other words, "the future" has no relevance without an intense gaze upon the present. Stated differently, belief in "the future" without proper planning for its unfolding is quixotic, a fairytale that begs for a happy ending that has no guarantee of fulfillment. Of course, Whitney sang a lyric. Sure, it was simply a song. Yet, that lyric became a quote that has been overused and in my estimation abused.

Adults have spewed those seven words ("I believe the children are our future") in sermons, graduation speeches, keynote addresses, you name it. Now, it's quite possible, in fact, I opine that most folks had and have benign intentions when they draw upon that lyric for oratorical usage. But, I was always taught that we should be careful of what we say and to make sure that we actually mean what we say. As an educator and a father, I have serious concern with utterances such as the above, especially when there's abundant evidence that suggests otherwise.

The truth is that our children are our *now*. With respect to biology, they will grow and get older. They will become adults. We pray, trust, and believe that they'll have families, become gainfully employed, and obtain statuses of leadership.

This is part of the cycle of human life. However, as their for-bears, as their leaders, we are responsible for leaving them an inheritance and a heritage worthy of their respect and replete with dignity. Sadly, for many youths, particularly youths on the margins, this is not the case. In his book, *Youth in a suspect society: Democracy or disposability?* (2009), public intellectual Henry Giroux argued that America has drifted away from the core of its democratic ideals and, consequently, the social contract that once prioritized the weal of children is currently defunct. Giroux (2009) made the case that youth-life in America is viewed with contempt.

> *"But as the United States, particularly under the Bush regime, became increasingly more authoritarian in its role as a national (in) security state, its use of surveillance, its suspension of civil liberties, its plundering of public goods, its suspension of basic social services, and its increasing use of torture and pure thuggery on the political level, it became clear that the current generation of young people was no longer viewed as an important social investment or as a marker for the state of democracy and moral life of the nation."*

Giroux (2009) went on to assert:
> *"Young people have become a generation of suspects in a society destroyed by the merging of market fundamentalism, consumerism, and militarism. Instead of a federal budget that addresses the needs of children, the United States has enacted federal policies that weaken government social programs, provide tax cuts for millionaires and corporations, and undercut or eliminate basic social provisions for children at risk."*

Assuredly, Giroux's (2009) critique of America's governmental and fiscal priorities as it pertains to children is disturbing. But, one needn't examine the conditions of adolescents per se to discover Americas' trend of dereliction as it pertains to the welfare of youths. The genesis of a child's life reveals the value that America has placed on youth well-being. Current United States FMLA policies permit expectant mothers up to 12 weeks of unpaid leave once their child is birthed, during which their job is purportedly secure. Essentially, the federal government has esteemed work over the weal of the mother and her child. Is three months really enough time for a woman's body to recoup to the point of her being able to render consistent service and exhibit thoroughgoing productivity (which is what the employer will expect)? What about her psycho-emotional state? Will she be able to be fully attentive to the needs of the beautiful new human being that she ushered into the world without being concerned about her work position? What about the increased expenses that accompany child-rearing? Babies are expensive. What is to be said about a nation that is willing to help a company skimp on its payroll while a mother is beleaguered by an expanded household budget? Is she in effect punished for having a child?

In contrast, European nations seem to excel as it relates to assisting women with child-rearing. In Germany, mothers receive 14 months of paid parental leave. The government subsidizes daycare expenses and provides a "child stipend" of about $200 per month. According to Hilfiker (2002), Scandinavian nations feature an approach to child and family support that exceeds government spending in America. For example, the Finnish government provides every family with allowances for each child up to age 17. Since the Finnish government favors a high birth rate, per-child allowances increase with each child that is birthed. About $90 is allotted for families with one child. Total child support allowances for a family with three children is about $330.

Single mothers in Finland fare even better as it pertains to government support. The Finnish government provides about $44 a month per child. The state also guarantees child support payments in the event that it is unable to collect payment from fathers. A payment of nearly $107 each month is provided for child support. Besides receiving financial support for the children, parents in Finland are compensated for staying home to raise their children. In the case of a two parent household, the spouse who opts to stay home and "work" receives a monthly allowance of $250. In addition, the parent that "works" in the home receives another $85 each month per child up to age four and $50 each month for older children. Single parents who decide to be stay-at-home caregivers are eligible to receive another $170 per month, with consideration given to family size and actual income. Similar to Germany, the Finns subsidize childcare. If a parent decides to transition back into the workforce, childcare is $200 per month for the first child and $200 for the second child. There's a $40 charge for each additional child. Charges are reduced for low-income families. Families with an annual income of less than $12,000 are eligible for *free* childcare.

Marian Wright Edelman, noted child activist and founder of the Children's Defense Fund, once declared that budgets were moral documents. With this in mind, it is entirely appropriate to call the morality of the United States into question. Sure, there's much to laud when it comes to American society, but there's also much that is flagrant and downright embarrassing. How can an "advanced" nation such as the United States be so Neanderthal as it pertains to taking care of its children and supporting its families? How can this be? Perhaps those with decision-making power only regard children as products rather than potential producers of ideas and innovations. Needless to say, the lack of sensitivity to the early development of children, with respect to financial support for mothers, contributes to the onset of despair and the subsequent need for hope. What we're seeing is contradictory to the Founding Father's intent to "secure the blessings of liberty and freedom for our progeny". Too many youths are born into situations laden with uncertainty and volatility with regard to basic needs and survival. Hence, it begs the question, "who is the progeny that the Framers spoke of?"

To my mind, it's quite possible that the Framer's statement didn't include all children, only those of a particular social class and ethnic group. If this is true, then it makes sense that millions of American children are at risk. It makes sense that millions of America's children are denied healthcare, denied adequate education, and consequently bereft of the foundation required to launch into a pursuit of "life, liberty, and happiness". This scene unfolds with extreme clarity in historically disadvantaged communities. Sure, youths in general, or the notion of "youth" is increasingly viewed with disdain and all youths are subject to the manipulations and predatory tactics of money-hungry entities, ethnicity notwithstanding. However, as Giroux (2009) pointed out, the suffering of youths of color is even more despicable:

> *"Youth marginalized by class and color can no longer inhabit public spheres that allow them to take refuge behind their status as developing children worthy of adult protection and compassion. Whether it be the school, the community center, the street corner, or their*

place of residence, the most powerful and influential forces shaping their lives emanate from the security state and the criminal justice system…the racialized spaces of oppression that poor youth of color inhabit make a mockery of the much vaunted claim that the election of Barack Obama to the presidency suggests that institutionalized racism is over. In a neoliberal political order, with its celebration of radical individualism, privatization, and deregulation, any invocation of race can only be affirmed as a private prejudice, decoupled from wider institutional forces. This depoliticizing and privatizing of racism makes it all the more difficult to both identify the racialized attacks on poor youth of color and take the kind of action that would dismantle the systemic conditions that promote such practices of exclusion and disposability." (p.18)

With such ominous life-prospect, should we be surprised to hear the harrowing stories of rampant thuggery and violence among youth, particularly youths of color in American urban centers? Should we be surprised to see the uprisings in places like Ferguson, MO and Baltimore? We shouldn't be shocked. Granted, it may be counterproductive to destroy businesses in your own community, but it's very possible that the ire and deviance of some youths of color, specifically the African American youths in those most recent sites of human rights violations, is "an appropriate response to an absurd situation" (West, 2008, p.295).

To the natural eye of the millions of virtual onlookers, many of those involved in violent protestation in Ferguson, MO and Baltimore were clearly adults. Yet, there were adolescents involved as well. And, it is plausible that youths who refrained from releasing their tensions and frustrations in the streets did so in much safer places such as school. It's difficult to make sense of life in a world when the deaths of Michael Brown, Eric Garner, Tariq Rice, Dontre Hamilton, Freddie Gray, Philando Castile, Sandra Bland, Alton Sterling, Terrence Cruthers, Stephon Clark, Botham Jean—all at the hands of police officers—are ingrained in your mind with haunting affect. The emotions associated with the fact that, "it could've been me" can potentially becloud the thinking of an observant young person who already exists on the margins. And, although a youth in this position may not be directly involved, the communal connection (e.g., African/African American ancestry) can produce what Jenmorri (2006) referred to as "secondary traumatization". In other words, the remembrance of the incident and the attempt to cope with its ramifications, and possibly help others, can have a negative, exhausting psychical effect. Youths can descend into languor as they try to grapple with the rawness of their social realities and the grim prospects of their future. Hence, schools often become the sites where their energy, emotion, and anger is released.

The matter is compounded when in addition to the pressures of society, schools themselves are unsafe spaces, quasi-plantations where compliance prerogatives and pedagogical incongruence keep African American youths bound. Is the disproportionality in discipline rates and the overrepresentation of black boys in special education part of the natural order of things or is it evidence of something much more insidious? Is the synchronic reality of black youths in cities across the United States performing at the bottom with respect to achievement a sign of their innate deficiency or an indicator of an educational system unconcerned with their academic development? Though generally regarded as safe places, schools have morphed into sites where spates of displaced aggression and flagrant rule violations create hazardous conditions, and perhaps rightly so. Never would I condone school violence and student misconduct, but the notion of remaining unfree, no matter where you go, would drive even the most civil and lettered individual bonkers.

The Death Game

Ta-Nehisi Coates (2015) discussed his observations of the similarities between the dangerous streets of Baltimore and the city's schools.

> *"The streets were not my only problem. If the streets shackled my right leg, the schools shackled my left. Fail to comprehend the streets and you gave up your body now. But fail to comprehend the schools and you gave up your body later. I suffered at the hands of both, but I resent the schools more...I came to see the streets and the schools as arms of the same beast. One enjoyed the official power of the state while the other enjoyed its implicit sanction. But fear and violence were the weaponry of both. Fail in the streets and the crews would catch you slipping and take your body. Fail in the schools and you would be suspended and sent back to those same streets, where they would take your body. And I began to see these two arms in relation—those who failed in the schools justified their destruction in the streets. The society could say, "He should have stayed in school," and then wash its hands of him."* *(pp.25, 33)*

Where shall the youth stuck in this complexity so poignantly described by Coates (2015) go? What and where is their sanctuary? These questions reflect the ponderings of many urban youths of color and those concerned with securing justice on their behalf, especially those in the American black community. The situation is as malevolent as the twisted schemes and deadly devices that terrified victims in the *Saw* (Lionsgate, 2004) horror film series. To many oppressed African American youths, the United States is the house that Jigsaw built (Jigsaw is the name of the villain in the Saw film series.). Youths get free and flee one tortuous machination only to find themselves heading into a different room with an equally wicked trap. And akin to the vile nature of Jigsaw's plots, the victims end up killing themselves or killing someone else in their effort to get free. It's a death game for sure. Even then, if one manages to survive mortal combat, absolute freedom isn't guaranteed because the house is rigged so as to continually deny freedom. In other words, Jigsaw wanted his victims to die in the house. Once inside, they were consigned to imminent death. Incidentally, the victims in the *Saw* films, weren't randomly selected. They'd committed some "sinful" act that Jigsaw deemed punishable by death. He was the arresting officer, prosecutor, judge, and jury. Unlike the victims in the *Saw* films, the only "sin" committed by oppressed African American youths in America is being born with a hue that isn't white.

Should blackness be deemed a socio-cultural marker that qualifies one for death and destruction? Of course not! The mere notion is absurd...if you are black or a person of color who can identify with the sting of race and class politics and inner-city realities. But, for those who espouse the logic of neo-liberalism and white supremacy, blackness or any other colored reality is grounds for exclusion and disposal (Giroux, 2009).

This immoral theoretical, political, intellectual, and economic stance informs social planning and arrangements that create conditions that lead to the slow deaths of the marginalized. Similar to Jigsaw, the system doesn't kill you per se; it generates policies and programs with strictures that pummel you mentally and emotionally. It makes survival nearly impossible. Then, it gives you the guns and pills so you can opt for self-destruction. To add insult to injury, the same system will order the creation of a commission to study the reasons why you opted for death and release a 1,000 page report that ultimately blames you for the conditions and tools that led to your demise. That's the Jigsaw effect, and that's life in the United States for far too many African American youths in the inner city.

With such wizardry confronting them, it's no wonder that African American males are atop statistics pertaining to expulsions and suspensions. Especially, when the argument can be made that schools aren't equipping African American youths with the knowledge and skills they need to destroy Jigsaw's house. In Milwaukee, a city currently regarded as the worst city for raising black boys, the public school district reported that the number of expelled African American males has increased since 2004-2005 (Milwaukee Board of School Directors, 2010). For example, during the 2008-2009 school year, African American males accounted for 84% of the over 260 students expelled that year. In comparison, their white non-Hispanic male counterparts accounted for four percent of the expulsions and Hispanic males accounted for nine percent of expulsions. Statistics for the following year were equally alarming. The number of expulsions in the district increased to 400. Of that number, African American males accounted for 86% of expulsions compared to seven percent and four percent for Hispanic males and white non-Hispanic males respectively (Figure 1).

Figure 1
Milwaukee Public Schools Student Expulsions, 2004-2005

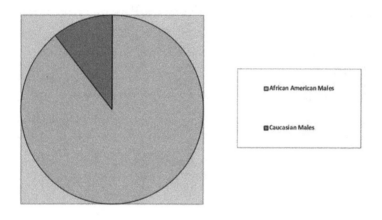

□African American Males

□Caucasian Males

Note. Adapted from "Student Expulsion Statistics", by
Milwaukee Board of School Directors, 2010, Regular board
meeting. Copyright 2012 by the Milwaukee Board of School
Directors.

Obviously, each expulsion case has its specific details and
in defense of the guilty, I'm sure they have reasons, whereby
they feel justified, that led to the administration's disposition.
What we do know for sure is that the above statistics do not
bode well for the future of a historically disadvantaged populace that is already hemmed in by oppression. If African
American children are indeed crying out—consciously or sub-
consciously—through disruptive acts in school, then educators ought to be individuals capable of hearing their cries and
discerning their needs. While consequences may be in order,
the children shouldn't be demonized and then disposed of with
no opportunity for redemption. Maybe their behavior—albeit

unacceptable—was a harbinger. What if in educators' efforts to exact discipline, they missed the subtext of these students' acts? What if there was something prophetic in their deviance?

Dr. Jeff Duncan Andrade, professor at San Francisco State University made the case that the plethora of frustrations, concerns, and dilemmas that afflict youths requires schools to become milieus where their burdens can be shared, addressed, and perhaps removed (2010). Further, Duncan-Andrade (2010) argued that the way educators respond to student suffering can and in many situations will determine academic and socio-behavioral outcomes. The *longing* youths that hail from American ghettos and barrios, demand—albeit secretly—that schools be safe spaces where they can sort out the myriad personal, family, and environmental challenges that they face. Additional researchers (Asante, 2008; Duncan-Andrade & Morrell, 2008; Dyson, 2001; and Rivera, 2009) concur that schools are sites with boundless potentiality for supporting the holistic development of children and have suggested that the majority of schools are missing the mark in this regard due to a self-serving agenda that promotes social reproduction over social transformation. In other words, it is possible that schools hurt more than they help; that the American public school system has glorified high-stakes testing at the expense of the development of children, race notwithstanding (Delpit & White-Bradley, 2003). In fact, Duncan-Andrade and Morrell (2008) pointed out that the curriculums offered in most American schools espouse and require teachers to facilitate pedagogies that are in effect diametrical to the urgent needs of oppressed urban youths and their communities. Abu-Jamal and Hill (2013) further decried the delimiting effects of urban schooling arguing that teachers are, "hamstrung by pre-figured scripted curricula that essentially de-skill them, reducing them to assembly-line workers."

These authors also stated that these same teachers train children to "become cogs in a machine, to become alienated workers, to become beings acted upon rather than actively functioning as agents in the world." (p.108, 110)

Currently, the dearth of competitive test scores in many states has pushed their education departments and school districts to fervently explore culturally relevant pedagogical approaches. To my mind, this shift in approach is not an acknowledgment of wrongfulness on the part of the governing bodies and corporations that decide on school curricula. Rather, this change is a knee-jerk reaction to the often deplorable test scores in urban centers. In other words, lest states and districts face the possibility of a decline in notoriety and federal funding, they must make adjustments so that youths of color don't "mess things up". In other words, by helping "them", states and school districts intend to help themselves.

Now granted, my aim in divulging my thoughts on these matters is not to paint all educators with a broad, insensitive or sinister brush. Many folks in education want to do the right things. Yet, this doesn't dismiss the fact that many practices and policies are rooted in old world ideologies that have given rise to the disparities that are so problematic today. Unless the underpinning values and principles are extirpated, the results will remain the same.

In his classic treatise, "The Miseducation of the Negro", Dr. Carter G. Woodson argued that the American public education system perpetuated the oppression that African Americans were faced with in the larger society (1999). Not only did black youths have to battle irksome Jim Crow policies outside of the school house, but inside the school house, black youths were further reminded of their inferiority. The curriculum rarely, if at all, exposed them to information about Africa or even references to the African contribution in America. If they were lucky black youths were offered scant historical facts in textbooks. During attempts to implement multicultural celebrations, schools mentioned Africa with insulting brevity. In contrast, black youths were inundated with information about European history and the exploits of white American men in particular. Black youths were saturated with the philosophies, worldview, epistemologies, and sensibilities of the dominant white culture. Hence, this essentialization of white American culture and its concomitant European history added to the burden of what it meant to be black in the United States. These youths had no means to interpret the content and ideas through their own cultural lens because the experiences of their people were excluded.

It is arguable that contemporary black youths are suffering from a precedent that was established during the era that Woodson (1999) discussed. And, it is further arguable that the lack of an educational experience that consults the wisdom, knowledge, and understanding of oppressed communities contributes to the academic underdevelopment of oppressed youths. They are disconnected from the teaching and learning experience because the core of their identity, their cultural and communal selves, is marginalized and at worst ignored. Thus, the educational experience for many oppressed youths impedes their ability to maximize learning. In other words, these youths have no authentic "opportunity to learn".

Opportunity to Learn

After securing his first administrative term in 2008, President Barak Obama and his team turned their attention to the infamous educational achievement gap. In essence, the achievement gap, the term given to address the disparity in standardized test scores between black youths and their white, non-Hispanic counterparts. The Obama administration announced that by the year 2020, the United States would lead the world in post-secondary education. This meant that the United States would produce more college graduates than any other nation. In order to accomplish this feat, the United States would have to produce more high school graduates than any other nation. For this to occur, all youths, regardless of race or class, would have to have access to a quality educational experience.

According to the Schott Foundation (2010), the term access means, "the odds of historically disadvantaged students enrolling in a high school where nearly all students graduate on time and are college ready, when compared to the odds for students not historically disadvantaged" (para.5). To further clarify the notion of access, the Obama administration declared that all American youths must have an "opportunity to learn", which is described in four key components: "high quality early education; highly qualified teachers and instructors in grades K-12; college preparatory curricula that will prepare all youth for college, work and community; and equitable instructional resources" (para.7).

Despite the lofty and good-spirited aim of this educational initiative, national data reveals that many students, particularly those from historically disadvantaged communities (namely black and brown communities), sorely lack an "opportunity to learn" as defined by the Schott Foundation (2010). Most of these youths don't have access to high performing schools. They typically encounter novice teachers who are not highly-qualified, or they receive jaded, veteran teachers whose "my way or the highway" approach is unappealing (to put it mildly). Equally appalling, many schools attended by youths from historically disadvantaged communities have meager resources with which to provide a meaningful learning experience that is on par with that of their more affluent, mainstream peers. Sadly, the corollary has been and continues to be the perpetuation of a vicious cycle. These struggling communities produce and send away youths with urgent needs who return home with more needs. Few overcome the asperities of their lived experience to become agents of change that can contribute to the socio-economic improvement of their communities (Kafele, 2004).

National data published by the Schott Foundation (2013) revealed that African American youths suffer from gross inequities more than their historically disadvantaged Hispanic or Asian peers when assessed by several education measures including graduation rate, suspensions, percentage of students designated Mentally Retarded or enrollment in Advanced Placement courses. In 2013 the National Assessment of Educational Progress released test results that gave further credence to lack of an "opportunity to learn" among black youths. The study indicated that only 12% of black eighth graders scored at or above proficiency in Reading compared to 38% of their white, non-Hispanic peers (Figure 2). In regard to Math, 13% of black eighth graders scored at or above proficiency compared to 45% of their white non-Hispanic peers (Figure 2). Other data provided evidence of disparities including national suspension rates, expulsions, and Special Education classification data. Specifically, black youths are overrepresented in Special Education, underrepresented in Gifted/Talented programs, and disproportionately the recipients of out-of-school suspensions and expulsions (Kunjufu, 2005; Schott Foundation 2013).

Figure 2
2013 Percentages of Black Male and Caucasian Males at or Above Proficiency

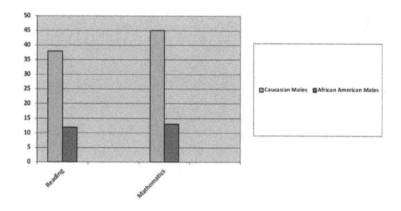

Note. Adapted from "National Assessment of Educational Progress (NAEP) Evidence of Inequities," by The Schott Foundation for Public Education, 2013, The Schott Foundation 50 State Report on Public Education and Black Males. Copyright 2017 by the Schott Foundation for Public Education.

Further compounding the issue of underperformance among youths from historically disadvantaged communities, the Schott Foundation (2013) reported that African American and Latino youths have only half of an "opportunity to learn" compared to other non-white students. According to the "Opportunity to Learn Index", 15% of black youths attend or have access to high-performing schools compared to 32% of their white, non-Hispanic peers. A startling 42% of black youths attend low-performing schools compared to 15% of their white non-Hispanic counterparts (Schott Foundation,

2013). African American youths seem to fare the worst amongst youths of color. This same report revealed that compared to their Native American, Latino, and Asian American peers, African American youths are more likely to attend poorly-re-sourced, low-performing schools.

Figure 3
Percentages of African American Students Attending
Well-Resourced, High-Performing Schools Compared to
Caucasian Counterparts

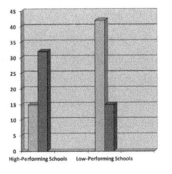

Note. Adapted from "Opportunity to Learn Index," by The
Schott Foundation for Public Education, 2010, Opportunity
to Learn 50 State Report. Copyright 2012 by the Schott
Foundation for Public Education.

The above statistics are but a modicum of evidence that underscores the notion that education is not providing sufficient support to those who need it the most. While oppressed, urban youths may not articulate their angst with academic jargon, it's quite possible that their actions are argument enough. Drop-out rates, suspension rates, and expulsions abound. It's not hard to conceive that many oppressed urban youths have low belief in their ability to acquire critical academic literacies (e.g., computational, linguistic, etc.). It's not difficult to believe that they feel powerless to change the harsh realities of their lived experience and existential situations (Britner & Pajares, 2001; Duncan-Andrade, 2008).

Origins

An individual can walk into any public space where people gather for social exchanges (e.g., coffee shops, parks, barber shops, beauty salons, etc.) and hear a variety of conversations relative to life. Although most of the kibitzing is full of opinion and conjecture, there are occasions when someone may reference facts and/or research to make their claims. Today more than ever social media sites have become cyber-spaces for these kinds of conversations. It usually begins with a picture or video with an accompanying caption. Then, viewers weigh in on the subject. Facebook in particular, has become a platform for socio-political debate. In the aftermath of the incendiary white-on-black murder cases that afflicted the African American community post-Trayvon Martin (e.g., Michael Brown, Eric Garner, Jordan Davis, Walter Scott, Dontre Hamilton), I'd scroll through Facebook posts and observe users broach information, mostly historical, to try to provide perspective on why these incidents occur. On more than one occasion individuals posted information about the systemic nature of oppression in the United States, essentially asserting that holding the immediate perpetrator(s) accountable is only part of the solution. These contributors suggested that the structure of the criminal justice system needs to be thoroughly examined, possibly dismantled, and reconstructed before real change can occur.

In regard to acts of violence against blacks by white police officers, one contributor in particular pointed out the origins of the police force. During American enslavement, white males were hired by plantation owners to track fugitive slaves, apprehend them, and return them to their owners. After the 13th Amendment—which abolished slavery—was enacted, Vagrancy Laws were introduced that made it illegal for any black person to be engaged in non-working activities. This meant that if a group of black males was simply sitting on a porch or walking together in a field, they could be arrested for violating Vagrancy Laws, imprisoned, and made to work per judge sentencing. It was quasi-enslavement since the 13th Amendment permitted enslavement as punishment for a crime. In either case, white males comprised the group that would "police" locales and enforce the laws and restrictive policies. Ironically, the Reconstruction era featured disgruntled ex-Confederate soldiers as police officers. They were called "pater-ollers". They'd move about plantation grounds in wagons or on horseback. It's very interesting that today police departments refer to police vans as "patty wagons".

Thus, contributors of this kind of information aimed to shed light on a much larger socio-political issue using the contemporary cases as points of departure. In similar fashion and in reference to the present condition of African Americans youths in education, I found it necessary to consult history to discover the origins of the inequity that to my mind have spawned the marginalization of black children. Some authors (Cesaire, 1965; Karenga, 2002; Memmi, 2006) Wilson, 1993) have argued that any query into the nature of oppression in America must begin with an investigation of European hegemony manifested through imperialism and colonialism.

During the historical time period that writers of many middle and high school textbooks refer to as, "The Age of Exploration", people of color suffered tremendous devastation at the hands of what can be termed, "leading European nations". Over a timespan that ranged from the late 15th century well into the mid-to-late 19th century, France, Great Britain, Spain, Belgium, Portugal, and the Netherlands entered into a race for wealth, power, and expansive territory. At the behest of monarchs, the armed forces of these nations, along with less official sailors of the mercenary ilk, set out on countless jaunts across the vast seas of the world. Many of the excursions led to the development of the pirate tales that thousands enjoy today (It's interesting how a period of filled with theft, pogroms, and other skullduggery is glorified today, even in the form of cartoons for children—Disney's *Jake and the Neverland Pirates*.). The "soft" story is that these brave men overcame treacherous waves and storms to reach lands with beautiful flora and exotic animals. They befriended and made pacts with tribal leaders and chiefs in the distant locales who through barter supplied the explorers with indigenous gifts that were addictive (e.g., spices, precious metals, herbs, etc.).

Upon the explorer's return to their homelands, they lavished their monarchs and leaders with goods that ultimately enriched the local culture. But, access to goods from exotic lands wasn't enough. The monarchs wanted to own the lands: they wanted to control the people of the lands. The result for Europe was great. France and Great Britain evolved into rich, poly-cultural societies. Even today, the cohort nations of the European Union enjoy a variety of ethnic presence, expression, and contribution because of colonialism. Sadly, these benefits came at the expense of the nations they colonized.

According to Fanon (1952), colonialism decimated the lands and people groups of countless lands and territories. Specifically, Fanon (1952) argued that colonialist governance and military power and its concomitant violence, domination, and exploitation; had a severe psychological impact on indigenous populations. There was a clear false binary. The colonized suffered, while the colonists thrived. Kane (2007) confirmed the false binary established within the tenuous social context of colonialism. In other words, the intimation made by those who'd prefer to romanticize the era of colonialism is that the end justified the means; that there was no other way that indigenous populations could become culturally advanced apart from the influence of Europe's children. Granted, through colonialism concepts, technologies, and philosophies may have been introduced that helped enhance certain aspects of daily living amongst the affected populations. However, as Kane (2007) stated, any recognizable boons came with a great price.

Cesaire (1965), similar to Fanon (1952), contended that the dehumanization brought upon Native American, Asian, African, and Latino people of color—through colonialism— culminated in a legacy of misery, pain, and despair. Ankara (2004) indicated that one reason for the simultaneous advance of Europeans and the demise of people groups of color is the notion of race. A classical means of distinguishing humans, race was a by-product of colonialism created by anthropologists and biologists. "Scientists" began to associate behavior with race (i.e., skin color, physical features, and geographic location) often without authentic understanding of culture and certainly without contextual insights. Behaviors that were benign, noble, and virtuous became linked with the character of Europeans. Meanwhile any deviance and pathology was linked to indigenous populations, despite the onset of these behaviors being clearly related to the injustice, violence, exclusion, and domination inherent in colonialist milieus. The corollary was a taxonomy that featured a ranking order of "races" with Europeans at the top. Resultantly, Europeans were regarded as being culturally and biologically superior. And, it was this notion that influenced all interactions between colonialists and colonized people (Cesaire, 2001).

Further damage was inflicted upon the colonized through what I term a "psycho-cultural reprogramming" process whereby the history, epistemology, ideology, and philosophy that they esteemed was deprecated and discarded in favor of all things European or American (Adams, 1995). The goal of the colonialist was to forge a new man, a more corrigible being that would think and act in alignment with the dictates of the homeland of the colonialists. As Kane (2007) contended, "the task of the colonist was to replace indigenous histories and cultures and replace them with newly constructed racial ideologies".

With respect to the trials and tribulations faced by Africans during American enslavement, "psycho-cultural reprogramming" occurred with all deliberate speed. Africans across the diaspora had shattered psyches (Asante, 2003). Youth in particular became targets of this Euro-American regeneration process. According to Perkins (1995), slave traders considered youths more easy to control and groom for the benefit of the slave institution. The effect was devastating. Generations of individuals were forced to literally lose their natural minds and develop new, alien minds that would render them helpless against any indoctrination tactics and subjugation maneuvers. Enslaved Africans became cultural zombies, dead to their true selves though they were fully alive and useful in the hands of their oppressors. Everything that they knew to be sacred was ground into grains of nothingness by insular dogmas, pejoratives, and image distortions (Adams, 1995; Woodson, 1999). Cesaire (1972) commented on the conquest of Africa by imperialist nations:

"An entire generation of 'enlightened' European scholars worked hard to wipe out the cultural and intellectual contributions of Egypt and Nubia from European history, to whiten the West in order to maintain the purity of the "European" race. They also stripped all of Africa of any semblance of civilization using the printed page to eradicate their history and thus reduce a whole continent and its progeny to little more than beasts of burden or brutish heathens. The result is the fabrication of Europe as a discrete, racially pure entity, solely responsible for modernity, on the one hand, and the fabrication of the Negro on the other." (p.22)

This inverse approach to relations among the oppressed and their oppressors was promoted through education. During the Reconstruction period, education in the United States became the vehicle of choice to apprehend specific political objectives, guarantee economic outcomes, and maintain pre-antebellum social arrangements (Watkins, 2001). Both European and American intelligentsia introduced and corroborated notions of racial hierarchy and ethnic inferiorities. These "experts" presented what they regarded as hard evidence to support the propping up of occidental philosophy, sensibility, and epistemology and the degradation of the culture, philosophy, and linguistics of non-European people groups. Hence, education became the preeminent means to civilize the improvident and culturally-retrogressive blacks and integrate them into what was widely believed to be a progressive white society (Watkins,

2001). Northern financiers who were interested in maintaining the balance of power between the races gave vigorously and generously to found and support schools that would teach blacks skills amicable to their elitist socio-political and economic imperatives.

According to Woodson (1999), this approach to educational development led to the systemization of fallacy that produced "mis-educated" blacks who were unable to articulate the beliefs, values, and hopes of their native land; powerless to resist oppression and exploitation brought about by dominant, mainstream American society. Moreover, the "mis-educated" blacks would be bereft of the critical insight and tools needed to reclaim, reconstruct, and revitalize the African cultural traditions, understandings, sensibilities, and philosophies pertinent to the advancement of the African community. The mass effect was a populace that felt displaced even though America was their home; a group devoid of authentic personhood and mired in despair.

For years, prevarication was the norm. In other words, white Americans believed the falsehood that was promulgated in schools. And, since black inferiority was accepted as "gospel truth", over time the ideology influenced policy that promoted separation of the races. Thus, school districts emerged that were identifiable by race. Persons with segregationist platforms advocated for curricular, funding, transportation, and construction guidelines that advanced claims for separation. In wasn't until the famed Brown v. Board of Education Supreme Court ruling in 1954 that the harmful effects of segregation were nationally exposed. Even still, states, particularly southern American states, and many school districts—some in the North—remained steadfast in their segregationist policies. And, even when they did relent, the threads of racial superiority were so finely woven into their cultural fabric that injustices continued to occur that squelched hope for students and communities of color.

Restoring the Land

Today, all youths need hope. Duncan-Andrade (2010) maintained that President Barak Obama put forth hope during his 2008 presidential campaign and won largely because the American populace resonated with that message. Obama's proclamation of hope for America provided psychologically wounded and emotionally jaded citizens with an intangible anchor of sorts. It was near magical. Obama's presence alone seemed to reify the notion of hope in a country that has long been led and dominated by white, "land-owning", men. In other words, Obama didn't necessarily need a long political record of triumph over social issues and evidence of his authorship of bills that brought about significant economic change or improvement in foreign relations.

To some degree, in Obama, the word hope became flesh. Never before in the history of America had a man of color with a "Muslim name" been named leader of the American empire. Never before had a man without the traditional antecedents been exalted to the highest seat of power in government. Obama's political ascendancy alone was "change that the American people could believe in". For so many families, the keepers of the old guard promoted agendas that aimed at exclusion for most and improvement for an infinitesimal portion of the population. Surely, this man—Obama—could make a difference. This was the overall sentiment. Princeton professor and noted author Eddie S. Glaude, Jr. conveyed the perception of Obama among many African Americans who voted for him:

"Obama was supposed to be different. He was supposed to care about black people...We've been duped, and we're angry with ourselves. Many progressives "green-screened" him. We made Obama whatever we wanted him to be. If we wanted an antiwar candidate, he was it. If we wanted someone who supported universal health care he was it; someone who would challenge Wall Street, he was our guy; a candidate committed to the poor, Obama was our man. He was our political Play-Doh. And he obliged our fantasies all the way to the White House." (p.147)

I can even recall pressure being exacted on my conscience by friends and loved ones who dared me to cast my vote for anyone other than Obama; as if my one vote could snatch our collective hope away. Fast forward to 2016 and some of the same folks who cried tears of joy during Obama's inauguration were crying tears of sadness and/or regret. The hope they'd longed for never materialized beyond symbolism. Eight years after Obama's coming, America became a nation in mourning because the sun had set on the hope that many so desperately believed in. Under Obama's watch, racial oppression has intensified; academic performance has continued to wane in most urban centers; market forces have invaded education and brought tremendous fiscal pressure to bear on public schools; many children still don't have insurance; and unfair practices yet loom in housing.

Clearly, Obama won victories, but that's typical of any presidency. Furthermore, victories are at best subjective conclusions. But, Obama was supposed to be special. As Glaude (2016) poignantly shared, "Obama was supposed to be more". For blacks in particular, Obama was our "Neo" (triumphant character from the movie *The Matrix*). He was supposed to be "the one" to deliver the black community out of the American wilderness of oppression. Instead what most have been left with is the realization that the notion of messianic leaders is superannuated; that the change that we want doesn't rest in the bowels of one fascinating man or woman. Perhaps the takeaway from the Obama administration should be the power of collective will. Millions seized the opportunity to let their voice be heard through the ballot and something unprecedented occurred. What if the same logic and fervor could be directed towards today's pressing issues? What would happen in an America in which citizens rallied together on agreed upon problems and co-labored to create change?

Glaude (2016) underscored the power of the collective will and argued for a broader vision of political engagement,

> *"Elections are important, but they are hardly the only work of democracy. For too long we've been sold a bill of goods that this person or that one will do what we need, if only we can get them elected. This promise wants us to believe that voting is democracy. But that's only half true. Sure, we must work overtime (sadly) to ensure that no one rolls back the gains of the Voting Rights Act and that everyone has access to the ballot. But the work of democracy does not end with elections." (p. 224)*

Perhaps we missed the point with Obama. Perhaps his idea of "change you can believe in" was directed at the populace the entire time. Perhaps his loyalists were too awe-struck. Just maybe Obama has been attempting to furtively explain his limitations, now realized, and the real way to exercise political power and, as it were, government by the people.

I can't help but think about the children in the wake of Obama's administration. They were heavily invested. More youth voters turned out than ever before in any elections. Was their hope decimated?

As we walk dangerously during the era of President Trump, one can't help but wonder if the underwhelming impact of Obama's final days and leave-taking has given rise to swelling apathy? Have millennials and teens, particularly those of color, completely given up on the vote and rejected institutional power? Do they now feel powerless and worse yet nihilistic? While it's very plausible that youths are sinking, mind-first, into quagmires of despair, I argue that they can be restored. I submit that the "valley" moment that currently exists for many in historically disadvantaged communities is temporary and will be such as long as righteous indignation and faith are propagated and modeled by socially aware and compassionate adults. To my mind, it's up to adults to reveal the prospects of hope when it comes alive in our hearts. I agree with Glaude (2016) who contended that, "we should turn our attention to efforts like the Forward Together moral movement and the Dream Defenders and #BlackLivesMatter, or to mobilizing around public school closings in our neighborhoods. Some issue, concrete and right in front of us, should be our focus. A collateral effect, although not the main objective, would be the election of men and women at the state and local levels who aren't about symbolism and celebrity, but who put forward a strategic vision for our communities."

Adults bear the responsibility of finding hope a home and inviting youths in for communion. Adults can help youths, namely black youths, discover their "Wakanda" (fictive African nation depicted in the 2018 Marvel/Disney blockbuster movie, *Black Panther*). The exhalation of adults in the form of knowledge, wisdom, and guidance can engender the type of radical imagination that leads to socio-cultural blueprints that go beyond the borders of our present social demarcations and lifts us up to higher planes of possibility. To my mind, Wakanda represents the hope that many long for. In Wakanda tradition is romanticized, cherished, respected, but not at the expense of technological innovation and the creative genius of blossoming generations. Wakanda represents a place where black life matters; a place where youths only know of oppression from a spectators lens because their parents, the community rejected the lethal seductions of colonialism. It represents a place where one's success isn't subject to lottery systems and the whims of bipartisan discourse. What's more is that aside from its cosmic evolution, Wakanda is an idea. And, in most cases, <u>ideas are incubators for hope</u>.

Glaude (2016) and others with a critique of the current political landscape suggested that the way things are going; hope is fleeting and in effect being run out of town. The fact that young people—namely college students—have asserted their citizenry, raised their voices, and put the best of their skills and creativity to work is a marker of hope in the prospect of youth. And, the support of more seasoned adults (in age and life experiences) only serves to boost the possibilities of their political insurgence. When adults open their eyes, open their ears, and extend their hands to youths, we generate a sense of positive anticipation. We convey the idea that we are for youths and that we stand in solidarity with them. Put differently, each of us represents the potential for housing hope, but it's not only in our words. Action is required. Commitment to life-affirming values is mandatory. Capacity for building healthy relationships is essential.

Hungry Souls

Over the years, Hollywood has released several movies that depict stories of men and women in schools who make a difference in the lives of youths. Some of the classic films include *Stand and Deliver*, *Lean on Me*, *Dangerous Minds,* and perhaps *Coach Carter*. In these films the male or female protagonist has the herculean task of motivating African American or Latino high school students to overcome the plight of their neighborhoods and go after high school graduation. Naturally, part of the stories focus on the personal life and inward and social challenges that the adults have to address while simultaneously assisting their students. In the end, the youths in each of the listed films succeed. The male or female protagonist is hailed a victor. Audiences who view these cinematic depictions of educator-student or coach-student interactions are typically left with feelings of inspiration; that one person can make a difference; that ordinary people can affect change. To my mind, tales of this nature serve a purpose. We need 'feel good' stories. They're fun. They provide an element of suspense and excitement. Yet, when I consider my experiences as an urban educator and I reflect on the issues facing this millennial generation, I can't help but think about the film, *Hunger Games*.

Hunger Games is a 21st century American film that depicts the dynamics of human interaction in a post-apocalyptic, dystopian society. The milieu of the tale is a super-state called Panem that maintains a seemingly impenetrable system of "haves and have nots". The affluent live in the capitol city: they represent the minority. Affluent Panemians enjoy the best in fashion, cuisine, transportation, and housing. The rest of Panem citizens are spread across 12 districts (so they're told) and are stratified by class, with the majority dwelling in abject squalor. Every year, the capitol city, hosts an eerily celebratory event called the "Hunger Games". During the "Hunger Games", Panemians remember their nation's history and rejoice in its prowess. Much of the jubilation and genuflection emitted from Panemians is related to state victory in a type of civil war. The celebration culminates in a contest that features youth representatives from each of the 12 Panem districts. Only one winner is crowned. Ironically, winning the Hunger Games comes at the expense of blood, not one's own necessarily, but the blood of other contestants.

More than a test of will and fortitude, the "Hunger Games" is in effect a conflation of contempt, derision, and punishment exacted upon Panem citizens due to the infamous revolt that led to the war. After squashing the uprising, government leaders issued an edict that each year the 12 districts that comprise Panem must participate in an annual "reaping" whereby they offer two children—one male and one female—as "tribute" to compete in a gladiatorial fight to the finish. Worse yet, this sadistic sporting event is televised for all Panem citizens to see including the parents and immediate loved ones of competitors, who are made to watch the contests on large screens. Forlorn and emotionally jaded, district residents are forced into merciless jeering and cheering as they support their tributes, knowing their youth's survival means death for someone else's child. Amid a miasma of alienation and anomie, a glimmer of optimism for change appears when the film's protagonist, an adolescent named Katniss Everdeen, volunteers as tribute to protect her younger sister who has been selected. What began as a demonstration of a sister's love evolves into an inadvertent protestation of hegemony as Katniss ultimately wins the contest armed with compassion, conviction, and courage; virtues that defy the rules of the games. The manner of Katniss' victory poses problems for the leadership of Panem. It sends a message to the on-looking masses that Panem's totalitarian regime and impermeable social arrangement does not define the character of an individual; that despite the repressive realities of their era, good can overtake evil; that the oppressed still have vision, virtue, value, and voice.

In many ways, the conditions of Panem mirror current American society, particularly in post-industrial urban centers. Elements of neoliberalism such as privatization of public goods and services, deregulation, and reductions in government spending have marginalized many urban residents, especially people of color (Giroux, 2009). High rise condominiums flank city business districts in grand array while vacant lots and dilapidated buildings fleck the landscape in historically disadvantaged neighborhoods that are ironically within two to four miles of these towering representations of opulence. Unemployment persists. Public school districts highlight few shining examples of progress in the midst of numerous examples of failing and under-educating schools. The latter, as a matter of consequence, ensure that the number of unemployed or unemployable residents will increase as high school graduating classes shrink. And, in an age when information struts about with monarchical heft, myriad urban youths of color who hail from historically disadvantaged communities where under-education persists, are bereft of the creativity, critical thinking, and communicative skills needed for college entrance and professional marketability.

The corollary of these phenomena is a crippling economic and political marginality. The response to economic and political marginalization often makes the front pages of leading metropolitan newspapers and headlines television news coverage: drug dealing and abuse; crime; violence; poverty; welfare dependency and infant and youth mortality. The consequence of both economic marginality and the ill-response is despair, alienation, frustration, and fear (Anderson, 1999). Hence, a disdain for mainstream American life and its inhabitants develops. A *hunger* for quality of life emerges. Some resort to tyrannical and gladiator-like measures (e.g., gangs) to secure it. And, similar to the environs of "Hunger Games" urban youths in these settings find themselves beset with ineluctable social arrangements and issues. They are involuntarily set at odds with each other and various districts (e.g., neighborhoods), faced with the challenge of surviving with limited resources. Sadly, many don't survive. They become victims, sacrifices in a nasty struggle for the most basic of substantive human rights—life.

Although such suffocating conditions persist, public school districts and their officials have the enormous task of providing viable educational opportunities and preparing children for effective citizenry in the future. Schools in these urban environments are responsible for leading children to educational achievement and social development despite the threat and weight of obvious peril (Shade, 2006). Because of prevalent dangers and traps, youths in these metropolitan settings cannot be risk-averse. They must negotiate life amid constant hardship and disappointment, yet still attempt to seize their aspirations. Those who "hunger" for achievement are akin to Katniss Everdeen, opting in to the quest for one reason, but fortuitously becoming a paladin of a different cause to which they find themselves inextricably connected—freedom. And as such, their valor and perseverance inspires their peerage. The "hungry" in this sense instantaneously transmute into symbols of hope, proof that there is a way to overcome dire circumstances. Thus, their educational journey evolves into a learning experience that equips them with tools and knowledge to transform their world (Asante, 2008).

The Relational Advantage

Interestingly enough, youths of this ilk, despite their personal exploits, are social creations. In *Hunger Games*, Katniss Everdeen was enabled and empowered through several critical relationships. Two relationships in particular made a significant difference in her ascent to triumph: a mentor and a sponsor. Haymitch Abernathy (played by actor Woody Harrell), Katniss' assigned mentor, was a previous winner of the "Hunger Games". He understood the general and hidden curriculum that had to be mastered in order to survive and win. Through a lens filled with mostly sardonic critique of the games, Haymitch saw Katniss' potential to not only win but establish both a trend and legacy. Haymitch provided pearls of wisdom and strategy that proved invaluable as Katniss endured the chilling asperity of the games. His mentorship provoked Katniss to broaden her social perspective and reject any lurking feelings of anomie. Haymitch revealed to Katniss that among the posh capitol city residents watching, were sympathetic viewers—sponsors—willing to open their coffers and supply critical resources. Sure enough, at a point in the contest when Katniss faced imminent death, a sponsor sent her a healing balm to take care of a severe wound. This gesture saved Katniss' life and debunked any notion that no one cared, that she was doomed to die in insolation.

Similarly, inner-city youths who thrive and achieve in spite of the hazards of their environments do so with help. They benefit from critical relationships (Arrington, 2014); from connections with individuals, primarily adults, who have open hearts and panoramic vision. In other words, these helpers see the bigger social picture. Though they may observe crudeness and/or crassness among some inner-city youths, they do not attribute either to personal, familial, or cultural deficit. No, these individuals recognize the socio-political factors that create the oppressive conditions under which many inner-city youths must live (Akom, 2009; Asante, 2008: Cress-Welsing, 1990; Duncan-Andrade, 2008; Wilson, 1991). Beyond the simple espy, these individuals offer their time, wisdom, and expertise so that the youths they encounter can be liberated from the throes of inner-city plight and emerge inspired to pursue their life-goals. As such, these helpers introduce and nurture hope. Helpers can be parents, extended family members, even peers (Arrington, 2014). In many instances, teachers help significantly, providing the mentorship and sponsorship that nourishes the "souls of young folk" and breathes life into their dreams.

Chapter 2

REACHING YOUTHS ON
THE MARGINS

*"I'm tired of this @#$%! My momma don't care. These
n#*&%s out in these streets don't care. It seem like the
majority of teachers that I had don't care. Why should
I care? I feel like saying @%$# it half the time. I feel
like giving up half the time. This girl is gettin' on my
nerves...I gotta a baby on the way. I don't know what
to do. The way I feel, anybody can get it! "*

Imagine that you were an adult having a conversation with a
young man who uttered the words above. What would you
do? Would you be offended because of the profanity? Would
your first thought be to correct his poor grammar? Or, would
you simply listen? What would you do?

For over six years, hearing emotional and sometimes explo-
sive rants of this nature was my reality. It didn't occur each day,
but often. I served as an administrator in an alternative high
school that was designed specifically for older children who
lived on the margins. Many of these youths had been through
numerous trials of life, the likes of which scores of adults may
not have been able to endure. Akin to their non-marginalized

peers, the youths that we served pursued traditional American ideals such as freedom and happiness. Unfortunately, they were born with a hue and into a social class that seemingly relegated them to a disadvantaged lifestyle, one in which freedom and happiness were difficult if not impossible to grasp.

These youths were not necessarily helpless. All of them possessed intelligence. In many cases, their academic records contained evidence of prior proficient or advanced performance in both reading and math. Some youths were gifted in the arts. I was often amazed at the talent that sadly remained hidden, unexposed because all anyone could generally see was their academic underperformance. Their grade point average and attendance records became their badges of recognition; numbers of identification, unwanted veils that malevolently ensconced their true potential, their true selves. Hence, these youths were unable to be true to self. They remained hidden, immured by numbers and considerably angry because they knew that deep down in the depths of their souls there lay treasure that simply needed to be unearthed. Part of the problem was that they hadn't encountered archaeologists, or in this sense adults willing to use their professional and humanitarian tools to engage in the act of excavation. But, at Woodson-Newton HS, we prided ourselves in and considered ourselves expert educational archaeologists. In fact, we pursued "buried treasure" in the same manner that Indiana Jones and his cohorts sought after ancient objects of tremendous value. See, we believed that within children lay virtue and valuables of immense worth. Valuables such as poetic ability, mathematical genius, oratorical agility, deep kindness and compassion, vision, and artistic skill were buried—we believed—underneath hurt, pain, devastation, mistrust, depression, self-doubt, alienation, self and group hate, and despair. Our task was to help remove the dirt. Yes, we were helpers. In other words, we never perceived that it was our sole responsibility to do the heavy lifting. To do so would assume a level of deficiency on the part of the students. No, we rejected deficit-thinking and avoided the hubristic notion that we were all-powerful because of our age and credentials. Instead, we assumed that our students were powerful and that they only needed to be awakened to their true potential.

When the dirt was removed and the treasure was revealed, it was a sight to see! There's nothing like seeing a child, six years old or seventeen, light up with confidence and joy because they're proud of their academic or behavioral growth and subsequent accomplishments. There's nothing like the smile of a young man or a young woman who's made it through the storm and lived to tell about it. I can recall one of our graduates poignantly sharing remarks that helped me understand the pivotal nature of our line of work. Her name was Amber, and she said, "I was dead before I came to Woodson-Newton." Amber had no clue, but her words had the impact of a gale-force wind. I couldn't show it at the time, but I was thrust into a state of shock. Amber's remarks were brief yet bursting with substance and profundity. I'd served at WHNS for several years, but I never fully grasped the importance of the educational experience that we provided. I never realized that the programmatic focus and the ethos that had been established was bringing young people back to life.

Later on I gained insight into Anique's choice of words. Prior to her enrollment at WNHS, Anique was visionless. Attending school was at best a perfunctory exercise. Her experience at WNHS helped her to Believe in her own abilities. It renewed her confidence in people, and resurrected her dreams.

The Initial Inquiry

While serving at WNHS, I became increasingly curious about the ways that many of the youths were able to keep at the pursuit of educational and life-goals despite unfavorable socio-ecological factors. My inquiry was further fueled by the observations that I made as a school leader. With respect to context, WNHS was an alternative high school in a major urban school district. WNHS provided educational services for a variety of non-traditional high school students in grades 9-12. Of the 170 students that were enrolled at the time of my inquiry, 98% of the students were African American, 1.5% were Latino/Hispanic, and 1% were Caucasian. Twenty-two precent of WNHS students were adjudicated, 3% were expelled, 50% were chronic truants, and 25% were categorized as "other", i.e., students who do not necessarily meet the identified criteria for enrollment, yet have unique academic and socio-emotional needs that require perhaps alternate services and service delivery in a setting more suited to their needs. With respect to specific enrollment criteria, WNHS endeavored to enroll adjudicated youths and those returning to the larger school district from expulsion. WNHS also admitted students who were considered at-risk, i.e., in danger of not graduating from high school. Many of these students were challenged with credit deficiency, chronic truancy, and repeated behavioral misconduct. In order to meet the urgent academic and socio-emotional needs of such a unique population, WNHS featured online learning, low teacher-to-student ratios, and consistent interaction with community-based educators who provided educational services that primarily addressed life and social skill development through social, cultural and political discovery.

This rich blend of academic and support services was provided to WNHS students throughout each school year;

however, student enrollment was temporary. Most WNHS youths were enrolled for one school year (two full 18 week semesters). In some cases, students were granted an extension of stay whereby they were allowed to remain at WNHS for another semester. Upon completion of their time at WNHS, youths were either transitioned into another suitable learning environment via the WNHS Enrollment Process (The WNHS Enrollment Process was facilitated by the school Enrollment Specialist. This individual was the school representative that initially enrolled youths and monitored student progress during their time at WNHS. As student time of completion neared, the Enrollment Specialist contacted potential schools to arrange for subsequent student enrollment.), or students/parents had the option to select their next school.

My primary administrative tasks involved student enroll-ment and academic monitoring. Since I was typically the first WNHS staff member that prospective students encountered, I gained some insight into their backgrounds. Often students or adults who accompanied the students would discuss family and/or social issues as reasons for their recalcitrance, poor aca-demic performance, truancy and other foibles (Some of the sto-ries were laden with plots, twists and turns that would make Hollywood marvel). Essentially, it was unofficial deductive research. As we conversed and I asked questions, the reasons "why" became more clear, I understood how the students ended up in need of WNHS's services.

Most remarkable in my observation of student matricula-tion at WNHS was student perseverance amid harsh urban real-ities. Some students braved treks through combat zones (Akom, 2009) just to get to school. Some students lived in group homes with little to no contact with their biological parents. A few students lived in gender-specific shelters, uncertain about what their immediate future held. These and other examples of the details of students' lived experiences informed my assumption that these youths must have hope; that somehow they believed that success was attainable regardless of the tenuous circumstances they were met with. Thus, I embarked on a journey to probe WNHS students' experience with hope.

The Woodson-Newton Way

Before delving more into the revelations shared by students, it's important at this juncture to provide insight into the underpinning philosophy of WNHS. The aim of WNHS was to be a locus for transformation that resurrected ancient principles for human growth and development and community vivification. These elements were infused into embraceable, contemporary forms. Ergo, it is important to explicate the means by which this occurred and the means by which the school accomplished this most astonishing feat, particularly in an ever-increasing post-modern, automated society. WNHS featured an ethos that was a compilation of guiding values and beliefs that drew upon the best of African sensibility and aspiration. The subjacent principle within this construct was the West African Proverb, "I am because we are and because we are therefore I am". This principle propagated interdependence, community, and reciprocity. It contended that no one in the WNHS learning community obtained success on their own, but rather success, when achieved is a collective win based on collective effort.

Values that guided WNHS and contributed to its ethos included those offered in the Nguzo Saba, also known as the Seven Principles of Kwanzaa that govern Black/African social life (Karenga, 2002): collective work and responsibility, unity, self-determination, and purpose. When asked about the fabric of WNHS, Principal Malik Stokes stated, "in addition to our school's guiding principle and values, we want to contend with dualisms that repress potentialities and stymie adult and student expression". To this end, students and staff critiqued societal constructs, mores, laws, and trajectories that delimit or deny the augmentation of adult and student psycho-cultural and socio-emotional competencies. The intended corollary of WNHS's studies, explorations, and evaluations was redefinition of purported notions of prosperity, family, manhood, womanhood, and authenticity that allowed all members of the WNHS learning community to "practice the possibilities" in life, in family, in community; versus accepting too often erroneous, culturally irrelevant, oppressive societal prescriptions (Friere, 1970).

Whenever he was asked, Principal Stokes often described WNHS's operation as "rhythmic". He suggested that a rhythmic operation at WNHS was necessary to accommodate what he referred to as, "embedded, infused, transferable principles", also known throughout the learning community as Woodson-Newton DNA or "wDNA". Per Stokes, this liberating gene consisted of hope, rigor, passion, authenticity, and urban youth anthropology practiced in a relevant contextual organism. The power of this gene manifested in its ability to penetrate human integument and somatic boundary and become imbedded in the human heart willing to embrace emancipatory thought and practice.

When asked what the notion of "wDNA" meant for staff at WNHS, Stokes addressed some of the challenges that WNHS staff were faced with.

"As a leader of this institution/organism, I challenge adults to evolve into critical consumers of educational paradigms and pedagogues who possess outstanding psycho-cultural and socio-emotional competencies."

Heart and Soul

Truthfully, WNHS, though not completely the brainchild of Principal Stokes, was largely a physical manifestation of his genius and creativity. An attribute that Principal Stokes consistently encouraged WNHS staff members to cultivate was the notion of urban youth anthropology. In other words, Principal Stokes maintained that the success of WNHS's mission rested on the notion that the adults that served youths possessed superior insight into the identities of the youths. Stated differently, Principal Stokes implored staff to "know their audience". A former Africology student, Principal Stokes, was certainly qualified to devise and publicize this expectation, especially as it pertained to African American youths and African/African American culture.

According to Principal Stokes, this notion of being an urban youth anthropologist was enriched after hearing educator and activist Roberto Rivera (2009) articulate the complexity of urban youths. Rivera called the uniqueness of urban youths, *"tri-dimensionality"*. He argued that they have an American identity, a cultural identity, and a hip hop identity. Rivera referred to these youths as *"tri-cultural youths"*. Rivera's (2009) perspective inspired Principal Stokes to expand Rivera's thoughts about the complexity of the contemporary urban African American adolescent to include an existential and a more specific cultural aspect. Hence, the "tri-cultural youth" evolved into the "penta-cultural youth": American, African, Hip Hop, Postmodern, and Post-Soul. Once, in a staff professional development, Principal Stokes made the claim that shameful educational outcomes continue due to the failure of many educators to

acknowledge, accept, study, and analyze the multi-dimension-
ality of urban youths. He further urged WNHS staff to commit
to a regiment of study that was inclusive of research of history
and culture, critique of policy and curriculum practices, and
vetting of traditional pedagogy, deconstructing it where necessary and retrofitting it to meet the edification specifications
of millennial youths. For Principal Stokes, African American
youths were worthy of such devotion and cognitive labor, worth
the extra time, and worth the sacrifice.

Woodson-Newton's DNA

The core values and principles of any institution provide
insight into the manner of its operations as well as key objectives and aspirations. Core values and principles are the elements that give organizations life and explain their reason for
existing. As indicated above, the work at WNHS was largely
rooted in love, rigor, hope, urban youth anthropology, passion, and urban youth anthropology. Per Stokes, a thoroughgoing educational experience for millennial African American
youths was incomplete without an emphasis on and exploration of Africanisms (cultural components and markers from
the African continent taught to them by village elders and parents); cultural values; post-modernist thought; and post-soul
perspectives.

Africanisms
The tragic experience of enslavement and racial oppression in the Americas left Africans and their descendants in
cultural shambles. Due to deliberate acts of dehumanization
and intolerant attitudes towards and acts against the African
ethos, Africans became psycho-emotionally lost. They literally

couldn't find their way back home. But, this reality was true as it pertained to remembrance of their communal way of life. They were stripped, tortured, and beat out of their African personage and coerced to become an "other" that they genuinely had no connection to. Africans were forced to morph into a different species called niggers. And, their white oppressors were determined to make sure that niggers had no connection to their true identity except in the cases where the niggers' cultural remembrance bolstered their oppressors' coffers.

Yet, countless Africans endured the whirlwinds of wickedness endemic to plantations, and they survived. Their fortitude was evident as cultural retentions began to spring forth in different forms. Though most often comprised of a mixture of tribes and tongues, enslaved Africans retained the gift of song, spirit, and sweat (Dubois, 1903). They also retained the tradition of caring for their young in a manner that ensured the transference of key aspects of African heritage. In respect to African culture, this phenomenon is called "kindezi" in the Bantu language, the care and cultural transmission provided by elders. Kindezi included nurturance of emotion, intuition, and physical precocity. It celebrated oral tradition and the sharing of critical knowledge among family and community members. Non-verbal cues and interpersonal orientation were among the communicative skills taught and promoted through. Communalism trumped individualism. In fact, elders were particularly concerned with helping youths to learn the difference between personal expression within a collective and personal agendas that deviate from the aims of a collective. To this end, individuality was encouraged, and African youths learned what it meant to "code-switch" (Kunjufu (2001; 2004; 2005); to exhibit the essence of who they were while steadily adjusting to the behavioral codes of the village. In other words, the interplay between expression of self and reverence of the norms of the community was a "both/and" proposition that helped to advance, preserve, and maintain societal progression.

Cultural Values

Besides the iteration of Africanisms, certain building blocks of Black/African social life were embraced and retained by the descendants of enslaved Africans in America. These building blocks took on the form of more contemporary pre-integration versions of ancient Africanism including the importance of family, religious centers, schools, and community centers; racial awareness; solidarity; and tenets reflective of the Nguzu Saba. Cultural values of this nature run counter to the preponderant market values common in the post-integration era. Sadly, values such as rugged individualism and extreme consumerism obtrude upon all youths. African American youths are even more victimized due to the appeal of mass media (e.g., television, internet, social media) and the devious manner in which it promotes the notion that consumption can alleviate the burdens of oppression (Wilson, 1991). The corollary of such a perspective is the elevation of class concerns and interests over community concerns and interests and consequent race unconsciousness.

Postmodern youth

The complexity of urban youth adolescence is revealed in blends of what can be termed postmodern urban youth sensibilities (Rogers, 2010). During our tenure of service at WNHS, we grappled with the notion of the urban African American postmodern adolescent. It is critical to carefully unpack the observations that were shared, in this regard, by Principal Stokes.

The following commentary reflects some of his ideas about this phenomenon as well as my current understandings.

In respect to what Principal Stokes termed "postmodern urban youth sensibilities", (Rogers, 2010), it's important to note that these entail social and cultural preferences that typically defy or ignore the predilections of older generations of citizens. One example is the homage that millennial youths pay peer networks and friendships. Unlike their parents and grandparents who came of age during the prime and latter times of modernity, postmodern youths generally avoid the tenets of traditional societal institutions (e.g., school, family, religious centers, government,). Or, they make insertions and contributions based on their perception of what is right. Essentially, this socio-cultural angle and psycho-emotional view amounts to revulsion of absolutisms and a desire for relativity (e.g., religion/spirituality, morality, ethics). Stated differently, *the postmodern youth questions everything*. Consequently, it becomes necessary to deconstruct all social phenomena (e.g., cultural traditions, mores, values, institutions) and investigate — using youth-approved measurements — to determine meaning. Within this frame of thinking, movies, music, and symbols provide inspiration for socio-cultural creation and communicating.

Youths who subscribe to this mindset have in effect repersonalized and reappropriated notions of religion/spirituality to fit their ever-expanding worldview. To the structuralist mind, their reappropriations are no more than sacrilege sometimes dressed in fancy or furtive terms (i.e., urban youth vernacular). The intent of the postmodern youth — in most cases — is not to offend. Nonetheless, their attempt to gain meaning, their existentialist stance, is viewed as an affront to traditional forms of spiritual reverence. Put differently, a portion of what informs urban youth postmodern sensibility is a new-fangled idea of what is life-affirming, true, and wholesome. Religious/spiritual interpretation remains "in the gray", subject to the whims of crude adolescent apperception and sweeping pop culture promotions. In some cases the "faith of their fathers" is put on trial as youths wrestle with the concept of otherworldly interventions. The movie franchises of Marvel Comics and DC Comics have added fodder for the already dubious youth with its slew of hero depictions such as X-Men, Avengers, The Green Lantern, Iron Man, The Dark Knight, Incredible Hulk, Superman, and their super contemporaries (According to reports both entities have plans for additional releases that depict the exploits of classic comic heroes.).

Whether it was intended or not, youths have accepted Hollywood as a locus to explore spiritual/theological ideas. For instance, in the 2016 film, *Batman v. Superman: Dawn of justice* (Warner Bros. Pictures, 2016), the villainous character Lex Luthor Jr. likens Superman to a messianic figure that always comes to the aid of humanity. When Luthor Jr. would refer to Superman, he'd often say, "God". In fact, in one scene Luthor Jr. says, "God is good as dead…" This he stated in reference to his plot to destroy Superman whom many in the famed Metropolis esteemed as their savior.

Furthermore, pop culture hero themes create a context within which urban youths can leverage their perceived powerlessness and become a "superhuman" as depicted in the hero-burlesque *"Kick-ass"* (Universal, Lionsgate, 2010). It seems as though this notion of "hero conversion" is especially important among urban African American youths whose perspective of success is often squashed by paternalism. They are constantly bombarded with symbolism, ideas, and messages that convey African American inferiority and European-American superiority (Wilson, 1991). It's as though African

American limitation is transcribed onto their consciousness. Consequently, unhealthy psychological states manifest such as "ego-defense orientation", "fatalism", and "chronic conflict and ambivalence" (Wilson, 1991, pp. 11-14), all of which lend to proclivities for fantasy and creation of unrealistic life-scenarios. In a very twisted manner, many urban African American youths, males in particular, seek to emulate the characteristics of oppressive forces; rather than the Hollywood delineation of a middle-class White teen accosting unsavory characters to fight crime, as seen in the movie *Kick-Ass*.

Instead of using their "powers", their gifts to end the violence and roguery that plagues their neighborhoods, many African American youths (again males in particular) embrace violence and acquire the requisite tools to implement violence (e.g., guns). As in the case of a Lex Luthor Jr., some of these youths self-deify in an effort to resist being controlled. They instead seek to control their lives and the lives of others through fear and intimidation. In doing so they elect themselves to "god status"; whimsically making determinations about who lives and who dies; who wins and who loses. Incidentally, socio-economic status determines the currency utilized to negotiate life. Lex Luthor Jr. was wealthy. He bought people, including their allegiance and service. For some inner-city boys, it could be money, but in many cases ultra-machismo via the threat of physical harm carries great weight. In other words, it's a "do what I say or else" kind of vibe that garners allegiance. And straightway, residents in their neighborhoods submit to what amounts to a code for living that guides social interaction (Anderson, 1999). But, in either case, violence is chosen as the means to conduct business when money and respect fail. Certainly, this approach is pathological. It's a reaction that fails to reflect any connection to liberating values and is actually the natural corollary of an oppressed, crestfallen generation that has willfully removed cultural landmarks.

Now granted, criminologists and other researchers may argue that the inner-cities of post-industrial centers and towns across the United States are rife with urban African American male miscreants. Yet, normalization of this character as authentically African or indicative of the African American community is offensive and should be avoided. The truth is that community despotism and domestic terrorism is despised by most urban African American youth.

At a deeper psychological level, it can be surmised that postmodernism in the typical urban youth manifests in their ability to determine what is real and what is right. Thus, the interrogation of traditional doctrines and institutions; the promotion and regard for self as sole authority; and the contradistinction and appraisal of conventionally sacred associations based on market rationale is the attempt by youths to understand the course of social, cultural, political, theological, ecological, and economic phenomena. Perhaps they are depicting personally and socially what they consider to be the way of the world. Only, for some of these phenomes, their version is dangerous and imposes on the freedom of others.

Could it be that they see people, namely older European-American males doing what they want without consequence? Could it be that they are attempting to play out what they've been shown to be the American way? Consider the frontier depictions of cowboys. Or, think about the mafia movies that glorified money and violence as the necessary means to success. Maybe, just maybe the postmodern youth—in the inner city—is creating his or her own epic adventure; their own rags to riches narrative. It can be easily interpreted from the western and mob examples shared that a person can determine their own fate if they acquire the goods and the tools to do so. In this way there is little distinction between a Lex Luthor Jr. character and "Raheem" from the block. Both feel alienated from mainstream society, access to finances notwithstanding. Both place no confidence in state-sanctioned authority. They possess oppositional values, promulgate cynicism, and harbor embitterment.

Another interesting aspect of the Luthor Jr. character was his very vocal disdain for his father. At times in the movie, Luthor Jr. made reference to abuse he suffered and the sting of his father's absenteeism. Again, despite the wealth, Luthor Jr.'s story rings true for many African American young men. Many trudge mean streets with father wounds that seem to never heal. The corollary of it all as evidenced by Luthor Jr.'s sociopathic disposition and lust for power is the need to be free. Life without boundaries...a world in which anything within their reach is able to be dominated and commodified as needed is their dream. It's delusional at best, but for these characters, *their* truth is all that matters. It's freethinking in perhaps its most fearsome form. Moreover, it seems as though this aspect of freethinking is strongly linked with the notion of the "impossibility of being wrong" (Rogers, 2010).

Searching for Identity

Traditionalists would probably acknowledge this description as mere adolescent rebellion, but in reality it's a paradigm indicative of the postmodern youth's trek towards meaningfulness. It's as if this youth (not all but many) is foundationless due to the absence of the primary identity-agent, the father. Disney's *The Lion King* (Buena Vista Pictures, 1994) illustrates the discovery of identity and meaning in superb fashion. There's a scene in *The Lion King* in which young, adolescent Simba (the story's protagonist), has a conversation with Rafiki, the local guru. Simba asks Rafiki if he knew his father Mufasa. Rafiki tells Simba that he *knows* his father and leads him to a place where he claims his father is. An excited but flummoxed Simba follows Rafiki to a river bank. Rafiki tells Simba to look in the river and he sees a reflection of his father staring back at him. Up until that time in the movie, Simba's life was upset by the awful and untimely demise of his father. The threat of premature death at the paws of his green-eyed and power hungry uncle drove him away from his home. He wandered aimlessly through the jungle in search of safety, sustenance, and solutions. Simba was a lost soul in search of an anchor, something that could harness him to purpose and significance. Interestingly and very similar to millennial youths, Simba found solace in his peer group. Their friendship was vital to Simba's well-being. His buddies influenced Simba's worldview to the degree that he became content with being just another member of a rag-tag jungle bunch that liked to eat, sleep, and have fun. The problem was that Simba was born to be great. He was not just another feline. Simba was a lion cub and heir to his father's throne. He was destined to lead. And, after being thrust into a tailspin of sorts, Simba had a most transformative experience at the river.

Upon seeing his dad's reflection in the water, Simba heard a voice call his name. The next thing he knew he was having a preternatural encounter during which a bundle of clouds swelled and unfurled in the image of his father. Suddenly, the image came alive and his father literally began to speak. Mufasa had the following to say to his son:

"Simba you have forgotten me. You have forgotten who you are and so you have forgotten me. Look inside yourself Simba. You are more than what you have become.

You must take your place in the circle of life…Remember who you are. You are my son and the one true king."

Simba's father, or his father's apparition, reminded him that he had a higher mission to attend to. He was not just Simba, Nala, Timone and Puumba's buddy. No, he was Prince Simba, and he was destined to be King. His father Mufasa's image gave Simba a point of reference, a standard to aspire to, and a snapshot of the future. Mufasa's image provided boundaries, definition, and demanded accountability. The experience with Mufasa's revenant renewed Simba's sense of meaning. He realized that he had a heritage to honor, one that didn't include gamboling with his peerage.

Now, if seeing Mufasa's image in the water and encountering Mufasa's revenant can have such a powerful impact, how much more would Simba had gained if Mufasa would've been alive? Fathers, when present and engaged, provide the substratum for the development of purpose and identity in their children's lives. No father, no sense of identity. Considering the millions of millennial youths who are fatherless (father not present in the home or active in the child's life), it makes sense that some, like Luthor Jr., would operate on the periphery of morality, breaking rules and simultaneously making their own. An argument can be made that such a mode of being is cathartic considering the psychical void that afflicts them. Instead of their character being shaped by a father's wisdom, instruction, and admonition, these youths tell tales of success (often fabricated) that place them in superior positions to mask the chagrin of being in what customarily is viewed as a subordinate status—fatherlessness. The stories are, in a word, desperate attempts to fill emotional and psychological gaps.

To my mind, this is one reason why social media is so popular. Youths can create profiles full of superlatives that garner respect in that cyber-space. In the late 1990's and early 2000's MySpace became a social media stronghold. Contemporarily, youths take to Facebook, Twitter, Instagram, and Snapchat. These sites allow them to forthwith evolve into social kings and queens, giants and titans, monsters and beasts. They mythologize their accomplishments and/or exploits. Since they understand the currency of youth culture, they can, "give the people what they want". Truth notwithstanding, the number of "likes" and followers that they accrue generates a false sense of celebrity that they relish. In regard to self-deification, their personally exalted position(s) feed the notion of the "impossibility of being wrong" that in their mind renders them god-like. It's a type of ego defense mechanism that assuages the postmodern youth's conscious and emotions and affords them a sense of hope that habitually revered institutions such as the family have failed to deliver. Rather than wait for the arrival of socio-culturally respected occasions for affirmation of development or transition into adulthood such as bar mitzvahs and coronations, postmodern youths generate their own encounters and celebrations. Tattoo and piercing parties, even dreadlocks (traditionally an African cultural expression, but increasingly growing in acceptance and trial among Caucasian youths) have become physical indicators of maturation, coming of age, peer acceptance, and religious/spiritual enlightenment.

Making Sense of It All

With regard to our evolving ideas about the postmodern youth, I observed that Gardner (2011) offered great insight with his recent addition to his theory of multiple intelligences—existential intelligence. Existential intelligence goes beyond the scope of what can be understood through sensory stimuli. It's one's ability to observe, comprehend, and explicate the presence of phenomena that surpasses their natural ability to perceive (Gardner, 2011). The theories and postulations of post-modern youth related to things ethereal or naturally incomprehensible can be unnerving for adults of older generations. Yet, their ideas offer postmodern youths a healthy neurological approach to confront prevailing social, political, and economic contradictions. In other words, this youth observes the world and concludes that some things just don't make sense. It's cognitive dissonance at a hyper level, especially among urban youths from historically disadvantaged communities. Cone (1997) argued that this state of mind is "existential absurdity", the disparity between the universe as one wishes it to be and as he sees it. A few examples of interrogatory postmodern considerations include but are not limited to the following questions:

Is there a such thing as universal truth?

1. Does God exist?
2. If religion is a good thing, then why has it influenced so many conflicts and wars?
3. If countries know the threat of nuclear warfare, then why is there a race to build nuclear weapons?
4. Why do rich countries have poor people?
5. Why do cities have dozens of vacant buildings and thousands of homeless people?

To some degree the postmodern youth is a 1960s child reincarnate. Akin to the flower children, this youth rejects the notion that what's always been is right because it's always been that way. The Occupy and #BlackLivesMatter movements are examples of millennials opting out of traditional ways of viewing institution and success and seeking other pathways to wholeness and social equilibrium. They've formed opinions and platforms. They've articulated and applied interpretations of rightness and wrongness. They've generated tenets and have determined to live according to their truth despite the consternation or criticism of those in the main. Besides, to their mind, the irrationality of their worldview is no more ridiculous than the "existential absurdity" (Cone, 1997, p. 24) of the present reality they were born into and are required, by default, to accept.

Post-soul

Another aspect of complexity related to urban African American youths is what Stokes (2010) referred to as a "Post-Soul" outlook. This dimension of the urban African American youth is similar in nature to the detachment observed with regard to the spiritual irreverence discussed previously. The deportment of the urban African American youth can often be attributed to a lack of esteem for the socio-cultural anchors that have long been part of their heritage. This stated, the "soul" tradition of African Americans is essentially an immixture of black Southern church religious values, black Southern hospitality and care, and the cultural expressions and nuances of black life in the Southern states (e.g., Tennessee, Mississippi, Arkansas, Louisiana, Georgia, etc.). The willingness to leave the old landmarks of African American heritage can be viewed as the result of failed cultural transmission. Or, very simply it could be that many urban African American youths perceive that the "stuff" of their parents' and grandparents' era is useless to help them negotiate urban life in the 21st century. Old school perspectives lose out to new school notions of family, freedom, right, and wrong.

For example, traditionally elders were viewed as community members worthy of honor. They didn't have to necessarily perform some great feat. Parents raised their children to show them respect for their role as senior members of the broader African American family. Presently, numerous parents allow their children to accord respect only to those who give respect. Hence, if an elder fails to show a youth respect, based on the youth's personal definition of respect, then that youth isn't obligated to respect the elder. This is but one example of a long-standing tenet in the unwritten social contract of the African American community. It hasn't been completely erased, but even that is debatable.

In sum, the lack of understanding of the dynamics of youth identity has created an ever-widening relational chasm and generational divide that threatens the prospects of collective action needed to improve our communities. Some scholars and teacher-researchers (Kafele, 2010; Rivera, 2009; Starratt, 2004) have even argued that failure to account for and address the cultural and community identities of urban youths has contributed to awful academic performance and other woeful statistics that reveal the psycho-social condition of urban youths of color in America. The collective at WNHS, at the behest of its leader, made a concerted effort to gain insight into the nature of the youth that it served. There were numerous discussions conducted. At times thought leaders in urban education were invited to share the latest in research and expound upon their observations and revelations. And of course, there was the daily interaction with the scholars. The WNHS collective engaged the same youth that was the object of their discussions. Thus, there was inquiry, conjecture, and action followed by analysis, evaluation, and eventually more discussion. Our aim was transformation. We intentionally focused on what was possible rather than immure ourselves in the limitation of what was obvious. Our students needed help. They were talented, but it many cases emotionally tattered. They had ideas about success, but were bereft of the insights needed to really make progress. They had energy, but they didn't always expend it in socially responsible ways. To reference Tupac Shakur, our scholars were roses mercilessly bound by tristful concrete realities (1999). It was our privilege to use our knowledge and compassion to help set them free.

Chapter 3

CLARIFYING HOPE

"Hope is being able to see that there is light despite all of the darkness."

-Archbishop Desmond Tutu

The literature related to hope is vast. In fact, this book could be an extensive elucidation on hope, associated factors, and its influence on various subpopulations. However, in an effort to help the reader acquire a useful definition and description of hope, I've decided to focus on the rudimentary aspects of hope theory. And, for the sake of this hope narrative, I've opted to share insights from the field that address the impact of hope in schools and among marginalized youths. The following literature review will provide the reader with a substantive introduction into the realm of hope.

Hope Theory

Snyder (2002), leading hope theorist, described hope as both a cognitive and an emotive phenomenon that provides tremendous aid in one's pursuit of a desired goal. Snyder further argued that hope is a reflection of "individuals' perceptions regarding their capacities to clearly conceptualize goals, develop the specific strategies to reach those goals (pathways thinking), and initiate and sustain the motivation for using those strategies (agency thinking)" (Snyder et al., 2003, p. 123). Snyder et al. (2006) described pathways thinking as "a person's belief that he or she can produce the mental routes or pathways to desired goals" (p. 90). Agency, per Snyder (2002) includes positive thinking or "the perceived capacity to use one's pathways to reach desired goals" (p. 251). Agency reveals itself attitudinally and verbally. Snyder (2002) indicated that agency thinking or agentic thought enlivens goal generation and implementation and is itself bolstered by self-affirming thoughts or positive self-talk (e.g., "I will succeed"; "Nothing can stop me"). Persons with immense hope frequently engage in agency thinking. They project strength in conversation and disposition. Moreover, individuals with a strong sense of agency are persuaded that their established goals are attainable because of the reasonableness of their selected pathway and their perception of capacity to succeed via the chosen route.

Interestingly, Bailey et al. (2007) found that agency was a strong predictor of life satisfaction. Further, Feldman et al. (2009) reported that agency strongly influences actual goal attainment more so than pathways thinking. Since individuals generally consider themselves successful when goals are attained; it is plausible to suggest that the finding by Feldman et al. (2009) supported Bailey et al.'s (2007) finding regarding agency and life satisfaction. All in all, goals, pathways, and agency produce hope and lead to attainment of a desired outcome (Howard, Butcher, & Egan, 2010; Snyder, 2002; Ward & Wampler, 2010). Snyder et al. (2002) expounded on the complex nature of hope:

"Hope, however, is not only a goal-oriented cognitive process. It also is a hierarchically organized system of beliefs regarding one's ability to successfully engage such a thought process. These beliefs are organized into three specific levels of abstraction: global or trait hope, domain-specific hope, and goal-specific hope." (p. 300)

Global or trait hope involves an individual's perception of their capacity to achieve a goal. It is the belief in the attainability of a goal, accurately expressed in the phrase, "I can do it if I want to". Domain-specific hope is the perception of one's ability to successfully achieve a goal in a certain life arena. For example, Olympic athletes may possess high global hope, but have low hope concerning marriage or family. Goal-specific hope is the belief that a particular goal is achievable. Persons with goal-specific hope may boast of being hopeful is a given context, yet express low hope regarding certain feats within that context. For example, an Olympic athlete may have high global and domain-specific hope, but believe that competitors from a certain country have an advantage because they train in high altitudes. Thus, the Olympic athlete may express low goal-specific hope.

In further discussion of the nature of hope, Snyder (1994; 2002) and others in the field (Chang & Banks, 2007; Meisenhelder, 1982; Shade, 2006; Smith, 2005; Yohani, 2008) maintained that considerable progress in understanding hope has been made, yet there's so much more to ascertain. Some (Grewal & Porter, 2007; Meisenhelder, 1982; Snyder, 2002) have argued that hopelessness—the antithesis of hope—helps to clarify the essence of hope and perhaps demystify some its less discernible features. For instance, individuals who have no goals and make no effort towards transcendence can be categorized as those in despair or self-consigned to hopelessness. Ironically, these individuals at times may suggest that they "hope" to do well, succeed, or have positive results in life. Smith (2005) considered this kind of verbalism obvious passivity that reduces the announcement of hope to fantasy due to the individual's refusal to act to bring about desired outcomes. Hence, they may have a wish, but not hope. Meisenhelder (1982) contended that those without hope, in this regard, embrace an ontological perspective that is more accurately defined as faith. Meanwhile, Snyder (2002) argued that an individual with this outlook may be a low-hope person, but not necessarily hopeless.

In respect to measurements of hope, Snyder (2002) observed that individuals with low-hope may possess a goal-orientation, but lack the requisite agency to fuel their pursuit of identified goals. Or, these individuals may be devoid of iterative pathways to reach the goals. In any case, no goal is attained because one or more elements of the hope triad [goals, pathways, and agency] are absent (Snyder, 2002; Snyder et al., 2006).

Myriad characteristics of individuals with low hope support this argument and provide insight. For example, Snyder (2002) observed that individuals with low-hope are generally inflexible to change and pessimistic about the future. They generate unclear or undefined pathways. Other characteristics of individuals with low hope include: emotionally negative, lethargic, apprehensive, easily encumbered by problems, avoidant of challenges, lonely, delusional, and incapable of unaided psychological adjustment. Conversely, Snyder (2002; Snyder et al., 2002; 2006) reported that individuals with high-hope are confident, decisive, buoyant, focused, constant, emotionally positive, and zealous. Individuals with high hope also readily embrace challenges and necessarily adjust to improve chances of attaining goals (Feldman et al., 2009; Snyder, 2002;

Snyder et al., 2002; 2006). Additionally, individuals with high hope demonstrate a propensity for confronting stressors and an ability to cope with serious illness and/or stress (Folkman, 2010; Snyder et al., 2006).

Ward and Wampler (2010) contributed to the discussion of individuals with low-hope and high-hope from a clinical and psychotherapeutic perspective. While investigating the utility of hope in marriage and family therapy, the authors found that individuals with high hope displayed a willingness and ability to overcome relationship challenges. Thus, Ward and Wampler (2010) concluded that several properties can help to determine an individual's level of hope: evidence, options, action, and connection. Evidence is a sign or marker in a marital relationship that suggests that a spouse is willing to adjust their behavior to achieve better relational outcomes. In this sense, evidence provides reason to develop or persist in hope. Options are related to pathways thinking in that it is the existence of and access to ways to reach desired outcomes. Action is the pursuit of a goal via a selected pathway or strategy. Connection highlights the element that brings two parties together and sustains their interaction (Howard, Butcher, & Egan, 2010; Grewal & Porter, 2007; Snyder, 2005; Yohani, 2008). Hence, hope is strengthened through "connection with other human beings" (p. 216).

Hope and Social Contexts

Social contexts influence hope (Folkman , 2010; Grewal & Porter, 2007; Yohani, 2008). With respect to race, Chang and Banks (2007) observed that ethnic groups experience hope differently. In an effort to accurately understand this finding, the authors compared the sense of agency and pathways thinking among Caucasians, Latinos, African Americans, and Asian

Americans. They also examined three other measures besides agency and pathways thinking: problem-solving, positive and negative effect, and life satisfaction. Chang and Banks (2007) reported low levels of life satisfaction among Latinos compared to the three other racial/ethnic groups and high levels of life satisfaction among African Americans compared to their Caucasian, Asian American, and Latino counterparts. African Americans, Latinos, and Asian Americans did not experience lower levels of hope when compared to their Caucasian counterparts. From this standpoint and parallel to Snyder (2002), the authors opined that this finding could be indicative of the need for historically disadvantaged groups to prepare for encounters with manifestations of systemic and racialized oppression (e.g., discrimination, language barriers, and limited medical services). Awareness of historical impediments and the anticipation of contemporary impediments prompt individuals from these communities to evade goal-setting, pathways thinking, and agentic thought. Incidentally, Caucasians reported low levels of hope compared to their Latino, Asian American, and African American counterparts. Chang and Banks (2007) suggested their report could be linked to perceptions of race-based privilege.

In further reference to the social dimension of hope, Yohani (2008) found that immersion into hope-filled environments can help children from oppressed minority communities transcend the horrors of their prior experience (Chang & Banks, 2007; Meisenhelder, 1982; Shade, 2006). Grewal and Porter's (2007) observed the opposite, that hopeless families often produced hopeless children. Snyder (2002) too investigated the influence of parents and families as it relates to the presence of hope in children. Snyder (2002) found that lack of parental/caregiver structure kills hope. In addition, Snyder (2002) noted other parent/family related "hope killers" among children including: imposition of goals by parents or caregivers; abandonment, physical abuse, and loss of parents/caregivers. Shade (2006) added that a community that fails to address the negative stressors that impact their lives (e.g., drugs, gangs, police brutality) kills hope among and within its children.

> *"A community that allows great disparities in the well-being of its members sends a sad message to children that they are not beneficiaries of the community's opportunities and so have little reason to trust the community or even identify themselves as its members." (p. 205)*

Adults also face hope killers. Among these are: loss of spouse, job loss, and victimization. Despite the gut-wrenching impact that these hope killers have on individuals both young and old, the literature (Davidson, Wingate, Slish, & Rasmussen, 2010; Howard, Butcher, & Egan, 2010; Moulden & Marshall, 2005; Shade, 2006; Snyder, 2002; 2005; Snyder et al., 2006; te Riele, 2010; Ward & Wampler, 2010; Yohani, 2008) advances the notion that healthy relationships (e.g., counselors, therapists, teachers, loved-ones) and healthy environments (e.g., community centers, schools, treatment facilities, places of worship, hospitals) introduce and nurture hope (Folkman, 2010).

Hope in Schools

Students with hope tend to excel academically across all levels of learning (e.g., K-12 and post-secondary) (Howard, Butcher, & Egan, 2010; Snyder et al., 2002; Snyder et al., 2003; Snyder, 2005; 2006). Teachers with hope develop hope in students through specific behaviors: enthusiastic instruction, listening, thoroughgoing planning, establishing clear objectives, and working with students on developing their own goals (Howard, Butcher, & Egan, 2010; Snyder, 2002; 2005; Snyder et al., 2002; Yohani, 2008). In respect to hope theory, Snyder et al. (2003) offered that K-12 teachers can introduce the practice of pathways thinking through a technique referred to as "stepping" (p. 129) or breaking down large goals into smaller, perhaps short-term goals.

Post (2006) made an equally cogent argument in favor of classrooms as sites for hope development. Drawing upon Snyder's (2002) earlier contention that teachers were purveyors of hope (2005), Post (2006) added that liberation is compatible with hope. Thus, teachers who supply hope are liberators. Further, Post (2006) stated that supplying hope in the classroom. First, students are able to see themselves as resources whereby they utilize their own skills and abilities and contribute to their own growth. Second, classroom conditions are created that help students recognize their own ends and means for pursuit. Third, teachers begin to understand the needs and desires of students and how to lead students in negotiating these with present realities. Fourth, students develop a desire to utilize what the talent and knowledge they possess.

Additional findings relative to K-12 educational spaces revealed that school support staff (e.g., social workers, psychologists, counselors) also contributed to the development of hope in students (Snyder et al., 2003). Specifically, Snyder et al. (2003) suggested that school psychologists can leverage their expertise amid external and internal school-community challenges by generating and promoting hope awareness in school environments. One strategy, noted the authors, is encouraging the development of agency thinking by facilitating or helping with journaling activities that emphasize the construction of self-affirming notes and thoughts. School psychologists can also foster hope in classrooms by working with teachers to create peer-learning opportunities that pair or group students together who otherwise would not choose to collaborate on their own. School psychologist commentary and contribution strongly influences the creation of sound student Individual Education Plan (IEP), particularly as it pertains to the facilitation of IEP goals.

Besides findings from the field regarding K-12 educational settings, researchers (Snyder, 2005; Snyder et al., 2002; 2006), reported higher achievement among college students who had hopeful instructors or instructors whose practice(s) made goal attainment easier. Examples of practices that fostered hope among college students included: "spending time and caring"; "setting goals for the class"; "creating pathways to class goals"; and "raising agency to pursue class goals". Listening was another hope-related instructional practice that influenced high achievement among college students.

Marginalized Students

Theory and literature related to student achievement suggests that inner-city students who live under deleterious conditions, particularly those who hail from historically disadvantaged communities, benefit from hope (Anyon, 1997; Duncan-Andrade, 2010; Shade, 2006; Yohani, 2008). Duncan-Andrade (2010) argued that educators who serve youths on the margins should be seriously committed to educational justice and supportive of the development of hope in the classroom. A stance of this magnitude asserted Duncan-Andrade (2010) helps many youths from historically disadvantaged communities withstand the poisons of toxic environments and thrive.

In further exploration of hope's complex nature, Duncan-Andrade (2010) articulated the notion of "critical hope", a transformative phenomenon revealed in three expressions: "material, Socratic, and audacious" (Duncan-Andrade, 2010, p. 185). Material hope is hope that is accessible to an individual in need. In educational settings; "material hope" richly enlivens the learning process. An example of such hope is teaching that connects curricula and pedagogy to the lived experiences of students (Duncan-Andrade, 2010; Duncan-Andrade & Morrell, 2008). Educators who exhibit this sort of leadership actually become "material hope", or as Snyder (2005) posited, "purveyors of hope" (p. 75) for students in desperate need of education that identifies with and responds to their urgent needs. Parallel to Duncan-Andrade's argument, Shade (2006) offered insight into educators and curriculum as ensamples of "material hope":

> *"Teachers can provide a telling example of a hopeful person by demonstrating habits of hope. A teacher's character, illuminated by the choices and actions he or she performs, sets a powerful example for students to follow...teachers can also deliberately integrate hope into the curriculum through the reading, writing, and telling of stories, especially those involving protagonists who overcome hardships." (pp. 207, 208)*

"Socratic hope" is the willingness of educators to "practice what they preach". It is the decision to critically reflect upon the "winters" (Palmer, 2000, p. 102) of one's life and endure the consequent pain produced by such contemplative moments. Further, "Socratic hope" compels individuals to grow, advance, and affect change personally, communally, and societally in response to their contemplation. It views misery, pain, and wrath as useful teachers—whether in unison or

separately—capable of catalyzing agency and radical transformation (Duncan-Andrade, 2010). Students' belief in a brighter
future is strongly linked to educators with "Socratic hope".
These are educators who recognize that their ability to engage
students in "winter" (Palmer, 2000, p. 102) fuels growth and
eventuates in transcendence.

"Audacious hope" is the readiness to share in the plight
of suffering communities despite the threat of personal loss
(Duncan-Andrade, 2010). "Audacious hope" resists policies,
structures, and institutional apparatuses that delimit human
potential. Educators with "audacious hope" are determined to
pursue justice and liberation in spite of inevitable danger. They
are willing to pay the price for student healing and student
freedom, knowing that the investment will yield tremendous
outcomes for students, in and out of the classroom.

te Riele (2010) also maintained that hope is a critical
resource for students from the edges of society, those who are
"marginalized, disadvantaged or excluded", (p. 35). te Riele
(2010) explained that schools in historically disadvantaged
communities and/or schools that serve children from historically disadvantaged communities should adopt a philosophy
of hope. According to te Riele (2010), a philosophy of hope
is an approach to education that canonizes hope and seeks to
infuse it into every aspect of school culture, operation, and
practice. To this point, te Riele (2010) expressed concern that
hope is oversimplified in schools, too often limited to narratives
of individuals who overcome tremendous socio-ecological dis-
advantages (Duncan-Andrade, 2010). In lieu of providing scant
doses of hope, te Riele (2010) argued that a philosophy of hope
in schools should be robust and rich, providing marginalized
students authentic opportunities to obtain hope and utilize its
features for personal ascent and social justice.

Akin to Duncan-Andrade (2010) and te Riele (2010), Shade (2006) argued that urban students who constantly face violent and impoverished living conditions benefit from environments that embrace and promote hope from a pragmatic standpoint. According to Shade (2006), schools can be communities of hope that empower students from communities trammeled by structural and materials inequities to stand in defiance of the status quo. Shade (2006) defined a community of hope as, "one that is committed to promoting the development of habits of hope in its members...when its activities and structures promote hopes, students themselves become participating members of a community of hope, helping to foster hope in the next generation." (pp. 199-200). And, as inherently relational contexts, schools can cultivate hope by weaving habits of hope into their culture, curricula, conventions, and customs. Specifically, Shade (2006) explained that persistence, courage, and resourcefulness are hopeful habits. Characteristics associated with persistence include: patience, self-control, trust, attentiveness, and humility. The willingness to act is associated with courage. Characteristics associated with resourcefulness include flexibility and enthusiasm for exploring personal intelligence and novel ideas. Per Shade (2006), hopefulness emerges from the union and interplay of these three habits.

"The habits of hope we develop and coordinate in pursuing particular hopes can thus enable us to transcend antecedent limitations and failed ends. Pragmatic hoping, then, is practical both in promoting realizable ends and developing the sustaining powers of hopefulness." (Shade, 2006, p.198)

Encapsulation

Hope is a human phenomenon that is often and easily misunderstood. Most people presume that hope is a mere feeling or a belief. But, in reality hope is much more complex. Snyder (2002) argued that hope is a bi-dimensional phenomenon that includes intellect and emotion. And as such, hope can be reproduced, studied, measured, and assessed. With respect to teaching and learning, Snyder et al. (2006) observed that hope, as a human strength, can be taught to students. How? Well, Snyder (2002) articulated that hope is distinguished from other social-emotional manifestations due to its necessitation of action relative to some present impediment. In other words, hope is not passive. It is not simply a desire for a good outcome to overtake a bad circumstance. Hope includes the belief that a good outcome is possible and the will to pursue steps that will lead to the realization of a favorable outcome.

Shade (2006) asserted that children who hail from impoverished, crime-stricken, violent neighborhoods must overcome the hazardous realities of their environments in order to succeed in school and in life. In this instance, the obstacle is the toxic social environment. And, hope is required for transcendence. Snyder (2002) would argue that children in this instance need to be taught how to hope. He'd argue that teachers can introduce and raise hope by teaching these children how to: a) set goals; b) devise pathways or strategies to reach those goals; and c) exhibit agency or the conspicuous belief in their selected pathways. Additional scholars in the field (Duncan-Andrade, 2010; Post, 2006; te Reile, 2010) attested to the value and impact of raising hope among youths on the margins. I too advance the notion that hope works for youths beset by myriad socio-ecological impediments. I too make the claim that youths should be taught the concept of *hoping*.

Chapter 4:

THE PEOPLE

(Part One)

"Those who are hopeful experience as many frustrations and disappointments as anyone else, but they're better equipped to withstand them and thus keep on for the long haul."

—Paul Loeb

I n this book's introduction, I provided a brief summation of the research process that I engaged in during my quest to understand hope from the viewpoint of the scholars I served. To help connect my subsequent revelations with the work, I've provided a recap of the research process. My intention in this chapter is to reveal the primary and secondary themes that emerged and to expound upon certain findings that were especially striking.

The purpose of the research study," *Never Giving Up: A Phenomenological Study of Hope in African American Students in a Small Urban Public High School*", was to examine the influence of hope in the lives of several urban African American high school students who attended an urban public high school that served predominantly marginalized urban African

American youths. The objectives of this research study were to develop a more accurate understanding of the characteristics of students with hope and to determine if student's enrollment at the school contributed to how they experienced hope. The related research question was: In what ways do students who attend WNHS experience hope? Three subquestions supported the investigation and paved the way for more incisive discussions:

- What are the characteristics of students who experience hope?
- How do students at WNHS describe their experience as it relates to hope?
- What aspects of WNHS do the students attribute to their experience with hope?

With regard to methodology, I opted for phenomenology, the investigative attempt to describe the meaning of a phenomenon based on the accounts of multiple individuals' lived experiences (Creswell, 2010). Interviews were utilized to collect data from 10 students, five African American boys and five African American girls. Each student participated in one interview. Interview questions were structured to gain insight into student definitions of hope; descriptions of individuals with hope; life-goals; and experiences while attending the small urban public high school, which listed hope as a core value of the school program.

The interview participants were identified, recruited, and selected based on completion of a routine WNHS critical thinking assignment—"Conscious Reflections". "Conscious Reflections" were designed to sharpen student's comprehension skills and draw upon their lived experiences to encourage social awareness and reflection. In the "Conscious Reflection" used for this project, students were asked to define hope, describe a person with hope, and to discuss if/how they were raised to think about hope. Following Snyder's (2002) treatment of high-hope individuals, I generated a rubric that listed 15 different characteristics of high-hope individuals to help determine which WNHS students were hopeful and which students would subsequently be intriguing candidates for recruitment into the research project.

Student responses were vetted based upon three categories: present, not present, and unclear. If a student's response mentioned or had traces of a high-hope characteristic, the researcher placed an "X" in the "present" space. Students whose responses indicated the presence of eight or more high-hope characteristics were targeted and recruited for interview participation. Thus, the students in this study were among those whose responses indicated the presence of eight or more high-hope characteristics.

Concerning post-interview data analysis, I utilized Creswell's (2010) phenomenological method which by his admission is derived from an analytic approach followed by Moustakas (1994). I initially completed a reflection that whereby I described my experience with hope. This activity, also referred to as *epoche* or bracketing, is a step in the analytic protocol where the researcher attempts to identify and suspend any biases, assumptions, and prejudgments that can hinder objectivity. The reflection also included mention of concerns or fears (Creswell, 2010). Next, I thoroughly read and reviewed all interview transcripts and generated a list of significant statements from each. Statements recorded during this phase of analysis, referred to as horizonalization of the data, were derived from the text or direct interviewee quotes.

Once a list of significant statements was developed, I reviewed the statements and translated them into formulated meanings which were then used along with interviewee quotes to craft subthemes or "meaning units". After examining the meaning units, both a textual description (what happened when the interviewees experienced the phenomenon) of the informants' experience and a structural description of the informants' experience (where, when, how often) began to emerge. The revelations were recorded in the form of dominant themes and subthemes. Together, they comprised a narrative of the essence of students' lived experience with hope.

Findings

The students in this research project provided significant insight into the way in which some urban African American high school students experience hope. Although the context and concomitant scenarios varied, several themes emerged from student discussions. (All but one of the ten students who participated in the research project self-identified as an individual with hope. One student was unsure if they were genuinely hopeful.) Initially, students discussed hope in terms and phraseology that suggested a perception of hope as an emotive and cognitive phenomenon that motivates individuals to pursue a desired end. Specific terms or statements shared that were related to human emotions included: "feeling"; "boost"; "power"; and "positive outlook". Students expressed the cognitive dimension of hope through the use of action phrases such as "sticking to it"; "keep you going"; "never giving up"; or "striving for the best".

The students also spoke of individuals who they considered hopeful and described some of the glowing characteristics that these persons possessed. Though not expressed in explicit terms; the sum of students' remarks about hopeful individuals revealed twelve specific characteristics: motivation, encouragement (social support), optimism, resilience, focus, constancy, awareness, vision, determination, sense of urgency, adaptable, and goal-centered. These discussions produced the first theme of the study—**"Disposition"**. All of the study participants voiced and demonstrated an intransigent attitude when they discussed their understanding of hope and their relationship with hope. It became clear that students with hope, particularly urban African American students on the margins, possessed a specific disposition. For the purpose of this study, the researcher defined disposition as "an inner strength or attitude that gives an individual impetus to advance, particularly when faced with opposition" (Arrington, 2014, p.395). In fact, the trials and impediments that the students reported or alluded to helped to explain why a distinctive disposition was necessary.

A second emergent theme in the study was, **"People and Places Matter"**. Examination and contemplation of student descriptions, recollections, and explanations revealed that these students experienced hope through interpersonal relationships and relationships with, or access to, institutions. In reference to interpersonal relationships, students discussed the influence of parents, siblings, extended family members, peers, and educators. Characteristics exhibited by these individuals included: fortitude, listening, transparency, goal-oriented, optimism, consistency, authenticity, growth-mindedness, and life-affirming values. Additionally, students explained that when interacting with their persons of influence, they observed hope in/through specific elements including: conversations, listening, stories, lifestyles, and successes. For these WNHS students, the behavior and attitude of those deemed hopeful, particularly in the midst of hardship, provided examples of what it meant to possess hope. Students also discussed the importance of access to institutions. Institutions that were mentioned included: church, college or universities, community centers, and a non-profit organization. Resources and benefits associated with these institutions included: partnerships, programs, service opportunities, recreation, links to careers, and safety.

While students praised the value of the aforementioned institutions as places with critical resources that could assist them with their pursuit of life-goals, some expounded on a particular place that could potentially hinder the apprehension of their life-goals—the ghetto (In this context, ghetto is used in reference to inner city neighborhoods mired by poverty and violence. A subtheme that emerged within the context of the second theme, "People and Places Matter", was "Avoiding Negativity". Some of the students perceived their neighborhoods as hazardous spaces. Elements associated with the ghetto included: deviant people (i.e., bad influences), poverty, crime, drugs, and destructive retail (e.g., liquor stores). More than personal weaknesses, these students perceived the ghetto as the most significant threat to their well-being and attainment of life-goals.

The third theme that emerged from the study was **"The Power of Reflection".** Two subthemes associated with this dominant theme were "Faith" and "Discovering Self". Interestingly, student discussions in relation to this theme maintained a relationship context. For example, when sharing on faith, a few students mentioned interpersonal relationships with parents or family. Church was discussed in reference to relationship or access to important institutions. Regarding "Discovering Self", students discussed the influence of family members and other key individuals citing critical conversations with these persons as a factor that prompted them to begin their journey towards change and experience with hope. In the study, I referred to this event as a "turning point". A "turning point" is a moment or occasion when an individual, based on the critical nature of their circumstance(s), decides to part with familiar ways of thinking and comfortable modes of behavior and instead opts for new ways of thinking and behaving that increase the prospect of obtainment of favorable outcomes.

"Elements of WNHS" was the final theme. Students discussed ways in which WNHS promoted hope. Two sub-themes associated with "Elements of WNHS" were "Online Expediency" and "WNHS Staff". First, students highlighted online learning as a modality that helped them to recover high school credits and obtain high school graduation (the primary goal). Increased concentration and accessibility were cited as the primary benefits of enrollment in online courses. Second, students repeatedly mentioned WNHS staff members (e.g., teachers, administrators) as individuals that helped them experience hope. Students perceived that WNHS staff genuinely cared for them. Besides students' perception of significant care from WNHS Staff, they discussed the value of lessons shared by WNHS staff. Examples of lessons shared by WNHS staff included topics such as healthy social interaction; building community; the power of self-determination; positive thinking; the necessity of change; regard for human concern; and self-regulation. Students also articulated specific messages that rang loudly as part of many of these lessons. They included: "believe in yourself"; "be the best you can be"; "anything is possible"; "stay focused"; and "don't doubt yourself".

Figure 4
Final Themes Related to WNHS Students and their
Experience with Hope

Theme	Subthemes	Commentary
Disposition of Students with Hope	1. *Facing fears* 2. *Unwavering optimism* *Refusal to quit*	*Students were resolute in their decision to pursue goals, impediments notwithstanding.*
People and Places Matter	1. *Significant relationships* 2. *Avoiding negativity*	*Each student linked their view of hope to a human or community resource.*
The Power of Reflection	1. *Faith* 2. *Discovering self*	*These two were crucial as it related to turning points in students' lives.*
Elements of WNHS	1. *Online expediency* 2. *WNHS Staff*	*Each student saw a connection between their current view of hope and their experience with these two aspects.*

(Arrington, 2014)

Sources of Hope

This research project confirmed the report from the field (Duncan-Andrade, 2010; Shade, 2006; Yohani, 2008) that marginalized youths benefit from social contexts that promote hope. More pointedly, this study advanced the notion that hope and/or experiences with hope are introduced and enhanced by key individuals as well as access to institutions that feature critical resources that meet students' needs. Though data were collected from a small sample of WNHS' students, the manner in which students conveyed their thoughts about hope suggested that many more inner-city youths of color could attest to their perspectives.

The People

Interestingly, within the conversation about experiences with hope, students consistently reified the construct by referring to an individual. It was as if they perceived that hope and these individuals were synonymous. In the study, I referred to these folks as persons of influence. Among the persons of influence were parents, siblings, extended family members, a friend, and an educator. Reports offered by study participants indicated that they had been witnesses of the ability of these persons of influence to withstand hardship and actually move forward towards life-goals. The behavior and attitude of the loved ones discussed was inspirational and in effect left an indelible imprint of what hope looked like in the minds of the students.

At the time of the study, I reviewed remarks shared by the study participants in relation to characteristics of people with hope. Specific attributes began to emerge that described their view of a person with hope. In total, 12 attributes were identified as being related to individuals with hope: motivation, encouragement (social support), optimism, resilience, focus, constancy, awareness, vision, determination, sense of urgency, adaptable, and goal-centered. Now granted, one doesn't have to possess all 12 characteristics to be deemed "hope-filled", but the study participants' commentary certainly indicated that an individual who hopes possesses more than one of the attributes. The figure below provides insight into specific phraseology shared by some of the study participants when they talked about hope and the kind of attitude or activity exhibited by one who hopes. These phrases are also linked to the 12 emergent attributes.

Figure 5

Characteristics of Persons with Hope

Student Name	Description	Characteristics
Brian	• *Faith in the future* • *Just keep going* • *Blank out everything*	• *Motivation* • *Encouragement* • *Resilience* • *Optimism* • *Focus*
Za'nya	• *Doesn't ignore the obvious* • *Set they sights on something bigger* • *Looks at the good in the situation*	• *Awareness* • *Vision* • *Optimism*
Tariq	• *A positive person* • *Always looking at the bright side* • *Keep the negative stuff away*	• *Optimism*
Casey	• *Willing to go through whatever* • *Get up and keep trying* • *Don't give up easily*	• *Adaptable* • *Sense of urgency* • *Determination* • *Goal-centered*

(Arrington, 2014)

Although the students provided generalities of people with hope, I interpreted their descriptions to be implicitly connected to their perceptions of self. In other words, I discerned that some of these students believed that they'd already incorporated the above attitudes and actions in their personal behavioral repertoire. Or, they had come to the realization that they needed to make the attitudinal and behavioral adjustments relative to the given phrases. One of the students, Brian, whom you'll learn more about later in chapter five, shared thoughts that support this claim:

> *"Uh, I went to jail a couple times. I'm still on probation. I'm supposed to get off in March...It just gave me time to think. You know I'm in here, with all these boys, all these people that ain't doing nothing. They ain't going to school. They in here with me and I'm just wit em'. So that got me thinking like man. Basically that's all it do. It just gave me time to think about where I'm at and how foolish I was to get in this predicament. I realized soon as I get outta here, I gotta get on my stuff... I'm confident in myself. I just, I know to get to where I want to be, I just gotta work out. It's just been times that I just slipped just put no effort into it. But, if I just choose to put effort into it and you know do what I'm supposed to do, I know I can do what I wanna do. I just gotta bring myself to want to work that hard."*

In respect to the "Power of Reflection", incarceration forced Brian to consider his ways. It also helped him to evaluate his life trajectory. Brian witnessed other young men who seemed to not engage in the same kind of reflection that he'd put himself through, and he resolved that change was necessary. Another study participant named Za'Nya also shared thoughts indicative of her recognition of the need to make significant changes. Unlike Brian, Za'Nya hadn't experienced incarceration, but she had sunk to depths of despondency and academic underachievement. In the commentary below, Za'Nya recalled the in-take meeting that I conducted and the contemplation that followed.

"Um, like I said before I was done with school as a sophomore, ready to give up and say, "I'm not doing this no more. I'm throwing in the towel. Ima do what I want to do from now on, no question about school and everything else like that. Um, then I came here. I had a meeting with Arrington and it's like a light clicked in my head. Like Za'Nya, what is you doing? You know this has to be done. You know that you have to graduate. You know that this is a must. Like, why you sleeping on yourself? And um, I mean when I got enrolled and I started coming I started believing that. You know you told me. You said, You smart and you don't need to not be in school and I'm like okay. I'm listening to him. I'm hearing him, but I want to see it for myself and then as the weeks went by I'm like yeah, this what I needed."

Za'Nya's revelation about what she needed and what she could possibly achieve underscores a major idea of this book; that hope is contagious and that it should be spread abroad. Moreover, her story as well as the stories of the other study participants confirmed that many youths on the margins want to succeed. They only need individuals, hopers, who can help them see themselves beyond their stains, warts, and wounds. These youths need to be surrounded by those who believe in them and who are equally willing to show them how to achieve favorable outcomes, no matter what they decide to pursue. The remainder of this chapter will provide insight into the impact that parents and parent-like figures had on these youths view of hope.

Parents

Among the 10 study participants, Casey, an African American female, was the only student that remotely mentioned the influence of two parents in her description of her experience with hope. Casey was an 18 year old African American female student at WNHS during the time of the research project. She entered WNHS as a chronic truant and academic underachiever.

One of Casey's older brothers, Malcolm, had graduated from WNHS. He also entered WNHS as an academic bottom-feeder. With lots of love, listening, and accountability, the staff at WNHS was able to help Malcolm complete high school. Knowing the depths to which he sank prior to WNHS, Casey's parents viewed the school as the answer for her situation. Malcolm was loud and at times obnoxious. Casey on the other hand was typically reticent. Malcolm was bothersome. Casey often moved in stealth-like fashion. Sometimes we didn't even know she'd arrived at school. Casey liked to sit in corner seats where she could have some privacy. When she did talk, she was usually soft-spoken.

Despite their participation at the time of her enrollment, Casey's parents became less and less involved over time. When Casey participated in the interview, she revealed that she was no longer living with her parents. Her commentary was not detailed at all so I couldn't discern the unique impact of either parent. But, what's clear is that Casey recognized her mother and father as individuals who encouraged her to succeed. When asked to talk about her experience with hope, Casey responded:

> *"How I was raised to think about hope is...oka, well, my parents never said stuff directly like this is what hope is. They told me stuff like believe in yourself, if you fail don't give up, stuff like that. And, that's how I*

*started believing in myself like okay if I believe I can
do it, I can do it, whatever it was."*

At this point in this report, it's important to engage in a brief
sidebar to again clarify the essence of Hope Theory. Remember,
according to Snyder (2002) hope requires three elements: goals,
pathways or strategies, and agency. It also includes the presence of some impediment or obstacle. Of course, the study
participants didn't know or understand this to be the case initially. And certainly, the folks that they regarded as having pivotal roles in their experience(s) with hope didn't have a clue
about Hope Theory. So, I'm not ridiculing their lack of knowledge. My intention is to more pointedly help readers understand the subjective nature of the forthcoming accounts. Sure,
Hope Theory has its aspect of empiricism and strict tenets, but
"everyday people" don't care about data and official academic
lexicon. The students didn't care about that. Could they apprehend the concepts? Absolutely. But overall, when people are in
crisis or overcome by issues of life, they want and need to know
that everything will eventually be okay. They need to know that
better is possible. They need to know that people can conquer
challenges similar to their own. And, in their lived experiences,
the people that these students talked about were purveyors of
consolation. For them, that was/is hope.

In respect to Hope Theory, the advisement of Casey's
parents was lacking. Yes, they provided encouragement and
attempted to stoke the flames of Casey's agency, but Casey
never discussed her parents' talks about goals and strategies.
Therefore, what her parents offered was a family-specific version of hope. That was fine because those conversations resonated with Casey. Those words were thought seeds planted in
the fertile soil of her mind.

Surely, Casey's scenario was the exception. Predominantly, *mothers* were mentioned whenever the students shared their experiences with hope. For example, Dawn, an African American female student at WNHS explained how she relished the ease with which she could converse with her mom. Dawn shared how she cherished heart-to-heart talks with her mother:

"Um, when she talks to me. Um, she just, it's just how and what she presents, what she's trying to tell us and whatever. So, it's in how she says it and her action that she has hope."

The guidance that Dawn received when she talked to her mother was refreshing to her. Specifically, Dawn reflected upon the "how" and the "what" of her mother's conversation. Her description drew upon—whether directly or indirectly—the old adage, "It's not what you say. It's how you say it". It was very obvious that Dawn found great value in the content of their talks and the manner in which her mother chose to speak to her.

Another African American female student, Za'Nya, passionately communicated the importance of her relationship with her mother:

"My momma. Without her I wouldn't even have life-goals. I would be just like any other bum on the street not doing nothing, not wanting to do nothing, not dreaming about nothing. Like I said, she really influenced me…"

I recall that during the interview with this scholar, tonality was a significant factor in her responses. For instance, the first two words, "My momma", were stated with a kind of emphasis that conveyed extreme gratitude towards and extreme need for her mother. When she said those first two words, there was a pause, as if that's all that needed to be said, "My momma". In other words, any discussion with Za'Nya about hope could be encapsulated in that simple phrase. Za'Nya's remarks put forth a binary of sorts when she stated, "Without her I wouldn't even have life-goals. I would be just like any other bum on the street not doing nothing..." Sure, her comment was laced with some assumptions about "bums on the street". Nonetheless, Za'Nya's words were rooted in a perception about those who are action-oriented and those who are stagnant in life. To her mind, you either have goals as evidenced by some kind of forward progress or you're a bum. Later on in the interview I gained more insight into the rationale that supported Za'Nya's "bum" reference. She specifically pointed out her sophomore year in high school (prior to arriving at WNHS) as a time when like a "bum", she was "not doing nothing".

"Um, like I said before I was done with school as a sophomore, wanting to be done with school as a sophomore, ready to give up and say, "I'm not doing this no more. I'm throwing in the towel. Ima do what I want to do from now on, no question about school and everything else like that."

Za'Nya revealed that it was her mother's idea to enroll her in WNHS. She convinced Za'Nya to give the school a chance. Za'Nya's success at WNHS and eventual graduation from WNHS contributed to her appreciation for her mother. Her mother helped Za'Nya help herself. She helped Za'Nya overcome "bum" status. Za'Nya's mother helped her keep her dreams alive.

Of the African American young men who participated in the research project, two commented on the significance of their mother, but only one directly commented on the influence of his mother as it related to the development of a sense of hope. Jameel was a 19 year old adjudicated youth. He didn't officially meet WNHS's enrollment criteria. He was not referred to WNHS because of recent incarceration, expulsion, chronic truancy, or extreme credit deficiency. Jameel was an "Other", but not in the offensive sense of the term. A relative who had a positive experience at WNHS told Jameel about the program, and it stirred his curiosity, "I had a cousin that went here and he told me about the school, so I just decided to come and see for myself." Although Jameel didn't bear the same "marks" (e.g., recent incarceration, expulsion, chronic truancy, or extreme credit deficiency) of many WNHS students, he hailed from a single-parent home which was very common among WNHS scholars. Jameel credited his mother and grandmother with helping him to rebound from past mistakes and focus on making healthy life-choices, "Yeah, I heard about hope from my grandmomma, you know she a church lady. My momma... just like my social surroundings I guess..."

When I enrolled Jameel, he stated that he wanted to attend WNHS because he believed the school could help him rebound from prior years of classroom carelessness and lack of academic productivity during his early high school years. During the interview, Jameel reflected on this time, "People was telling me that ain't nothin' gon come from what you doin' so when I actually seen it happen I'm like my family right. My momma always told me, but I was just hard-headed." Consistency in poor decision-making did lead to a period of incarceration for Jameel. While he was incarcerated, he came to a turning point…"Like when I first went to jail, I just had time to think. People tell you…I had time to think."

Jameel's interview was refreshing and insightful. Despite the frequent insertions of the colloquial, "You know what I'm sayin?", a phrase so common among many youth in the hip hop generation, Jameel's remarks represented what some may consider an urban contradiction. Jameel featured the classic look of a "boy in the hood" or a "dude from the block". Some may call it "ghetto aesthetics". He had numerous tattoos. He sported a grill at times. He had dreadlocks. And, he wore jeans, a T-shirt, and a hooded sweater. There was nothing fundamentally wrong with Jameel's fashion selection, but sadly his appearance would concern some citizens. Some would observe Jameel's attire and label him a thug. Isn't that what happened to Trayvon Martin? Didn't he have on jeans and a hooded sweater? Unbeknownst to those who would certainly prejudge Jameel and impugn his character based on his look, his aspirations and mentality surpassed the typical survival-based parameters of many of the inner-city boys that I'd worked with. Jameel understood the shallow nature of social interaction and observance in mainstream society, yet he rejected any notion of being limited because of his appearance. He commented:

"Like because how I look. You know what I'm sayin'? I got a lot of tattoos and all that. And everybody that look like me they think that they thuggin' or gang-bangin' so-called or drug dealin'. I mean I wanna be the person that little kids look up to even though I got a hood image. I still wanna have knowledge behind that, you know what I'm sayin?"

As I listened to Jameel's social analysis and what I perceived to be his desire for transcendence, I became excited. I couldn't wait to hear him talk about his mother and how she helped him experience hope. When Jameel shared, I discerned an emphasis on the emotive dimension of hope.

"She don't never give up on nothing. When she was...I mean she ain't never showed us that she was struggling, but you know I seen her you know what I'm saying. She always said, "hope for the best, wish for the best, pray for the best". She was always telling me don't give up and always hope for the best."

During the interview with Jameel, he described his mother as one who wouldn't give up. Interestingly, his observation of her moxie in the face of adversity was consistent with his definition/description of hope. He stated that having hope meant never giving up and continuing to move ahead. Watching Jameel as he spoke and listening to his choice of words, I sensed that Jameel and his siblings derived strength from witnessing his mother's drive. In particular, I was struck by his remark, "I mean she ain't never showed that she was struggling, but you know I seen her..." This comment from Jameel indicated that to some degree his mother attempted to disguise or hide the reality of the impact that tough times were having on her. Now, Jameel didn't mention how old he was at the time, but whatever the age, he was able to see that his mother, though successful given their circumstances, was worn in some psychological, emotional, or even physical manner. That, for Jameel, was hope.

The Faith of My Mother…and Godparents

Incidentally, in discussing the influence of mothers, a synonymous relationship between faith and hope was broached by one of the participants. Amber, a member of the WNHS graduating class of 2011, agreed to participate in the research project because she supported the mission of WNHS. Amber was by far the most engaging and bubbly student among the study participants. Amber was a true criteria student with the antecedents typical of many WNHS students (e.g., African American, single-parent home, poverty, adult-like responsibilities, etc.). At first Amber enrolled as a junior, but due to discrepancies with the validity of her credit status, she was officially regarded as a sophomore.

Amber's story is one of educational disengagement. Before coming to WNHS, Amber attended a couple large high schools, but she rarely went to class. Amber became a chronic truant. At one point, Amber ironically attended the same high school that her mother worked in, and she still had spotty attendance! Amber's extreme disinterest in school and concerns about the suitability of the school environment compelled Amber's mother to attempt home-schooling. When issues arose related to the state's grading protocols, the home-school plan was scrapped. Amber began to sink. In her mind, school was optional rather than obligatory. She didn't take it seriously. It became obvious that the traditional school setting was a mismatch for Amber. She needed a more appropriate learning environment.

> *"And something was wrong with me. I just didn't want to stay in a school. I just didn't find the school that was just…Stone Creek, nah, so I left in the middle of the semester thinking it was okay because Focus was going to accept me and so yeah Focus and KTI. Then,*

Piedmont came and I stayed there for a year and I like it, but you know it wasn't...I just didn't go to school. To be honest, I was mad. I knew I wasn't going to get held responsible if I didn't go to school. I could pretty much do what I want so why not stay home and talk to my boyfriend and do whatever else I wanted to do during the day cuz I'm already a year behind in school. And, I just felt hopeless (laughter), but I didn't realize I was feeling hopeless. I just thought it was me trying to be cool or something, but it was me feeling like dang is it even possible for me to graduate?"

Fortunately, WNHS was a space of respite for Amber. When asked what the school meant to her, Amber replied, "I was dead before I came to Woodson-Newton. This school brought me back to life". Admittedly, Amber had become an academic wastrel. Despite their love for her, Amber's family members weren't always reliable sources of accountability and inspiration. Thus, the staff members at WNHS became Amber's extended family. When reflecting on her pre-WNHS years, Amber considered her previous underachievement infantile and totally unacceptable, "I still don't know why I never really went to school. I just was...I just didn't, but Woodson-Newton literally changed that for me, literally."

Amber's discussion about her experience with hope was just as interesting and curious as her biographical informa-tion. Knowingly or unknowingly, Amber used language that suggested that hope and faith were the same phenomenon. Her experience with hope was largely enswathed in a context of religious activity and prayer. In other words, Amber wit-nessed her mother utilize prayer as a strategy to attain goals (prayer request).

"My mother and her mother, called out and prayed when they needed something from God. When it was tough you know? When somebody got locked up or somebody was sick, but I never heard them pray out when it was just a normal day, when everything was going good. Umm, I don't know how I feel about that because everything I know, everything I can think of about hope results in faith and I don't know like it kinda seemed like they did have faith in God like well they know who to call on like when I'm a baby I cry out to my mother because I know she's gonna be the one who picks me up and make sure my boo-boo is alright. But, it was something missing, and I still don't know how I feel about that honestly because it kinda taught me that I couldn't or I didn't have to lean on God all of the time as if faith wasn't needed every day. Like it wasn't needed. Like anything can happen, any day and I guess it's kinda easy to have hope…I don't know if I can say faith and hope is the same thing, I don't know…like when…even now I think it's a bad habit my mother and grandmother taught me… to pray when or like cry out when you need something and read the Bible, then go to church because I feel like I do the same thing now. I'm almost ashamed when it's time for me to pray to God because I haven't prayed in like two weeks and here I'm praying about this test…."

For Amber, having faith meant having hope. And, why not? A very popular bible verse, Hebrews 11:1 declares, "Faith is the substance of things hoped for; the evidence of things not scene." Further, both faith and hope require belief beyond that which is tangible and observable. And, it can be argued that there is interplay between the two constructs. In fact, Jenmorri (2006) and Myers (2009) reasoned that faith and hope are related, lexical siblings perhaps. When faced with the need to confront personal obstacles and surmount contextual impediments introduced or sustained by societal forces, both faith and hope are necessary (Jenmorri, 2006). For instance, in review of the literature regarding hope, despair, and trauma therapy, Jenmorri (2006) found that exploration of faith traditions and/ or spiritual philosophies can be stimulated by traumatic events. And in cases where persons allowed themselves to become grounded in hope, selection of a personally viable faith tradition or spiritual philosophy soon followed. Jenmorri (2006) also observed that, "a spiritual philosophy and spiritual practices may nourish a practitioner's hope and soften the intensity of despair and other aspects of secondary traumatization" (p. 50). Coincidentally or perhaps not, Jenmorri (2006) observed that work with the traumatized can impair faith, reduce the importance of spiritual philosophies, and/or cast practitioners into despair.

Since the literature revealed that hope and faith have a more symbiotic than antithetical relationship, Amber's interchangeable use of the words was understandable. Her purported philosophical flux about prayer as a pathway to a goal was also understandable. Inconsistency in the use of prayer caused Amber to question it's utility, "but I never hear them pray out when it was just a normal day, when everything was going good... it was something missing, and I still don't know how I feel about that honestly because it kinda taught me that I couldn't, I couldn't or I didn't have to lean on God all of the time as if faith wasn't needed every day". It appeared that prayer was always linked to a desperate appeal to achieve relief from some trial or tragedy. Again, since Amber viewed hope and faith in the same manner, her observational takeaway was that hope was only relevant when emergencies occurred. Once emergencies were addressed or mitigated, hope was no longer important. In truth, Amber wasn't with her mother and grand-mother 24/7, so it stands to reason that she was not privy to prayers offered during favorable seasons and moments. Yet, the impact of what Amber did witness left a major imprint on her mind and shaped her perception—albeit a bit twisted—of hope. Amber's experience strengthened the argument that parents have considerable influence as it relates to introducing hope to and raising hope among children.

Chapter 5

THE PEOPLE

(Part Two)

The ancient African proverb, "It takes a village to raise a child" is often quoted and appropriated when individuals discuss efforts to improve life outcomes for young people. From genuine, compassionate community activists to camera-friendly, campaigning politicians, leaders have drawn upon this wisdom. Whether the person uttering this truism is sincere or sinister, it remains true. Parents cannot successfully raise children alone.

Elite writer, Malcolm Gladwell, alluded to the influence of the village on the success of children by telling the stories of some of the world's best and brightest thinkers, entertainers, and persons of notable repute. In his book *Outliers: The Story of Success*, Gladwell (2008) spoke of the social context or social environment as a phenomenon conducive to the upward trajectory of current maven Bill Gates and the late Steve Jobs. For example, Bill Gates attended a middle school where parents raised money to pay for students to attend a summer camp where they'd learn computer skills. Did the young Bill Gates have tremendous acumen? Was his aptitude high? The answer may be yes in both cases. But, Gates had access to a camp where he could explore computers and build his affinity for technology. It could be that his experience at camp convinced young Bill Gates that his destiny was inextricably connected to computers.

Acumen and aptitude without access to experts and great resources often result in deferred dreams. Inner cities across the United States are full of African American children with acumen and aptitude, but no access. Although I discuss significant places in chapters six and seven, it's important to mention that *where* young people spend their time is in many cases linked to *who* they know or *who* their loved ones know. Either way, the notion of access is powerful. It is a difference maker. We'll never know how Bill Gates's trajectory may have been altered were it not for that camp experience, but we know for sure that it affected him in a very positive way. The opportunity, encouragement, and support he received extended beyond the purview of his parents.

Now, I know what some readers may be thinking. It's a bit sketchy to attempt to draw significant parallels between the youths of this study project and white males who happen to also be billionaires. The point again is that *who* youths have access to matters. And, the strengths, the resources, the stories of those who are accessible to youth matters even more. In this discussion of "The People", I highlight the influence of siblings, extended family members, a peer, and a dedicated teacher. As you'll observe, it's not necessarily about the influential persons having or giving money. Their example, their time, and their words were gold to this project's participants.

Siblings

For some reason, we are wired in such a way that we desire to emulate those who are closest to us. Oftentimes, we want to be like our parents. Or, those with older siblings attempt to follow their path(s). Tariq's story is more consistent with the latter path of emulation. He discussed experiencing hope through his relationship with his older sisters.

"Like the real reason I really came to WNHS cuz I seen how my sisters, how they loved this school, how this school really changed they life like and made em more positive. I had like four or five family members come to this school. And, I can really tell how this school helped."

Akin to many urban African American males from tough neighborhoods, Tariq's upbringing was difficult. He was not bashful in talking about the impediments that he and his sisters were confronted with on a daily basis. For example, he and his siblings had experience in the foster care system. In fact, Tariq was in foster care prior to the start of the research project. Nevertheless, Tariq began to believe that his situation could be improved because he witnessed the impact that enrollment at WNHS had on each of his sisters. In Tariq's words, "…this school really changed they life, like made them more positive." While he didn't express it explicitly, Tariq's remark associated his sisters with low motivation or possibly hopelessness prior to their arrival at WNHS. If nothing else, it was clear that something changed when they enrolled and continued at WNHS.

Three of Tariq's four sisters graduated from WNHS. Two of the sisters who graduated were teen moms. So, in addition to the challenges they faced, they were responsible for raising young lives. Besides observing the very conspicuous and serious responsibility of caring for a child, Tariq was privy to the less public struggles of his sisters. His observation of their triumph compelled Tariq to believe that he too could overcome obstacles and complete high school. Tariq saw his sisters pre-WNHS and post-WNHS. In his sisters' example, Tariq was able to identify some characteristics of people who have hope: optimism, growth-mindedness, and determination.

Extended Family Members

Besides mothers, a few students witnessed hope through relationships with other adult female family members. For example, Dawn also raved about her grandmother. When asked if and how she was raised to think about hope, Dawn shared,

> *"From my grandma and my friends. My grandmother, she...that woman, she just makes you want to have hope. She from what I've seen where they came from, she just makes me want to be a better person just in general and having hope in the future."*

Similar to her remarks about her mother, Dawn's commentary about her grandmother conveyed admiration and a deep appreciation. The phrase, "she just makes me want to have hope" suggested that Dawn's grandmother, in some way, displayed behavior or shared compelling words that were very inspirational. Another key phrase in Dawn's brief talk about her grandmother was "from what I've seen where they came from". This thought pointed to a historical reference about her grandmother and others in her family. It suggested that Dawn was told about days past during which adversity or hardship was prevalent. Although Dawn couldn't elaborate to share specifics, her remark indicated that her grandmother and others in the family are in a much better place compared to "where they came from".

Maurice talked about his aunt when describing his experience with hope. Maurice's relationship with his aunt is significant for two reasons. First of all, he hails from the embattled streets of Detroit. His aunt helped him out of that situation by allowing him to move to Kingstown to live with her. She was also responsible for researching schools and finding out about WNHS. Thus, Maurice perceived that his chances of pursuing and obtaining life-goals were already better simply because his aunt took notice of his situation and intervened.

> "Uh, I moved down here from Detroit, but I also started to lose interest in school when I came down here and I moved wit my auntie. She enrolled me here. She told me that it was a nice little school. So, she just picked me up one day and enrolled me in uh WNHS. My expectations was… I just wanted to see if it was different from regular schools cuz I know ya'll had a small setting or whatever, but, I found out it's a nice situation you know?"

Second of all, Maurice explained that he observed his aunt's perseverance despite a particular entrepreneurial setback. He took notice of the mettle she exhibited. When asked to provide insight into the way in which he encountered hope, Maurice remarked:

"Seeing people fail, that's all I can say is seeing a couple of people fail like my auntie. She actually had a cleaning business, and it kinda went down really fast. But, you know...she went back to school for business. So, she tryin' hard at it. You know just seeing people fail like that's the hard part. But, I learned that you just gotta try anyway, fail or not."

The willingness of Maurice's aunt to persist in her life-goal pursuit helped him to recognize the journey associated with having hope. Maurice never mentioned if his aunt intended to reopen the cleaning business after finishing school. But, her enrollment into a program that would provide her with additional entrepreneurial knowledge and skills was a definite sign that his aunt was "tryin' hard" to grow professionally. Maurice's aunt was still in school at the time of the interview. Her example of perseverance impacted Maurice and was reflective of the iterative nature of the pathways component of Hope Theory. Maurice commented, "...I learned that you just gotta try anyway, fail or not." If one pathway or strategy doesn't work, then an individual regroups, recalibrates, and selects a different and more feasible pathway or strategy that they believe will help them attain their goal(s).

While Maurice encountered hope through relationship with his aunt, Amber mentioned folks who were true extensions of her primary family unit—her godparents. Similar to her discussion about her mother and grandmother's prayer life, Amber revealed that her experience with hope was inclusive of her godparents' religious devotion.

"And, my godmother who basically helped raise me as well and my godfather they prayed every day, every

night, every morning, noon and night, breakfast, lunch, and dinner you know. And, so I got that. I don't know if that like relates. I don't how in my mind that relates to being faithful, but I guess that's how you build up your spirit in being faithful."

In respect to the sequence of Hope Theory, prayer in Amber's experience was linked to the pursuit of a goal. Whether direct or indirect, she observed prayer as a pathway. Amber described her godparents' conspicuous prayer life. Unlike her assumption that her mother and grandmother prayed consistently, Amber knew her godparents prayed on a regular basis (e.g., morning, night, mealtimes, etc.). To Amber, their prayer habit demonstrated a constant need for faith and hope. And, prayer as a family mainstay communicated a need for relationship with a supernatural being. In Amber's experience that meant God.

Growing up observing an obvious and consistent life of prayer among her godparents and what she presumed was an inconsistent commitment to prayer by her mother caused Amber to be dubious about prayer. During her conversation, Amber expressed somewhat of a lamentation over her current life of prayer,

"...I think it's a bad habit my mother and grandmother taught me, to pray when or like cry out when you need something... I'm almost ashamed when it's time for me to pray to God because I'm now kinda like I haven't prayed in like two weeks and here I'm praying about this test..."

Despite conveying a sense of inspiration in her talk about her godparents and prayer, Amber's comment revealed that she adopted the practice she observed from her mother and grandmother. Yet, the approach of her godparents was more desirable. Amber continued to aim for a relationship with God which for her would signify the prevailing presence of hope in her life. And, as her discussion below indicates, experiencing hope meant having faith. Faith in God helped Amber to overcome doubts and fears and accomplish her goal of high school graduation.

"Faith. I really can't think of it as being anything else but having faith. I mean you can have hope without believing in God, but for me personally it really comes down to just having faith. Whatever happens next, it's not up to me. It's up to that master plan for my life. It's my destiny, and I don't know. Sometimes that scares me, but it's always like man, I guess I gotta get through it, but it also makes me… uh like, graduating. I wanted to graduate, but I was scared. I was scared that it may not be possible that I could graduate on time. I had faith that I could, but I also was worried that I couldn't. I would be emotional and crying and stuff like that, but it happened. And, maybe because I did what I had to do. But, I also really believe that it was people that God put in my life to really steer me in the right direction. I mean I could say that it's because of my faith. I really can't take all the credit for what I did. I really don't wanna take all of the credit because I really feel like I graduated because of God, because I had faith in Him."

Peers

Nearly 30 years ago, Kunjufu (1989) described the peer group as being the primary influence in the lives of youth. The same case can easily be made today with the emergence of millennial youths who seem to innately embrace a group orientation (Womack, 2010). Even children as young as five or six years old understand the power of friends. Cartoons attempt to promote benevolence and care in friendships. Babies, toddlers, and pre-adolescents alike are inundated with themes about sharing and helping. Tons of shows feature a male or female protagonist who is flanked by a supporting cast of buddies. My biological children have watched or currently watch shows that present friendship in a very positive light: *Little Bill, Ni Hao Kia-Lan Kilan, Thomas the Tank Engine, The Backyardigans, Franklin and Friends, Paw Patrol, and PJ Masks.*

Even the idea of "super friends" has resurfaced and spread among older youths as DC Comics represents its famed crew of gifted defenders of good—the Justice League (Superman, Wonder Woman, Aquaman, the Green Lantern, Cyborg, Batman & Robin, and Flash). Marvel Comics' recrudescent X-Men and Avengers franchises also contribute to the promotion of friendship, team, and the ability of the *group* to overcome insurmountable odds. With so much media saturation of "team themes", it makes sense that the modern-day youth views success and friends in an inseparable light.

Now, the opposite of positivity can certainly spread amongst a youth peer group as well. My reference to "the good guys" is not meant to oversimplify the dynamics of youth interaction and adolescent bonding. No, my purpose is to highlight the benefits of healthy peer relationships. Moreover, I argue that the best relationships—youth or adult—offer inspiration. Dawn talked about the significant influence of a close friend. She discussed being inspired by her friend's refusal to cower and quit in the face of hard times. Specifically Dawn explained,

> *"Um, my friend and what she goes through and how she wants to do better and I see that she is. She makes me want to have hope just for myself so that I can to get to where. Like, how she is and how she thinks bigger."*

When Dawn initially commented on extended family members and hope, she said, "my friend". A particular friend became the focal point of the discussion. (Dawn explained that this friend actually resided with her and her family at the time of the study.) When I examined Dawn's remarks more closely, there were four striking phrases that support the notion of inspiration in a friendship and its importance: "what she goes through and how she wants to do better and I see that she is"; "makes me want to have hope just for myself"; "how she is"; and "how she thinks bigger".

Prior to elaborating on the revelations I unearthed in Dawn's comments, it's necessary to provide a brief description of the type of young lady she was at the time of the research project. When I met Dawn, she was a 17 year old junior attempting to overcome a couple semesters of academic mediocrity at another high school.

> *"My mom talked about it. At first I didn't know what this school was about and everything. I didn't know if I really wanted to come here. So, at the end of my sophomore year we talked about it like the whole summer and she was giving me options and everything and I just felt*

*like after I visited here that this was the best thing for
me. So, this is the school that I picked."*

Dawn and her mother met with me to discuss the possibilities at WNHS. I learned that Dawn lived with her mother and
sister, and that despite her very reticent demeanor during the
in-take meeting, Dawn could be quite loquacious when in her
comfort zone at home. Dawn was not the typical WNHS student. Her high school file lacked the typical descriptors that I'd
become accustomed to reviewing: incarcerated, expelled, and/
or chronic truancy. But, akin to most WNHS enrollees, Dawn
was credit deficient. She wasn't as far behind as many of WNHS
students I enrolled, but Dawn was in danger of not graduating
on schedule. More than anything, the interview revealed that
Dawn was an "Other". The term "Other" simply meant that her
reason for matriculation at WNHS didn't align with the actual
enrollment criteria. Nevertheless, I opted to invite Dawn to join
the WNHS family. I could tell that she lacked confidence when
it came to coursework: I knew that WNHS could help her build
the inner strength necessary to breakthrough whatever fears she
had and be successful.

Besides the attention and love she'd receive at WNHS, I
later learned that Dawn's turnaround was fueled by the example
set by a good friend. Dawn never fully expounded on details of
her friend's situation, but her remarks told plenty. Hardship of
some kind was clearly the potential source of discouragement
in her friend's life, as indicated by Dawn's words, "what she
goes through and how she wants to do better and I see that she
is". As Post (2006) commented, hope is related to seeing or
looking beyond the situation. Therefore, every encounter with
this friend was an experience with hope for Dawn. The remark,
"what she goes through", alluded to the presence of stress or

difficulty. According to Dawn, her friend didn't let the impediment sully her perspective. Instead, Dawn's friend conveyed and/or demonstrated optimism as revealed in Dawn's comment, "how she wants to do better".

One of the female participants, Za'Nya, offered a description of an individual with hope that aligns perfectly with Dawn's report of her friend. Za'Nya asserted that a person with hope "doesn't ignore the obvious" or sets their "sights on something bigger". Again, Dawn's friend focused on moving beyond the immediacy of her present reality. In line with Hope Theory's (Snyder, 2002) requirement of active engagement, Dawn's remark, "I see that she is", confirmed that her friend took steps to pursue more desirable life-outcomes. Since she was close to her friend, it stood to reason that Dawn had insight into her friend's situation, including the origins of the circumstance and the effect of the circumstance on her friend's psyche, emotions, and behavior. Thus, Dawn's statement that referenced an impediment and her friend's disposition helped explain why she broached her friend as a key figure in her experience with hope.

Two other phrases in Dawn's original quote about her friend supported Dawn's claim that she experienced hope through her friend, "how she is" and "how she thinks bigger". Now, these phrases were preceded in Dawn's comment by the statement, "She makes me want to have hope just for myself so that I can get to where". The ability of Dawn's friend to look beyond (Post, 2006) inspired Dawn to want to have what her friend possessed. In turn, Dawn's peer became her role model, a living, young example of what it meant to have hope. The phrase, "how she is", suggested that Dawn admired the characteristics in her friend that helped her to (e.g., attitude, emotions, behavior) endure her circumstance(s). Dawn's friend wouldn't allow that which was right in front of her to define her or determine what was possible for her life.

Reexamination of a statement Dawn made about her grandmother ("she just makes me want to be a better person") revealed a similarity with a comment she made about her friend. In both cases, Dawn implicitly drew a distinction between what she possessed compared to what her grandmother and friend possessed. Dawn believed that she didn't have *it*, ("…makes me want to have hope just for myself"), but her friend did. Altogether, the benefit of Dawn's experiences and observations was that she witnessed the *intergenerational* aspect of hope. By Dawn's measurements, both elders and teens in her life possessed hope. And, it was from these persons of influence that Dawn gained the strength to believe in herself, devise strategies, and pursue high school graduation.

A Teacher Like Momma

Although the prevailing subject with respect to individuals that the students perceived to have hope was an adult female family member; one student, Brian, expressed appreciation for an African American female teacher. Brian remembered the love for students that she displayed through high expectations, strictness, and accountability.

I can recollect that Brian was an interesting student. At the time of the research study, Brian was 17 years old. Overall, he was a quiet guy…never one to initiate trouble. In fact, Brian kept to himself most of the time. Compared to many young men at WNHS, Brian was very focused on attending school. Brian lived in the central section of the city where he was raised by his mother. The oldest among several siblings, Brian was responsible for helping out at home. His mother relied on him to look after younger siblings and/or relatives. Brian was a family guy in the truest sense of the term. He took his responsibilities serious, even running home at times after school to make sure he wouldn't be late getting home.

Brian was what I called a "true criteria student". Prior to enrolling at WNHS, he had been adjudicated and under state supervision. Most often students in these scenarios were referred by state probation and parole agents, but Brian actually came to be enrolled at WNHS through referral from a friend. During our time together Brian talked about the buzz in the community about WNHS. He heard that students who enrolled in WNHS had a real chance to turn their academic performance around and graduate. Brian attended a large public high school before he arrived at WNHS. And, according to Brian, he did everything but go to school.

"I was at Coolidge. Yeah, I stayed skipping. I ain't go to school. So…I forgot what happened, but somehow I ended up downstairs in the guidance counselor office and you know I was just looking at my transcript like man I been slipping for like two years. This ain't right. I gotta do something. Then I talked to Roland. He told me about this. He just knew what I needed, and this was it. So, he told my momma. We came up here. That's how it went."

Brian was a very subdued young man, melancholy even. I observed introspection in his comments. Brian wasn't verbose, but what he did share was insightful. In my experience with youths over a career of about 15 years, I've witnessed numerous students attribute their failure and/or deviance to external factors. This wasn't the case with Brian. No, Brian was honest as he recalled the road that led to his arrival at WNHS. He knew that *he* was his own problem. Brian also believed that *he* was his own solution.

> *"I just...I know how to get to where I want to be. I just gotta work it out. It's just been times that I just slipped, slipped up and put no effort into it. But if I just choose to put effort into it and you know do what I'm supposed to do, I know I can do what I wanna do. I just gotta bring myself to want to work that hard."*

When Brian began to expound upon the influence of his teacher, his remarks confirmed what Snyder (2005) and other scholars (Duncan-Andrade, 2010; Shade 2006) had discovered about the unique power of committed educators. Sure, Brian talked about the influence of his mother, but in a different light. Whether she knew it or not, this teacher became Brian's school-mother. He esteemed her that highly.

> *"Her name was Ms. Summers. You know she's the coolest teacher I ever had. I loved her like she was my momma. She the only one that like kept me pin-point on my work. I ain't never been a person that just do work you know. You know I was sliding a little. I still got my D's that I needed to get and you know she kept on til I got to 5th grade. She was there... Ms. Summers, she not fake and...you know what she want. She gon go after it. If she want the whole class to shut-up, that's gon be her goal. She gon make the class shut-up, but in a positive way to where you have no choice but to respect her. And, you know I didn't get a lot of them impressions off the other teachers."*

Brian's description of his experience with his teacher was extremely compelling. Being an African American male, I understand how important our mothers are to us. Our mothers are precious jewels. Therefore, when Brian accorded his teacher this exalted status, "like my mother", I knew that Ms. Summer had a very significant impact on his life. Moreover, Brian's tone and countenance was serious. There was no smirking, chuckling, or smiling that could suggest hyperbole. Instead, Brian was sincere. His expression conveyed a belief that this woman who wasn't his mother, touched his life in a manner that only his mother could surpass.

Initially, when Brian talked about his experience with hope, he described the value of his mother's conversations with him. Brian also mentioned that his mother was resourceful. She sought out external supports to help reinforce positive messages that could help him refrain from engaging in deviance. Brian's mother took him to church. Both her openness to conversation and effort to connect Brian with church indicated his mother's love and care; that she wasn't willing to give up on him, despite the poor choices he was making at the time. Since Brian explained that he loved Ms. Summers like she was his mother, he must have discerned genuine love and care through his relationship with her.

After listening to Brian's remarks about his mother and Ms. Summers, it became clear that the dominant similarity that they shared with regard to Brian was the refusal to give up on him. Both women persevered in their relationship with Brian. (Sure, one could contest and suggest that any mother would remain committed to the well-being of their child. Or, another could object and suggest that Ms. Summers only did what teachers are supposed to do. If only it were that simple! The sad reality is that numerous mothers and teachers grow weary, and they stop fighting for their children and students). An example of Ms. Summers's commitment and subsequent influence on Brian was revealed in the comment, "She the only one that like kept me pin-point on my work". The phrase "kept me" indicated that Ms. Summers held Brian accountable. Additionally, the phrase, "She the only one", suggested that other teachers didn't hold Brian accountable. That Ms. Summers was able to help Brian focus suggested that she had earned Brian's respect and trust and was therefore able to issue demands and elicit appropriate responses where other teachers were unsuccessful.

So far, one would probably imagine that Ms. Summers mirrored the remarkable heroes and heroines that we've seen in the feel-good movies about education. You know the movies where a savvy teacher lifts a despondent student or students out of the dung hill of low academic achievement onto mighty platforms of productivity and high academic achievement (Lean On Me, Stand and Deliver, Freedom Writers, etc). Well...that didn't happen in Brian's case. Actually, in a sort of humorous way, Brian confessed that he actually performed poorly, "I ain't never been a person that just do work you know. You know I was sliding a little. I still got my D's that I needed to get...". Brian barely passed Ms. Summers' class, but the impact of having access to a teacher who defied his desire to meander in academic nothingness was seemingly greater than achieving a "A" or a "B". What Brian received from Ms. Summers surpassed the importance of an elementary report card grade. The performance marks Brian received were indelibly written on his heart; marks whose impressions were full of authentic love.

For instance, Brian recalled Ms. Summers' passion and no-nonsense approach to establishing order in her classroom:

"...Ms. Summers, she not fake and she not finna just... you know what she want, she gon go after it. If she want the whole class to shut-up that's gon be her goal. She gon make the class shut-up, but in a positive way to where you have no choice but to respect her. And, you know I didn't get them impressions off the other teachers."

No cumulative folder can contain the lessons of loving rebuke and focus that Brian learned from Ms. Summers. In their book, *The Art of Critical Pedagogy: Possibilities for Moving from Theory to Practice in Urban Schools*, Jeff Duncan-Andrade and Ernest Morrell (2008) discussed the notion of access as it pertains to students and their ability to benefit from the assets that teachers possess:

"Students need access not only to the ideas and skills we seek to transfer. They also need to be able to access our love, and they need to be able to see how we draw upon that love to conquer our fears and to work with others for change." (p.189)

Indeed, Brian's recollection of his times in Ms. Summers' class may have revealed an individual who was tough on her students. But, to Duncan-Andrade and Morrell's (2008) point, there was a love element in play that Brian could sense; the kind of love that a no non-sense mother would display. In doing so, Ms. Summers earned the respect of her students. And, in relation to Hope Theory, this love compelled Ms. Summers to resist behavior that could impede her lesson objectives and the maintenance of a classroom environment conducive to learning. In this way, Ms. Summers raised hope among her students. She didn't allow them to do whatever they wanted to do. Shade (2006) acknowledged that this kind of predictability and expectation for order provides students with a sense of security which is critical to imparting and cultivating hope. Brian's experience supports literature related to culturally relevant classroom management as well. According to Brown (2004), successful teachers of students in urban settings utilize culturally responsive management practices that are inclusive of the development of personal relationships, mutual respect, culturally congruent communication processes, assertiveness and clear expectations.

You Feel Me?

Several years ago, a good friend of mine, Dr. Decoteau Irby, invited me to participate in a workshop that he was conducting related to urban education and making classroom connections with adolescent African American male students. Dr. Irby argued that African American youths must feel you before they esteem what you have to say (Irby, 2012). Almost without words, they have to viscerally connect with an educator's soul. This is undoubtedly a psycho-emotive experience, but it occurs in a socio-cultural context—the classroom. For some the connection is felt instantly upon hearing certain words or observing certain behavior. For others the revelation of realness may occur through an uncomfortable ordeal of some kind, but they connect nonetheless.

I find it very interesting that Brian made it a point to allude to the pretense of other teachers he'd worked with. His remarks, "she not fake", and, "I didn't get them impressions off the other teachers", indicated that despite his lack of engagement and focus, Brian did focus on teacher language. He paid attention to what was said and how it was said. In sum, the communicative style of teachers matters to children (Brown, 2004). And, given the context of this discussion, I don't think it's inappropriate to suggest that Brian could *feel* who was real.

Brian's recollection reminded me of the blockbuster movie *Avatar* (20th Century Fox, 2009). The film's protagonist, Jake Sully, had to select a creature to be his riding partner as part of a type of tribal rites of passage requirement. It was a rite that all potential warriors had to engage and conquer (Sully was really a U.S. Marine who'd been assigned to infiltrate the tribe and gather intelligence for senior commanders.). His companion told him that he couldn't simply make the creature submit to his leadership (ridership) through arbitrary commands. He couldn't dominate the creature. No, there had to be a connection. After days of unsuccessful attempts to mount and ride this beast, Sully relaxed, spoke calmly to the creature and made the connection. From that day forward—in the movie—the creature allowed Sully to lead him (ride him). Sully rode with tremendous precision and swagger as if he were a member of the indigenous group he'd infiltrated.

In essence, this is what Dr. Irby was addressing in his workshop. Once students feel you, they will allow you to lead them. When this happens, they'll want to know what you're talking about. And, they will want to understand it. Without the connection, without the "feel", attempts at teaching will be futile at best.

In no way am I likening African American male adolescents to beasts, and I'm certainly not calling Brian a creature, but I do argue that Brian's account of his experience with Ms. Summers is similar to Jake Sully in Avatar. Ms. Summers had to connect with Brian in order to fully engage him in the learning process. Obviously, she made the connection. Brian's remarks indicated that he "felt" her and that he didn't feel his other

teachers. In contrast to Ms. Summers, Brian detected disingenuous behavior and therefore regarded them as unworthy of his
trust and respect.

Zooming Out

An observation worth reiterating is the predominant conversational focus on the impact of African American women.
Casey mentioned her parents, and Amber briefly mentioned
her godparents when she described prayer as an element associated with hope. But, even with these two students' remarks,
no special attention was given to testimonials, conversations,
or activities that they observed through interaction with a father
or father figure. This is both noteworthy and alarming. Since no
other student in the study mentioned the influence of a natural
father or father figure, I've concluded that the majority of the
study participants had no significant relationship with their biological father or a father figure. If any of the students did have
a significant relationship with their fathers or a father figure,
hope-related characteristics may have been entirely absent or
sorely lacking at best. Is this an assumption? Sure. But, the lack
of student commentary about the significant impact of a male or
male parent makes it a plausible assumption. The figure below
highlights the study participants, the individuals that they identified as a person who influenced their experience with hope
and associated hope-related characteristics.

Figure 6
Characteristics of Persons of Influence

Student	Person(s) of Influence	Characteristics
Jameel	Mother	• Fortitude • Inspirational • Optimism
Dawn	Mother Grandmother Friend	• Listener • Goal-oriented • Transparent • Inspirational
Za'Nya	Mother	• Goal-oriented • Inspirational
Brian	Mother Teacher	• Listener • Resourceful • Consistency • Authenticity
Casey	Parents	• Inspirational
Maurice	Aunt	• Goal-oriented • Fortitude
Amber	Godparents	• Consistency • Faith
Tariq	Siblings	• Optimism • Growth-mindedness • Fortitude

(Arrington, 2014)

In the upcoming chapter, the reader will observe students mention male leaders in what I've termed "places of hope". However, the interview protocol at this point in the research process did not call for inquiry into contemporary individuals who were helping them. It simply required that the study participants discuss their experience with hope. Overwhelmingly, the students shared that a woman was—in their eyes—a paragon of hope. The example that these women exhibited motivated the students to grow and enhance their life satisfaction possibilities. For Maurice, his aunt inspired him to pursue entrepreneurship and service. He indicated that the experiences of his up-bringing and subsequent interactions with his aunt compelled him to reciprocate goodwill to other children who may suffer similar plight.

> *"Uh, like anything like uh, like a store or anything like a cleaning business and a couple of things. I can't really think of em but you know a couple of things, do anything positive you know to help kids out or something like you know just keep em out the neighborhood for a little while...stuff like that."*

Za'Nya explained that without the influence of her mother, she'd probably be a wastrel drifting through life, "...without her I wouldn't even have life-goals. I would be just like any other bum on the street not doing nothing." Dawn poignantly shared that her grandmother made her want to be a "better person". With respect to the initial dominant theme in the study, these students' remarks revealed a powerful result of their relationships with these women. The encounters they had with these significant women, whether through critical conversations or observation of resilience, influenced these youths to see themselves beyond (Post, 2006) the immediacy of their present realities. How? Why? Hope found a home. Hope found a home in the hearts of these influential women, each one amazing in her own way. And, the atmosphere within which they spoke and acted became overcome with the seeds of transcendence. These seeds were dispersed into the souls of the young folks who recognized their impact. The seeds began to germinate and eventually there was growth. I believe that the discussions I was so fortunate to be included in were evidence of growth. Hope was burgeoning and the study participants were rising out of the ashes of past failure and into the limitless skies of possibilities. Regardless of their lot, (e.g., social, academic, emotional, behavioral, or psychological) the participants thus inspired, perceived themselves as capable of transcendence. The points of view they espoused were full of elements and tones of intransigence, social awareness, and confidence.

Astoundingly, the students' introspections teemed with projections of a recrudescent self. Their remarks appeared to be inclusive of ruminations about whom and what they wanted to be as well as the pathway to "becoming". In a word, these students seemed to be simultaneously constructing a definition of hope and a futuristic image of self. Additionally, this notion of a recrudescent self, further explicated the impermeability of the disposition of students with hope. Their commentary suggested that no hindrance was immovable. They were impelled to vigorously pursue supports that could help them make their vision a reality. This, in essence, was the hope of the students in this research project...the hope of an alternate future with an alternate ending.

Chapter 6

THE PLACES

"We are at our best as human beings when we realize that we're all tied together in a labyrinth of interrelation that culminates in our collective destiny."

-M.K. Asante, Jr.

The inner-city streets that the study participants hailed from are rife with conspicuous hazards. They are teeming with all sorts of reasons why youths on the margins can't succeed or shouldn't succeed. Whether it's human trafficking, gang violence or drug wars, youths from violent and impoverished communities have much to avoid and navigate not only in their pursuit of life satisfaction, but oftentimes just to make it to school and back home safely. Instances of police brutality and malpractice against Tamir Rice, Walter Scott, Alton Sterling, Dontre Hamilton, Sandra Bland, Eric Garner, Jay Anderson, Philando Castile, Stephon Clark, Botham Jean and others snuff out any sense of consolation that inner-city youth are even safe among public servants who take oaths to protect them.

In such tenuous, suffocating social climates, it's easy to become trammeled by fear and doubtful thinking. It's easy to become consumed by negativity and allow your dreams to be crushed. And, the need for refuge, for protection from the array of ghetto perils, is much more pronounced. The amazing students in this study were critically aware of their immediate environments and were determined to beat the odds. They exhibited and articulated a kind of righteous defiance that nothing, not even "the hood" was going to stop them from achieving their goals. See, Hope Theory also advocates that the reason that hope is needed in the first place is because some obstacle or impediment is present that could potentially deny one's goal attainment. Hence, there's a need for pathways and agency. With this theoretical factor in mind, it's crucial to highlight the student's wisdom and recognition of delimiting factors in their lives.

For example, Jameel, a young man whom I previously introduced as being formerly incarcerated and in effect a victim of the streets, expressed disdain for what he perceived to be ecological and cultural elements that could trammel his pursuit of life-goals.

"Seeing the same thing everyday...same liquor store, same corner stores, same people. I cain't be around that especially if I plan on having kids and getting money. The only way of getting money out there in the hood is the illegal way. I ain't trying to..."I'm already labeled as a statistic...Like just because how I look. You know what I'm saying? I got a lot of tattoos and all that. And everybody that look like me they think that they thuggin' or gang-bangin' so-called or drug dealin'. I mean I wanna to be the person that little kids look up to even though I got a hood image. I still wanna have knowledge behind that, you know what I'm saying?"

Poignantly, Jameel recognized the power of stigmatization. Yet, Jameel remained self-determined, even if others couldn't see beyond his style. His comments suggested that he resolved to reject delimiting stereotypes associated with his urban aesthetic and hip hop sensibility. Still further, Jameel's remarks indicated a level of social awareness and responsibility to influence children in his community who may identify with his presentation.

Maurice offered thoughts that really painted a grim picture of the looming tragedy that many inner-city youth believe they have to evade.

"My life-goals are making it to see 30, having my own successful business at 30. Because even when you're doing positive things there's still always negative things around, like negative people. Like, for instance, you cain't beat the fact that you still live in the neighborhood or whatever, so them people are still gon be around and them things are still gon be around. It's just inside of you to you know, turn the negative into the positive. So, I just like to see 30 cuz 25 is pretty close. Thirty is a long time away, and I'd like to be here at 30."

I'm sure that there are people who assumed that making it to the age of 30 was a given when they were teenagers. But, everyone doesn't share the same expectation. The deathtraps in impoverished and violent communities are real and too often tangible. To highlight the sheer absurdity that thousands of inner-city youth are faced with, filmmaker Spike Lee drew a comparison between the murder rate in Chicago and battlefields in the Middle East. He found that the rate of killing in the streets of Chicago is comparable to that of actual combat zones. Thus, he was moved to create the film entitled, Chiraq; a moniker used to articulate the similarity between the streets of Iraq and the streets of Chicago. Although the movie contained some elements of burlesque, Lee undoubtedly attempted to draw mainstream attention to the repulsive murder rate that is growing in the margins of a major American metropole.

With such devastation and pain ever present, it's easy for those who call the margins home to contend that no one cares. It's easy to drift into despair. To this end, project participants offered insight into the places where they experienced hope. These spaces were instrumental in providing youths with atmospheres full of positivity and access to psychological and emotional sustenance. So, in contrast to Chapter 4, this chapter will focus more so on relationships with and student access to institutions that, according to their testimony, helped introduce them to hope. Institutions mentioned during student interviews included church, a college, a university, a non-profit organization, community centers, and of course a high school. Analysis and evaluation of the students' commentary revealed specific characteristics or benefits that were consistently observed and received in one or more of these spaces: inspirational, values-centered, resourceful, educational, multiple opportunities, accessible, youth-centered, recreational, educational, safe, inclusive, age-diversity, learning opportunities, and service-oriented.

Church

America has a long and intimate relationship with church. Most of us were taught about the pilgrims and Plymouth Rock. We were told about their quest for religious freedom. We were told that ours was a story of courage, community, and deep commitment to faith. We were told about their lifestyle of thrift and extreme reverence for the sacred. It became the quintessential model of Americanism. In fact, ideologically we refer to this as the "Protestant Work Ethic". As a traditional "Christian" nation, America has a long history of moral law that has been informed by biblical values. Many Americans' views on marriage, family, and citizenship have been shaped by the Ten Commandments of the Old Testament and the Golden Rule of the New Testament. And though postmodern thought has infringed upon and narrowed the moral landscape and is continually influencing our collective moral compass, the tension, that currently exist with respect to issues such as abortion and same-sex marriage confirm that millions of Americans still esteem the bible and its teachings.

While Christianity is very much a common thread in the colorful fabric of general American life, God and the bible has meant even more to oppressed communities. Boff and Pixley (1989) argued that God has always had a "preferential option for the poor" (p.22); that wherever people are suffering, He is present and provides a means of deliverance out of oppression. Further, Boff and Pixley (1989) contended that, "God is a savior of the oppressed..." (p.24). Cone (1997) along with Boff and Pixley (1989) cited the Exodus account of the Old Testament as evidence of God's willingness to draw near to those on the margins of society, dominated by hegemonic social structures, and bereft of pathways to self-actualization. The biblical canon reveals the story of the Hebrews (Jewish people). They were a nomadic people who through a combination of fortuitous events and fear became enslaved by the Egyptian empire. The pharaoh or king of Egypt was hard-hearted. His regime featured work mandates that pummeled the Hebrews physically and psychologically. Bondage was the perceived lot of the Hebrews. Toil and struggle was their inheritance. Year after year the narrative of oppression remained the same.

One day while tending his flock, a shepherd named Moses saw a truly astounding sight. He noticed that there was a bush that was aflame, but it was not consumed. Moses approached this burning bush and a voice suddenly called his name and required him to remove his sandals. The voice then shared the following with Moses:

> *"...I have certainly seen the oppression of my people in Egypt. I have heard their cries of distress because of their harsh slave drivers. Yes, I am aware of their suffering. So I have come down to rescue them from the power of the Egyptians and lead them out of Egypt into their own fertile and spacious land...The cry of the people of Israel has reached me, and I have seen how harshly the Egyptians abuse them. Now go, for I am sending you to Pharaoh. You must lead my people Israel out of Egypt." (Exodus 3:7-10, New Living Translation)*

The passage of scripture above is regarded as the commissioning of Moses. He was a Hebrew man who'd been raised in the ways of Egypt; taught their culture; taught their way of thinking and protocols of social interaction. The deity that the Hebrews or people of Israel called Yahweh, selected Moses to champion their cause for freedom. In the end, Yahweh or God used Moses to perform miracles and exact judgment on the Egyptian empire for their perennial cruelty and indifference to human suffering. Under the leadership of Moses, the Hebrews escaped enslavement. A gaggle of beleaguered souls, they hurried anxiously towards freedom, towards the Promised Land. Pharaoh and his army hotly pursued the Israelites with intent to destroy them. Skewered between a relentless despot and a natural barrier in the Red Sea, the Israelites thought that they had been led astray; that they'd been led into the desert to die a tortuous death. But, God supremely intervened. He told Moses to stretch out his rod. Moses obeyed and the great Red Sea suddenly parted. The Israelites miraculously ambled across its briny floor unharmed by the force of its swirling waves. Pharaoh and his army attempted to follow the Israelites into the Red Sea, but God caused the waters to close in on them. Pharaoh and his formidable army drowned. It's an epic account of the truly marginalized, the forgotten, the destitute overcoming a giant of an enemy.

Actor Charleston Heston popularized the Moses character with his depiction of Moses in the classic 1956 movie, *The Ten Commandments*. Each year during the Easter holiday season, one of the major television networks airs this film. I'm sure the value of the story is weighed differently based on the lens of the viewer. To my mind, the Exodus story is a cinematic representation of hope. There was a goal (liberation). There were pathways (Moses was chosen to lead. Moses and his brother Aaron consistently petitioned Pharaoh to release the Hebrews. God/Yahweh performed miracles and sent plagues to demonstrate His power.). There was agency (God/Yahweh constantly reminded Moses of His promise to rescue the Hebrews). In other words, it was God/Yahweh's goal to rescue His people. Moses was the vessel to carry out the plan. God/Yahweh knew what He was capable of. He never wavered in his belief.

During the ordeal of American enslavement, preachers amongst the oppressed Africans would tell the Exodus story and boldly proclaim that God was still in the business of deliverance. They'd encourage their brothers and sisters by telling them that God still listened to the cries of the oppressed and that one day they'd be free just like the Hebrews. This notion of God caring for the oppressed and the prospect of freedom on the horizon helped to sustain generations of enslaved Africans. Wilmore (1998) offered a perspective on the relevance of the exilic experience to blacks encumbered by oppression.

"But the preeminent relevance of the Old Testament for blacks, as many of the most famous spirituals bear witness, was found in the story of the Exodus. The Egyptian captivity of the people of Israel, their miraculous deliverance from the army of Pharaoh, and their eventual possessions of the land promised by God to their ancestors—this was the inspiration to which the black believer so often turned in the dark night of the soul. Whenever the Judeo-Christian tradition is made known to an oppressed people, the scenario of election, captivity, and liberation in the Old Testament seems to have a special appeal. The story of the deliverance of Israel from slavery has always been understood as the prototype of nationalistic redemption—the divine revelation of the transhistorical meaning of historical experience." (p.60)

Because of the expository genius of Black preachers, the church became a place of hope for black folks. It was a gathering that stimulated and nurtured their imaginations. Though their time of corporate worship may have been limited and in most cases surveilled (Bennett, 1964), it was a time nonetheless when the enslaved could shed their slave persona—albeit momentarily—and revel in the possibilities of freedom. Cone (1997) contended that,

"The black church was the creation of a people whose daily experience was an encounter with the over-whelming and brutalizing reality of white power. For the slaves it was the sole source of personal identity and the sense of community..." (p.92)

Surely, enslaved Africans attended church to receive their weekly infill of humanity for it was in that sanctum that they were reminded that they were part of God's creative act. And, amid a most dehumanizing enslavement experience, outpourings of encouragement and human affirmation were indispensable. Wilmore (1998) discussed the importance of church to the enslaved as well,

"Going to church for blacks was never as much a matter of custom and convention as it was for whites. It was rather a necessity. The church was the one impregnable corner of the world where consolation, unity, and mutual assistance could be found and from which the master—at least in the North—could be effectively barred if the people were not of a mind to welcome him." (p.102)

Interestingly, in the Exodus account, God tells Moses that He wanted the Hebrews to be free so they could worship Him. In other words, their bondage was preventing them from engaging in an activity that was uniquely related to their human experience—spiritual encounter. Through their ancestors, the Hebrews had come into relationship with Yahweh, but the plight of Egyptian enslavement created a chasm that seemingly could not be overcome. Thus, they needed to be rescued. In the same way, American enslavement deprived blacks of freedom, denied them the pursuit of happiness and the realization of personhood.

In a word, enslavement rejected the attempt of blacks to be fully human. To this point, Cone (1997) added that, "As long as man is a slave to another power, he is not free to serve God with mature responsibility. He is not free to become what he is—human." (p.39) So, the church, for generations, was a station where the oppressed received supplies of dignity, morality, meaning, love, and critical knowledge. It was the epicenter of the enslaved community and later the African American community post-enslavement. The white supremacist power structure still sought ways to maintain control of blacks and prevent their social and economic ascent throughout the period of Reconstruction, Jim Crow, and subsequent seasons of state-sanctioned segregation. Yet and still, black folks found solace and peace from the violent storms of racism through religious affiliation…in most cases it was the church. One only needs to consider the leadership and message of Dr. Martin Luther King, Jr. and his contemporaries to recognize that well into the 1950s and 1960s, church was a space of empowerment, community, protest, and hope. Dyson (2016) points out that, "For most of their history, the black pulpit has been the freest place for black people; the church has been the place where blacks gathered to enhance social networks, gain education, wage social struggle, and to express the grief and glory of black existence" (p.84). Indeed, despite its spots, wrinkles, and blemishes, the church has been home to hope and an abode for regeneration and restoration of the mind, heart, and soul of the black community.

Angel's Story

Just as going to church to hear the Good News about God's ability to rescue the enslaved and end the long night of suffering was medicine to the weary bodies and souls of black folks during American enslavement, Reconstruction, and the Jim Crow era; the oppressed still draw upon the inspiration found in church today. Though it is documented that millennials attend church less than their parents (Luce, 2005), many youths, regardless of hue, still respond to faith-teachings and enjoy the fellowship that church offers. One of the study participants in particular, Angel, mentioned having her spirit lifted whenever she attended church. Before I discuss Angel's experience at church, it's necessary to take a detour at this juncture to share how she became a member of the WNHS family.

Angel was the youngest of the study participants. Unlike the others, Angel had been a member of the Woodson-Newton Achievement Center (WNAC). WNAC was a middle school program that WNHS leaders launched to help struggling middle school students improve their academic and socio-emotional skills. Students were referred by their middle school administrators, counselors, social workers, or parents. The admission criteria were specific. Students had to be overaged 7th or 8th graders, chronic truants, significantly disruptive, and/or academically deficient. Similar to the WNHS admittance process, WNAC candidates had to participate in an in-take meeting with a WNAC Transition Specialist. If accepted, the student would be a member of a 20 student cohort. When the program began, each cohort attended school in the WNHS building. Eventually, WNAC was granted permission to move into a separate building.

WNAC was truly an alternative setting for middle school youth, but it wasn't restrictive in the manner that many alternative programs can be. The goal wasn't punishment: the goal was progress and promotion. The overarching theme mirrored that of WNHS—restoration. Seventh grade students who completed the program returned to their home school with a charge to be better than they were previously. The eighth grade students, many of whom had been previously retained, were eligible for promotion into ninth grade upon successful completion of the program.

Truly, WNAC was a different place. It featured a schedule with classes that were designed to uplift and edify students. All academic work was completed in the morning. Students received remedial support in Math, Reading, and English Language Arts. After lunch, students participated in either cultural exploratory classes whereby community educators or school staff led workshops and discussions that aimed to help bridge the gap between students' learned and lived experiences. There were discussions about race, class, globalization, even hip hop. Students also had access to experiential learning. Inner-city youths were exposed to outdoors activities such as snowshoeing, cross-country skiing, and hiking. To top it all off, their school day ended about an hour earlier than their non-WNAC peers. Hence, the majority of WNAC students loved the school. If there was a consistent negative aspect, it was the duration of enrollment. Each cohort remained for eight weeks. At the end of eight weeks, students had to defend a personal portfolio that included work samples and other documents that provided evidence of successful completion of the program. In other words, they had to make the case for their promotion. Some students went back to their former schools restored and ready to excel. Many of the overaged 8th graders who successfully defended were promoted to 9th grade. In some cases, they enrolled in WNHS for the remainder of the school year.

Thereafter, they enrolled in a comprehensive high school. This was Angel's story.

Similar to Casey, Angel was quiet and dare I say careful. As a WNHS student, Angel made few friends. Her attendance was sporadic at times. When she did attend, she worked diligently. During the interview, she appeared guarded to a certain degree, unsure about what she could or should say. I did my best to assure her that the process was easy and that she was safe. When asked to talk about her experience with hope, Angel maintained that she was self-taught, that her family rarely if at all discussed hope, "I wasn't really raised on hope. Nobody in my family really taught me anything about it. I taught myself that hope is never giving up on what you believe in." As I listened to Angel's remarks, I couldn't help but reflect on the definition of hope that she shared earlier during the interview. For a young lady who professed to not have any official hope-talk with significant others, Angel articulated a noteworthy perspective:

> *"Hope is never giving up, always striving for the best even when people say you can't do it. There is no so such thing as you can't do it. If you have hope, you have success and you have already overcome the obstacle that has came your way. Hope is never giving up on anything, even when people say you can't do it, you prove them wrong."*

Looking into her diffident eyes, I searched for understanding and clarity. Her statement about hope contained key components such as transcendence and agency. But I couldn't identify the connection. I couldn't figure out the origin of her insight, especially since she contended that no one at home really talked about hope. My curiosity was especially piqued because Angel had a very transparent moment during our conversation. She commented on a period in her life that for her was the equivalent of hitting rock bottom.

> *"Um, I had people you know tell me I wasn't gon make it. You know? At my pace, or the things that I'm doing, I probably won't live to see a certain age...It was certain things that I did in the past like um, hmmm...well I don't want to get into detail but I was doing some pretty bad things and people was just like girl you need to chill out before you end up dead."*

Perhaps after reading Angel's comment, one can understand the difficulty that I had in juxtaposing her insight with regard to hope and her background. Angel's comments contained elements of danger, fear, and recklessness. Of course, an argument can be made about whether or not a teenager can actually hit rock bottom. My response is that everyone has appetites and passions that if untamed, can lead to catastrophe, age notwithstanding. Moreover, subjectivity rules perceptions of pleasure and pain. We all have different thresholds. What is too much for one person may be a walk-in-the-park for another. If Angel acknowledged that people, not just one person, but people were telling her to make changes or else, then she truly had arrived at a point of no return.

Keep in mind, all of this thinking occurred in my mind in a matter of seconds. My dendrites and synapses were firing at a ridiculous clip. Then, Angel rescued me. She talked about church. Angel's revelations about hope weren't achieved by completely autodidactic measures. No, Angel was inspired in a space where faith in God permeated all social interaction.

"When I used to go to church, I used to always hear the pastor say have hope or it would be signs on the walls and stuff and it would have hope and maybe a little paragraph about what it means. Just something to lift your spirit up. I really took heed to that kind of stuff."

Angel's statement provided evidence that she wanted more for herself despite the oppressive situation that she was in. Going to church and hearing about hope was in effect supplementary. What she didn't receive at home amongst her biological family, Angel was able to receive from her spiritual family. In respect to the discussion about people who influenced students in their experience with hope, the argument can be made that the pastor of the church that Angel attended was a person of influence. She referenced him and his messages specifically. It's reminiscent of the enslaved preacher and his influence on the plantation. No doubt, the preacher was the most important person on the plantation. For, it was the preacher that reminded the enslaved that God hears the cries of the oppressed and always has a plan for deliverance. It was the preacher that would ingeniously weave furtive language in his messages to communicate plans for insurrections (Wilmore, 1998). The preacher was the leader in the one space on the plantation where "massah's" impositions were impenetrable. The preacher prophetically belted out a consistent and powerful message, that regardless of the brutal nature of the enslavement system, freedom couldn't be denied and God guaranteed its arrival.

Just as the enslaved looked forward to Sunday, when work was often suspended and family and community were enjoyed; I imagined that Angel too looked forward to Sundays. I imagined that attending church was therapeutic to her young, careworn soul. Her pastor always said, "have hope". That message, that exposition, that encouragement nourished Angel, to the degree that she was able to formulate her own understanding of hope, which she interpreted as, "never giving up". And, true to her comment, Angel didn't give up. She persevered while attending WNAC. She persisted while attending WNHS. Angel eventually transitioned from WNHS and enrolled in a comprehensive high school where she later graduated.

Youth Service

Besides Angel, Casey provided insight into her experience with church. Those who are familiar with ecclesial settings, particular in the Christian faith, know that in addition to the Sunday "main service" that is generally led by a senior pastor, many churches feature services for young people. Sometimes youth services are conducted on Sundays, while the adult service or main service is in session. Youth services are also conducted during the week. When asked how she was raised to think about hope, Casey responded, "My church. We had a youth group. So we had like youth services and stuff like that and we talked a lot about stuff like hope and believing in yourself and like that, don't give up. So, church."

Ever the unforthcoming one, Casey's elaboration was lacking, but her remembrance of the influence of the youth group revealed a couple critical insights. First, the presence of a youth group at church indicated a level of socio-cultural awareness on the part of church leadership. Principles of social learning consistently point to the effectiveness of youths learning together. Furthermore and in respect to pedagogy, young people need a Gospel experience that is laden with language, illustrations, and explanations that are relevant to youth culture. Sure, church mattered to Casey, but the youth group made church that much more significant in her eyes. Her remembrance of hope was linked to the youth group setting.

Second, Casey mentioned that, "stuff like hope" was a mainstay in the discussions in the young groups. According to Casey, messages related to "believing in yourself" were embedded within the content of the discussions in youth group. Casey and her consorts were frequently told, "don't give up." Incidentally, these messages helped to shape Casey's definition of hope ("...knowing you can do something no matter what or if something seems impossible to do that you can do it if you hope in yourself.") and inform her description of individuals with hope ("...get up and keep trying"; "...don't give up easy"). Further, what Casey heard in the youth group reinforced words she'd heard from her parents. ("They told me stuff like believe in yourself, if you fail don't give up..."). The corollary of these inspirational connections was an understanding of hope that was deeply enrooted in focus and intransigence. Whether it was the tacit remarks of her parents, or the youth group talks, a central message rang loudly in Casey's ear— "don't give up". Akin to her ancestors, Casey was admonished to move forward despite any challenges. Church, and namely youth church, offered Casey a consistent place for positive dialogue, edification, and motivation through discussions that addressed the concerns of their present realities.

A Different Experience

Brian also mentioned church, but as part of his discussion about his mother. Although Brian didn't explicitly link his experience with hope to church membership, he did acknowledge that his mother, in her effort to instill a sense of hope, required him to go to church. Brian made it clear that he wasn't a "church boy", but he understood the value that church attendance could add to one's life. Similar to Angel and Casey, Brian recognized the power of messaging. And in hindsight, he came to understand his mother's rationale. More importantly, Brian extrapolated an element of the church experience that he considered most useful — knowledge:

> *"She tried to keep me in church. That's what she tried to do with me…the most it did like I understood it, cuz I ain't never been the one to let go of knowledge, just blow away knowledge. I listened. I understood it, but it wasn't nothing that just really got into me, cuz I'm a whole different person. You know what people be trying to tell me about and telling they stories and stuff. You know I'm a whole different person. Stuff work different for me. You know I understand and take some kind of piece out of it, but you know just in case Ima need it, but I really don't get into that."*

As a churchgoer, Brian did the equivalent of eating what he perceived to be meat and spitting out the bones. While he appreciated the content provided at church, Brian's comments indicated that he didn't favor the culture. It was as if he wanted to be clear that church was his mom' idea ("Stuff work different for me"; "You know I'm a whole different person."). Yet, Brian was astute enough and possessed the wherewithal to recognize that the information that was shared was useful.

Unlike Brian, Za'Nya discussed having a present and continuous relationship with church. In fact, among the students in the study who mentioned church, Za'Nya was the lone regular attendee. When asked about places that have helped her to be hopeful, Za'Nya said very concisely, "Church like, um, most definitely helps me to stay hopeful." Interestingly, with the exception of Jameel who briefly described his grandmother as a "church lady", none of the students described significant relationships with persons of influence who attended church. Angel mentioned the pastor, but didn't provide a name. Casey and Brian referred to the content at church, but never broached the name of the provider. Even Za'Nya, the more frequent church attendee, spoke in generalities. It was apparent that these student's relationships with church was somewhat generic, peripheral even. Regardless, church attendance or membership was viewed as helpful rather than harmful or hokey. To my mind, the sum of the students' accounts of their relationship with church revealed two primary characteristics: inspiration and value-centeredness. And, in a society filled with harrowing tales of dissolute human behavior and declining moral regard, youth need a space where they can receive their fill of inspiration and significant impartations of pro-social values.

College & Universities

WNHS was a member of a broader network of schools that promoted college and career readiness School leaders, whether elementary or secondary, were expected to assiduously work with their staffs to orient students to habits and thinking that is suitable for post-secondary opportunities. Recent tuition spikes and the threat of government cessation of student loan programs have cast an ominous cloud over the post-secondary education landscape, yet leaders still promote college matriculation as a necessary step to career attainment and overall life satisfaction. The iteration of "college-speak" and the concomitant notion that the road to success goes through college, has convinced millions of youths that the realization of their dreams depends on college enrollment. Any inkling of hope for their future is linked to earning college degrees. Hence, colleges and universities are viewed by most youth as places of hope.

At the time of this project, two of the participants were actually enrolled in a technical college. Several students envisioned themselves as collegians. Therefore, I decided to frame the discussion about colleges and universities and hope within a context of pursuit of life-goals. The students had identified life-goals, and they accumulated knowledge of schools that offered programs and/or opportunities that could help them achieve their life-goals. Similar to numerous incoming college freshmen, a few of the study participants were undecided. They had not identified life-goals, but they believed that attending a college or university would help them achieve success. Thus, the thought of a future relationship with a college or university allowed students to expand their experience with hope.

Let's begin with Za'Nya, one of two collegians at the time of the research project. Za'Nya was in her freshman year at a local technical college. Although she enrolled at the local technical college for specific reasons, Za'Nya introduced her career aspiration and discussed her desire to attend a university.

> *"I want to be a psychologist. I want to go to a big university... Sometimes it's more opportunity after you graduate, you know a more known school is better. Better jobs. And, then I want the college experience. You know, living on the dorms and being around all the college kids."*

College life appealed to Za'Nya for both youthful and professional reasons. In a very forward-thinking way, she recognized the associated advantage of attending and earning a degree from a more mainline four-year university compared to the junior college that she attended ("Sometimes it's more opportunity after you graduate. You know a more known school is better. Better jobs."). It was obvious that Za'Nya had thought through her process of *becoming*. She considered the steps and concluded the pathway to her goal fulfillment would necessarily have to include a university with acclaim. For Za'Nya the addition of credentials from a university would improve her prospects of career attainment and bolster her sense of agency, the belief that she could successfully pursue psychology and join the field as a professional.

Grounded and Focused

Similar to Za'Nya, Amber graduated from WNHS and was enrolled at a local technical college at the time of the research project. Post-secondary education at a four year college or university was in her sight as well, but perhaps at a later date. Amber was an expectant mother, and she believed that her pregnancy required her to select an alternate route. Amber had the following to say about her post-secondary plans:

"I started Laketon in the fall and umm in the teacher education track. I've been taking five classes for this semester. Next semester I'm having my baby so I'll be taking two classes. They told me I shouldn't do that, but I really can't have too much idle time (laughter) but ummm, so after Laketon, after I get done with the four semesters at Laketon, I have the option of transferring to Prescott, Dwitt, or Milton. Milton is really interested in Laketon students that are especially in the teacher's track program at Laketon. They're offering scholarships and stuff too so I'm kind of thinking about Milton to be honest. It looks nice like oh, you graduated from

145

Milton? I kind of want to be challenged. I don't want to just accept having a bachelor's degree because I don't feel like that's challenging enough...so after I finish my four semester at Laketon, I'll end up transferring to one of the schools to get my four-year degree. I want to become a teacher."

Remarkably, Amber pointed out a benefit of attending a large university that Za'Nya mentioned, public perception of the degree ("I'm kind of thinking about Marquette to be honest. It looks nice like oh, you graduated from Marquette..."). Akin to Za'Nya, enrollment at the technical college was a decision born out of the need for an educational experience more amenable to her reality. Both young ladies regarded relationship with and access to a university as a pathway to life-goal attainment. Amber was even more strategic in her selection of local technical colleges. She selected Laketon because of its connection with Milton, the school of her then dreams, "Milton is really interested in Laketon students that are especially in the teacher's track program at Milton, and so, and they're offering scholarships and stuff..."

I was fascinated by Amber's resolve and focus. Yes, she was pregnant. And yes, giving birth to a child would undoubtedly change her entire life, but Amber's sense of agency was strong. Rather than take a year or so off to concentrate her strength and efforts on her baby, Amber planned to enroll in Milton at the same time. Why? Her life-goal. Amber was enthralled with the prospect of becoming a teacher:

"I want to become a teacher. I just don't know what type of teacher. I mean I just don't know what grade-level I want to teach. Ummm, my, I want to start with

the younger individuals, the children, but that's just not where my heart is at. It's something I feel comfortable with doing you know? Like I know I can count to ten with them, you know, (laughter), but I wouldn't, I don't feel like I would be fulfilled there. So, like when I was younger I always said I was going to teach seventh grade. I always wanted to teach..."

For Amber, it would only be a matter of time before she achieved her goal of becoming a teacher. She was ambitious and exhibited tons of optimism. Laketon was her space of hope. As a Laketon student, she participated in learning and interactions that allowed her to take steps closer to Milton and eventually her educational dream.

Angel also looked forward to enrollment in a college or university. Her life-goal was to become a real estate agent. Angel watched some of the cable television shows that featured real estate agents and was drawn by what the accoutrements that some agents amassed. She wanted the flash and the cash. Even though she was aware that the salary index among real estate agents varied, Angel was still convinced that real estate was her field. As such, Angel understood that enrolling in a college or university was a critical step towards achieving her life-goal:

"...Go to college and learn about that stuff. My plan right now to be honest... I really don't have a plan. I sort of just go with the flow right now...well really just to finish high school and go on to college, but I know it's going to be extremely hard because I'm going through a lot of stuff at the time. But, I believe that I can do it. I can really make it... Because I believe in myself, and I believe that I can make it to college."

The social impediments in Angel's life notwithstanding, she possessed strong belief in her personal capabilities. If there was any trepidation at all, it was related to the "stuff" in her life at the time. True to her statement about hope, Angel seemed poised to fight to obtain her goal. She was certain that if she could get to college, she could reach her goal of becoming a real estate agent.

More...Please!

Heretofore, I've referred to Casey as the unforthcoming student who provided painfully terse commentary. Humorously, I must add another adjective to her description—-restrained! Compared to her study contemporaries, Casey expressed no noticeable excitement about attending a college or university. She viewed college very mundanely and pragmatically: it was merely a means to an end. Of course, there was nothing wrong with her attitude. When discussing college, the stark contrast between Casey and the other girls' posture and expression was super-obvious.

Casey's eyes were focused on a career in Criminal Justice. She wanted to become a correctional officer. Casey did her homework. She knew the qualifications necessary to become a correctional officer. If there was a pathway that allowed her to put on a uniform without attending college, Casey would certainly select it. As it related to her immediate goals, her life-goal and college enrollment, Casey explained:

> *"Basically, now, as far as I can see, um graduating from high school, going to college. I want to be a correctional officer so I'll probably be in college for like four years. Um, then after that I want to actually start in that career. I'm not sure what would happen after*

that, but that's as far as I'm trying to look right now...
I've looked at schools. I haven't like looked into their
Criminal Justice programs if they had good ones. But,
I've looked at some schools."

Even with what appeared to be a dulled expectation for college matriculation, I was impressed with Casey's deliberate attempt to identify schools that provided the program that she needed for her career choice and life-goal. Her research efforts revealed how serious-minded she was about *becoming* a correctional officer. (Perhaps I was spoiled by the energy of Amber and Za'Nya. Maybe as a black male who'd benefited wonderfully from the college experience, I wanted Casey to appear to want college in a more demonstrative way. Maybe the very overt excitement expressed by Casey and Amber and Za'Nya was due to the fact that they were already in college. Casey was still a high school student attempting to recover high school credits. It was plausible that Casey was simply articulating her plan, but still grounded in the reality of her high school situation.)

Going After Knowledge
So far I've only discussed the girls as it concerns study participants and their relationship and/or their potential relationship with colleges and universities. The young men had thoughts about college enrollment and completion, but conveyed a greater degree of undecidedness. In comparison, the girls knew the names of institutions and knew specific fields that they intended to enter. Sounds typical huh? At any rate, though the boys weren't as direct in pinpointing where they wanted to attend college, they were assured of the importance of college enrollment as it pertained to their career dreams.

For example, Maurice hadn't settled on a specific career. It wasn't that he had no clue, Maurice simply had options. Evidently, Maurice knew that he possessed a skill-set that permitted him the privilege of being selective. Maurice shared the following when he articulated his thoughts on careers,

"I really have a couple of things that I would like to do in my life, a couple of careers that I'd like to try out or go to school for...like being a detective or just being a entrepreneur. You know just business overall. Anything that comes to my mind at the time."

Listening to Maurice, I discerned confidence and imagination. He could see himself functioning in multiple ways. Yet, there was something about entrepreneurship that attracted Maurice. At the time I presumed that Maurice's thoughts about owning his own business were influenced by his relationship with his aunt (an entrepreneur). Perhaps they were. But, as he elaborated, another source of motivation emerged. Maurice communicated a desire to engage in social entrepreneurship,

"Uh, like anything like a store or anything like a cleaning business and a couple of things. I can't really think of em but you know a couple of things, do anything positive you know to help kids out or something like you know just keep em out the neighborhood for a little while...stuff like that."

Maurice was open-minded. His flexibility as it pertained to career goals suggested that entrepreneurship was possibly a means rather than an end in itself. Maurice wanted to help people. Two phrases from the above commentary in Maurice's interview highlighted his openness, "Anything that comes to my mind at the time" and "...do anything positive". These comments suggested that his was a service-orientation. Maurice was concerned with the impact of his prospective venture(s) on the surrounding communities. Since Maurice's life-goal was meaningful service, he was also open-minded and flexible concerning post-secondary options:

> *"My plan is to finish school like completely and go to a four year school or two-year. It really don't matter cuz like I can really do both of em like go to a two-year and a four-year like just keep going to school and see how deep I can get in it and try to get to the end."*

Certainly, Maurice viewed post-secondary education as a critical step towards living his dream. Growing up in Detroit was no easy task. Maurice understood the importance of responsible citizenry. He knew that positivity was a premium in settings where misfortune and disappointment reign supreme. It was quite amazing. In lieu of pursuing college and an eventual career that could position him to make tons of money and move as far away from the haunting scenes of the inner-city, Maurice resolved that he would succeed so he could invest. This vision of responsible, pro-social entrepreneurship shared by Maurice typified the attitude that Duncan-Andrade and Morrell (2008) articulated should be part of the goal of education in the millennial era. The authors called for education that would challenge students to choose community investment over divestment, service to their neighborhoods rather than shallow self-indulgence.

A Way Out and Up

Inasmuch as Maurice leaned towards abnegation as part of his vision, Jameel regarded college enrollment as a critical alternative to the perils and problems of his environment. Jameel was not set on any college or university in particular. Unlike Maurice, he had no burgeoning career blueprint. In full disclosure, Jameel admitted that he didn't even know what he wanted to do after graduation. But, he was sure that he didn't want to live in his environment anymore, "I'm undecided about what I want to do when I graduate like what I wanna go to college for. I just know, I don't want to be in the ghetto for the rest of my life." After growing up in a milieu that he termed "the ghetto", Jameel concluded that it was a socially insalubrious setting and he wanted out. Thus, post-secondary enrollment at a college or university was Jameel's way out.

Jameel was convinced that the "normal" happenings of the ghetto weren't normal. Jameel's social assessment led him to a place of dissonance. He knew that what he witnessed daily wasn't all there was to life. Cone (1997) termed Jameel's state of mind, "existential absurdity", the belief that the world as one sees and experiences it is incongruent with the way that the world should be. During our conversation, Jameel asked poignant questions related to the inundation of liquor stores in the urban setting and the lack of viable employment opportunities. It made no sense to him. To support Jameel's position, I use the quote below, once again, because it is rich and encompasses multiple facets of the hope discussion (My apologies to those who lament its overuse.).

"Seeing the same thing every day...same liquor store, same corner stores, same people. I cain't be around that especially if I plan on having kids and getting money.

The only way of getting money out there in the hood is the illegal way. I ain't trying to do that. I'm already labeled as a statistic. Like, just because how I look. You know what I'm saying? I got a lot of tattoos and all that. And everybody that look like me they think that they thuggin' or gang-bangin' so-called or drug dealin'. I mean I wanna be the person that little kids look up to even though I got a hood image. I still wanna have knowledge behind that, you know what I'm saying?"

To my mind, Jameel wanted to break the mold and do something different. I never sensed that Jameel was ashamed of the environment that he grew up in. No, his attitude suggested more of a desire to go beyond. He was unwilling to accept the notion that what he observed each day was the extent of what could be seen in life. Hence, departure from the all too familiar scenes and sounds of the ghetto would allow Jameel to explore and confirm his postulates about life. In Jameel's case, enrollment in a college or university would be confirmatory for himself, not so much for others. It would afford Jameel the opportunity to study a field, obtain knowledge, and acquire skills that he could utilize to seek gainful employment, something uncommon, something lightly esteemed in his neighborhood.

Even though Jameel's thoughts on college enrollment differed a bit compared to Maurice's points, it was interesting to observe that both young men wanted to stand as role models. Jameel stated, "I mean I wanna be the person that little kids look up to even though I got a hood image." Similar to Maurice, Jameel wanted to be an ensample of what it means to surmount obstacles and succeed. And in both cases, the boys perceived that enrollment in a college or university offered the assurance that they can achieve and become emblems of hope for others.

In a nutshell, college and/or university enrollment was discussed as the critical link to career aspirations and life-goals for all of the highlighted students. Three students specifically identified their career choice: Za'Nya, Amber, and Casey. They had already begun to research and/or identify schools that have programs in the fields they intended to pursue. Maurice and Jameel hadn't settled upon career fields, but they knew that college and/or university enrollment was an essential step. Compared to his female counterparts, Maurice's motivation was more others-centered. While they relished the prospect of operating in a career field (e.g., education, psychology, criminal justice); Maurice eyed service to his community. Jameel's position was a bit more pragmatic. Part of his focus was survival. He refused to believe that he was helplessly bound to "ghetto life". Transcendence and transformation were Jameel's reasons for pursuing college enrollment. Regardless of the student's intentions, earning a degree was viewed as a pathway to life-goal attainment. Therefore, the college or university environment was a place of hope. Characteristics associated with colleges or universities included opportunities for career pursuit and access to multiple resources.

Community Centers

As a reminder, the nexus between the study participants and the places that they mentioned in association with their experience with hope is related to goal attainment. In other words, the institutions named featured an element that either supported a selected pathway or strengthened their agency. Church was a place that seemed to specialize in promoting an overall message of hope. This discourse helped to ground the affected students in their goal pursuit by inspiring them to reject any inkling of surrender to internal or external impediments. A critical aspect of Hope Theory, as it pertains to agency, is the belief that one's selected pathway(s) are actually viable. Agency also suggests that an individual has the ability to carry out any tasks related to the pathway(s). Study participants who spoke of the significance of colleges and universities focused on the acquisition of critical knowledge and skills—vis-à-vis specific majors or fields—that would enable them to obtain their life-goal. To this end, the college and/or university setting, in their estimation, functioned as a bridge to reduce or eliminate knowledge gaps and resource gaps. Essentially, enrollment in institutions of higher learning is and was a pathway for the study participants.

Besides church and post-secondary institutions, at least two students discussed their relationship with a community center. Community centers are generally mainstays in most cities, towns, and villages. Metaphorically, they are "watering holes" where community residents can be refreshed through a variety of programs such as academic tutoring, healthy meals, competitive sports, or arts & crafts. While examining the outcomes of the Clemente Program in Australia, an adult educational program "designed to engage the disaffected, isolated, homeless and poor in values-based education" (p. 92), Howard, Butcher, and Egan (2010) observed that community centers are places where innovative partnerships generate strategies and programs that meet the urgent needs of marginalized groups. The authors defined innovative partnerships as "the collaboration of committed partners from community, academe, corporate and government sectors" (p. 89). The key according to Howard, Butcher, and Egan (2010) is the installment of a shared vision and commitment to the enhancement of educational and learning opportunities for those on the margins.

Community centers are also hubs for social activism and political activity. For example, in my hometown, several of the Boys & Girls Club sites function as polling places and sites for town hall meetings where residents can receive important information and voice their concerns. Most importantly, community centers have long been regarded as sanctuaries where children can escape violence.

Maurice and Tariq recalled their membership in community centers when they discussed institutions that contributed to their experience with hope. Tariq mentioned a community center named the Rising Star Foundation. He recalled a memory from his experience, "Yeah, when umm...I used to go to the Rising Star Foundation. We used to have a youth program there. They used to teach a lot about like how to adapt ourselves to life, like being a part of life like not just being here." With respect to access, this community center that Tariq featured offered programming that resonated with youth. Though Tariq was unable to describe in detail specific lessons, I interpreted his remarks to suggest that the program facilitators encouraged he and his peers to thrive rather than merely survive; to have dignity and to be positively engaged in life. For example, Tariq's phrase, "like being a part of life..." may have indicated an attempt by program facilitators to help youths think about how they can impact their world. It may have indicated that the facilitators wanted students to expand their personal visions and see themselves beyond societal and family perceptions. I interpreted the latter portion of Tariq's comment, "...like not just being here" to mean that the program facilitators wanted the young people to think about purpose. While it cannot be proven, it stands to reason that the facilitators even wanted Tariq and his contemporaries to recognize the connection between hope and purpose. I surmised that the content included inspiration and the pursuit of higher aims because Tariq acknowledged that the messages in the youth program compelled him to think about hope.

Hoops and Hope

When I asked Maurice to talk about people or places that helped him to think about hope, he mentioned a more familiar organization—the YMCA. Maurice explained his relationship with the YMCA:

> *"Yeah, uh, I started school when I was three which actually was the YMCA at Pearson Rock here. That was the only school I ever attended in Kingstown. You know but I was raised in Detroit so that was the only school I went to down here. My moms used to work there. I used to stay up there. I played basketball and things like that, but I really wasn't in to the afterschool programs. I really just played basketball at school, but I really just, you know, grew up in the streets. I liked to be in the streets a lot."*

Initially, Maurice's connection to the YMCA was due to his mother's status as a YMCA employee (I understood this well because my mother was a public school teacher, and I spent many mornings and evenings in the school buildings that she taught in. And, similar to Maurice, I enjoyed playing basketball in the school gymnasium.). The recreational programs featured at the YMCA captured Maurice's attention. Unlike Tariq, he didn't recall inspirational lectures, lessons, or discussions. Maurice had a penchant for basketball. While pondering Maurice's remarks, I considered the possibility that playing basketball may have been an alternative to him spending time "in the streets". And, it is possible that what began as a convenience for his mother (having Maurice at the YMCA while she worked, i.e., free childcare), may have evolved into a deliberate strategy to circumvent Maurice's fascination with being "in the streets". YMCA membership may have been Maurice's mother's way to protect him from the hazards of the inner city. Whether it was planned or unplanned, the arrangement ultimately worked for Maurice because he always had access to the YMCA basketball courts.

In further reflection on Maurice's discussion, I concluded that the hope that Maurice sensed may have actually been his mother's hope; that perhaps YMCA membership was a pathway to attainment of her goal of preserving her son's life. Recall that Maurice was the student that transparently stated that his goal was to live to see age 30. Since Maurice only specifically mentioned age three in his comments, I couldn't determine how long Maurice enjoyed his relationship with the YMCA. This is an important detail because the ability to consider abstract constructs does increase with age. The fact that Maurice recalled his relationship with the YMCA suggested that his experience may have been over an extended period of time. Thus, it can be argued that Maurice began to see the value in YMCA membership from his mother's perspective. Ostensibly, her hope became his hope.

Neither Tariq nor Maurice mentioned having memberships at a community center at the time of the study. Their testimonials suggested that their previous preferred places of recreation (Maurice) and refinement (Tariq) factored into their recollection of hope. And though some critics may not perceive that their accounts fit perfectly within the framework of the hope construct, the subjective nature of personal experience renders any and all bashing inquiry powerless. Through the experiences of Tariq and Maurice, I identified certain characteristics associated with the community centers: accessible, youth-centered, educational, safe, and recreational. Again, for youth on the margins, each identified characteristic is desirable and contributes to ways that they can experience hope.

Non-profit Organization

At a cursory glance, community centers and non-profit organizations are indistinguishable. Right? I mean, for all intents and purposes, community centers are non-profit enterprises. However, for the purpose of clarity of the study, I opted to separate community centers and non-profit organizations. The details of student testimonials provided enough reason to report findings in different sections. Further, I deemed it necessary to help readers contradistinguish the experiences of the students. Maurice and Tariq described community centers as physical places that they frequented. In either boy's case, their community center experiences featured services related to the development of life skills and recreational sports opportunities. Although all organizations have identified missions and visions, the presence of community centers—along with their sustainability—is largely contingent upon the needs of the surrounding community.

Within the context of this study, a guiding mission gives non-profit organizations life. Fulfillment of the mission drives all organization operations and underpins its practices. Thus unlike many community centers, non-profit organizations may not be consigned to a particular locale. The work of the organization establishes relevance and viability. Therefore, non-profit markets may stretch to include local, national, and global locations. The argument then is that community centers are primarily associated with place, while non-profit organizations are primarily associated with performance. Amber's account helps to shed some light on this distinction.

The Emergence of a New Self

Becoming a team member of a trustworthy non-profit organization extended and strengthened Amber's experience with hope. Instead of enrolling in college directly after high school, Amber opted to join a program named, Public Allies. Public Allies is a non-profit organization grounded in the belief that everyone can lead, and it helps individuals discover their leadership capacity while training them to lead. In respect to the point alluded to in the above paragraph, Public Allies is a national effort to engage diverse citizens in community revitalization and restoration (Public Allies, 2013). Prior to interviewing Amber, I heard one or two people mention Public Allies in conversation, but I had no real understanding of the scope of their program. Amber explained the impact that being a Public Allies member had on her life:

"I was so miserable cause I just couldn't grasp it. You know, I couldn't… It was just something that I was just doing wrong, and I don't like doing wrong. I don't like being wrong or you know constantly having something wrong with me. And so, it was challenging, but it also let me know how far I can go and how good I can get and become if I want, if I chose to. I mean, the beginning…I was lost the whole time, from September until January, I was lost. I mean it was a lot of personal things going on. I mean not personal but like, just things going on that I didn't like, but also a reflection of me that I didn't like, like I couldn't get right you know, and I didn't like that. And so, when I started to figure out the

160

process, I didn't want to let it go because then I had it you know? Once I had it, I had it and I'll always have it; how to interact in social networking. I thought I was good at that in high school, but I wasn't. It just was like literally my self-esteem cuz it was like these are adults most of these people that I'm with are already gradu-ated from college or doing they master's. I was just get-ting out of high school. I'm barely 18, but I was there. I graduated from that program. A lot of people didn't. Was it easy? No it wasn't. Did I do it? Yes, I did. And, that's something I can count on and carry with me the rest of my life..."

Amber's experience with Public Allies was a trial of self-discovery. True to its mission, Public Allies, according to Amber, helped her come face-to-face with her potential. More importantly, Amber recognized that she had the power to deter-mine her trajectory. Through participation in/with Public Allies, Amber strengthened skills, "And so, when I started to figure out the process. I didn't want to let it go because then I had it you know, once I had it, I had it and I'll always have it; how to interact in social networking. I thought I was good at that in high school, but no I wasn't."

Amber was transparent in mentioning the challenges she met as a member of Public Allies. It was an inward journey of sorts during which see longingly gazed at her potentiali-ties while simultaneously running into her limitations (Palmer, 2000). In the vernacular of many of the students that I've served, Amber "kept it real". As a Public Allies participant, Amber worked with middle school students. She ran headlong into the roadblocks of difficulty that accompany relations with adolescents. Amber confessed that she was lost. It was culture shock. Facets of her personality and repertoire that worked well in high school were useless in her new domain. Yet, Amber rode the tumultuous waves of change and learned in the midst of feeling "lost" and eventually navigated the Public Allies realm with veteran-like ease. In her discussion, Amber shared a personal question and answer repartee that to my mind was most salient, "Was it easy? No it wasn't. Did I do it? Yes, I did, and that's something I can count on and carry with me the rest of my life..." Through her stint with Public Allies, Amber's sense of agency grew. She became convinced that obstacles can be surmounted.

Amber's triumphant finish at Public Allies amid what she perceived to be unrelenting rigor, highlights what I believe all caring, authentic teachers desire for their students. She got it! What is it? It is the realization of self; that within each of us lies the potential to do the extraordinary; that within each of us is often latent strength and creativity that simply needs to be joggled loose from the mounds of self-doubt and apprehension that weigh us down. Amber's experience underscores the reason that adults, especially teachers, tell students to try. Of course risk-taking is scary. No one relishes vulnerability, particularly in an unfamiliar context with unpredictable variables. But, there is beauty and sheer joy in realizing that you *can* when everything inside of you speaks to the contrary. Amber experienced this victory and observed that she possessed internal attributes that enable her be successful wherever she journeys in life. Recall that Amber discussed her desire to be a teacher, *"I want to become a teacher. I just don't know what type of teacher. I mean I just don't know what grade-level I want to teach. Ummm, my..., I want to start with the younger individuals, the children, but that's just not where my heart at..."* Essentially, Amber's intent to teach was tested. Her heart was vetted through her experience with middle school students. I am not aware of the protocols of Public Allies as it pertains to the manner in which they dole out assignments. Maybe her advisors had knowledge of Amber's desire. Maybe not. Either way, Amber was placed in a situation that allowed her to contemplate and determine if education was really her realm.

It made sense that Amber included Public Allies in the discussion about her experience with hope. Though she may have mourned the loss of the viability of old skills, Amber basked in the exuberance of birthing new skills. Moreover, Amber participated in another graduation ceremony, thereby reaffirming her belief that she could begin and complete a major program while caring for a child. Public Allies was not the destination for Amber. Instead, Public Allies was another pathway along Amber's trek towards self-actualization and career attainment. Public Allies was a home for hope, and as such, it featured several characteristics that helped Amber experience hope: learning environment, inclusive, service-oriented, and age-diversity.

Summary of Students' Institutional Experience with Hope

In Chapter Four readers observed the role that persons of influence have in youths experiencing hope. Plainly stated; people matter. Who you are, what you do, and how those two notions work together absolutely matter to observant, curious young people. As we've seen in this chapter, places matter as well. And, just as the value of interaction with adults will vary with the uniqueness of youth (e.g., needs, aspirations, prior experiences, etc.) and the context of the relationship, the significance of place is equally subjective and contextual. The students' discussions prove this point. Several different institutions were linked with student experiences with hope: church, college and universities, community centers, and a non-profit organization. Incidentally, generalities seemed to dominate the discussions. No student discussed a significant relationship with individuals who were members of the institutions. The experience itself was the focal point. After I reviewed interview transcripts, I culled several instrumental characteristics associated with each institution that contributed to hope-raising experiences. Inspirational and values-centered were characteristics associated with church. Colleges and/or universities were resourceful and educational. Community centers were accessible, youth-centered, recreational, educational, and safe. The non-profit organization was inclusive, featured age-diversity, offered learning opportunities, and was service-oriented. Each place was critical to these youths on the margins. Each place added to the construction of a home for hope in the inner sanctum of their hearts.

Figure 7
Characteristics of Institutions

Student	Institution	Characteristics
Casey	• Church	• *Inspirational* • *Value-centered*
Angel	• Church	• *Inspirational* • *Value-centered*
Amber	• *College* • *University* • *Non-profit*	• *Resourceful* • *Multiple Opportunities* • *Educational* • *Inclusive* • *Learning environment* • *Service-oriented* • *Age-diversity*

The Places

Tariq	• Community Center	• Accessible • Youth-centered • Educational
Maurice	• Community Center	• Accessible • Youth-centered • Recreational • Safe

(Arrington, 2014)

Chapter 7

EDUCATION THE WOODSON-NEWTON WAY

(Part One)

"The flowers of tomorrow are in the seeds of today."
                                        -M.K. Asante, Jr.

Our children are heirs of the world that adults, both past and present generations, have left in their hands. Somehow we've constructed a society that thrives on technology and the advance of intellect, but is too often bereft of heart and enduring compassion. Human beings are without question the quintessential creative act of God Almighty. No creature is comparable. But, in all of our wonder and brilliance, we've managed to bequeath to our children a world that is as unstable as it is great, a world that is on the verge of implosion unless there is a tremendous interruption of the course that *we've* chosen. For instance, our children cope with violence on a daily basis. It's ubiquitous. Children cannot even be amused through cartoons without some aspect of their viewing being influenced by malice and reprisal. News outlets report on violence in various parts of the world. Some sports are violent. Some music lyrics are violent. Social media has become an easily accessible and user-friendly purveyor of violent thoughts and acts. Each day, everywhere, violence confronts us and propositions our conscience. Will we acquiesce to its solicitations or refuse and subject ourselves to relative marginalization? This is but one heavy force of contemporary social interaction that our children—heirs of the great society—have to contend with.

The matter ultimately becomes one of legacy and impartation. Adults must interrogate their beliefs and values. Adults must grapple with the notion that that which we hold dear has philosophical and moralistic origins. As noted Christian apologist Ravi Zacharias (2010) argued, we have to question "how and why we make our individual and societal decisions" (p.17). Further, we must accept the reality that the absentmindedness with which we've allowed our culture to expand—without significant concern for moral consideration—has created a scenario that forces our children to contend with cultural behemoths and socio-economic quagmires that they are ill-equipped to handle. As Americans, our thirst for intellectual prowess and global domination has overshadowed any focus on developing the social vision and souls of our progeny. That said, too many youths are coming of age in an era of sprawling secularization that can only be countered by kind hearts and spirits that teem with humanitarian values.

So, how do we counter the current trend? How do we in effect attempt to undue or mitigate the effects of our hubris and lack of foresight? The answer lies in seeds. Adults must become expert planters of life-affirming seeds that support the development of inner strength. No bountiful harvest ever springs forth haphazardly. No, all fruitage gleaned is the result of the assiduous labor of farmers who plant seeds with intentionality and see to it that the conditions that contribute best to crop development are sustained.

In the previous chapter, we examined students' accounts of their experiences in places associated with their encounters with hope. The students discussed meeting and courting hope at church, in colleges and universities, at community centers, and while engaged in the noble objectives of a respected non-profit organization. Yet, the place of grandeur, the Taj Mahal of hope if you will, per the project participants, was none other than WNHS. The high school they attended at the time of the study or had graduated from in the cases of Za'Nya and Amber, was to their minds the residence of hope. The way of education in this space, from the physical layout to the imagery that bedecked the walls, contributed to the growth of hope in the hearts and minds of students.

Drawing upon the fourth major theme of the research study, "Elements of WNHS", I will highlight the critical features of the school and share the accompanying student reflections. The specific features of WNHS (elements) that emerged in the reports were online learning, staff, and lessons. All three components were crucial to the revival of these students' interest in school and post-high school ambitions. Moreover, these elements influenced the students to view WNHS as a bridge to obtainment of one of their primary life-goals—high school graduation (Very fittingly, the motto of WNHS is "building bridges over troubled waters".). And, as a bridge, WNHS became a safe pathway to their futures.

Online Learning

Each study participant entered WNHS deficient in graduation credits. They were in academic arrears and desperately in need of support to restore their credibility as students. More importantly, the students needed a medium that would enable them to recover multiple academic credits in a relatively short amount of time. Remember, the average duration of enrollment at WNHS was one to one and a half years. Hence, there was some pressure to perform. Thankfully for the students, WNHS featured online learning. Now, I will not expound upon the research related to online learning (For a more extensive review of the literature related to online learning, its pros and cons, interested parties can read my dissertation.). But, suffice it to say that online learning, in simple terms, is learning that features instruction and content that is primarily accessed online (Allen & Seaman, 2011). Balfour (2010) called online learning an educational approach that utilizes computer and internet technology to provide virtual classrooms that allow students to matriculate through traditional K-12 course requirements without the stressors and limitations of traditional school settings. To Balfour's (2010) point, nearly all WNHS students were inhibited by the limitations of traditional high school settings, and subsequently needed a setting more suitable to their needs (That was part of the major premise for founding WNHS.).

Recognizing the dilemma that the combination of urgent needs, low student self-efficacy and lack of motivation presented, WNHS partnered with online learning providers to deliver academic services. Consistent with Allen and Seaman's (2011) claim, about 80% of instruction, regardless of the subject, was delivered online. The other 20% was provided by an actual teacher. With the support of a real, live person, students were able to complete courses in three to five weeks in most cases. Since most students were *overage* (Overage means that students were older than the typical age for a particular grade level. For example, we enrolled a number of students who were sophomores by credits, but actually 17, 18, and in some cases 19 years old. Typically sophomores in high schools are 15 or

16 years old.) and generally 8-10 credits short of the academic standing that they were supposed to possess, the prospect of completing a typically 18 week course in less than a third of the time was considered a sweet deal. Thus, upon hearing the details and testimonials of successful credit recovery, prospective students became almost instantly suffused with vigor and expectation.

Such a seemingly exclusive plan for academic resurgence far exceeded the paltry plans of their former high school homes. Initially, comparison and contrast dominated discussion about online learning. Although the satisfaction with online learning varied among the study participants, it was very difficult to deny its utility as it related to obtaining their primary goal— high school graduation. All of the students recognized, objectively, that online learning helped them take advantage of their "opportunity to learn" (Schott Foundation, 2013).

Music Please!

Principal Stokes always spoke about the school being "home" for the children. In other words, he attempted to help the staff understand that children who previously enjoyed no significant connection to school and consequently were unimpressed with its requirements and features, needed a reason to *want* to attend school. And, according to Principal Stokes, it was up to the staff to shape the conditions of the school environment in a way that appealed to the students. Access to music was one of the features that accompanied the online learning experience at WNHS. Angel's commentary attested to this fact.

> *"It's been um awesome. I like it a lot. I can concentrate. I can listen to music too so that helps me you know get through my work more, faster, and easier. And*

171

*um sometimes you know be a little bit difficult, but I
have help. You know, teachers help me with the things
that I need help with. Other than that online learning
is pretty good."*

While listening to music, students were able to tune out
everything in their vicinity that could potentially distract them.
Remember, these youths had "fallen from grace" in a sense.
Many of them were tired of being academic bottom-feeders.
But, more importantly, they were ready to complete high
school. Online learning offered a fast track to course completion. The ability to listen to music while working sweetened the
deal. It was an amenity that students were initially unaware of,
but greatly appreciated. To some degree, access to music was
the initial way that WNHS staff attempted to eliminate distractions. As Angel shared, her ability to concentrate on course
content was enhanced because the music helped to increase her
attentiveness.

Of course, there are folks who'd argue against this musical
option. And, it was an option. Students didn't have to listen to
music. But, it was accessible for those who were interested.
Thanks to the genius of the school's technology coordinator,
Mr. Ricks, WNHS students could log into their computers and
access a musical database. It was our own streaming system.
Students could choose from a list of well over 300 popular
songs. Incidentally, Mr. Ricks was only a co-producer. WNHS
students were allowed to request or recommend songs for the
database. They'd bring in CDs (purchased music). Mr. Ricks
would download the desired songs. So, not only was music
available, but it was music that the students actually liked.
How's that for an incentive for working?

Even further, Mr. Ricks was capable of manipulating the "streaming activity" by embargoing certain songs. Principal Stokes frequently encouraged students to monitor their musical diets. He understood that the majority of WNHS students loved hip hop. In most cases the students preferred songs that contained references to misogyny, violence, and extreme materialism. Principal Stokes argued that such "food" was unhealthy and too much of it would certainly have ill social and psychological effects. Thus, he also provided Mr. Ricks with music. His selections were smooth, often inspirational songs. Principal Stokes also exposed WNHS students to what is termed conscience hip hop, songs that advance socio-political messages and offer critiques of American culture and global issues. To my mind, it was a brilliant move on his part. With his savvy, the staff honored the choices of the students, but also directed the student's attention to more healthy options that were amenable to the staff. We honored their stuff: they respected our stuff (Duncan-Andrade, 2010). The idea was strategically culturally responsive. And, to the delight of the teachers, they could control the situation, and it required no significant effort on their part. If a student became too engrossed in listening instead of working, Mr. Ricks could simply shut down their music access.

Clearly, the music feature wasn't available in traditional school settings. And, this uniqueness added to the cache that enrollment at WNHS was building among students. With this feature, Angel experienced a reduction in disruptions, and she was able to become more efficient with her allotted work time.

Improving the School Experience

Jameel drew a distinction between the traditional classroom and the WNHS classroom setting. Akin to Angel, he relished the ability to put on headphones and tune out everything around him:

> *"I like it cuz I can pay more attention to it cuz with my headphones I can just zone into the direct instructions. I can listen more and then when I'm at home, I can just do it cuz I got a laptop so I just do it at home whenever I got free time. It's different because we working on the computers and then in the regular school know what I'm sayin' it's distractions. If the teacher talkin', sometimes you don't pay attention. I focus here better than at the previous schools that I went to."*

While examining Jameel's remarks, I was drawn to a word that he used, focus ("I focus here better than at previous schools that I went to".). This notion was consistently broached regardless of the study participant. Again, increased focus contributed to faster course completion. Faster course completion contributed to faster credit recovery and eventual high school graduation. Online learning transmuted the school experience from tolerable or in some cases intolerable to enjoyable.

Consider Maurice. His was a totally different personality, but he expressed the same appreciation for online learning.

> *"My experience with online learning has been nothing but great like you know cuz when you sittin' in a classroom full of 30 people and it's only one teacher you know you really can't get the full attention that you need. When it's one computer and one of you, you know can just sit there and pay attention."*

Maurice's remarks certainly supported reduced class sizes. Maurice's remarks also pointed towards an equitable educational experience, one that gives students what *they* need rather than what's manageable for the school. Notice his comment, "…when you sittin' in a classroom full of 30 people and it's only one teacher you know you really can't get the full attention that you need." One of the misconceptions about youth on the margins or in the case of WNHS scholars, youths with "checkered past", is that they don't want to learn. This couldn't be farther from the truth. Maurice clearly wanted to pay attention while attending traditional school, or at least was willing, but the dynamics of the large classroom made it difficult.

Casey shared Maurice's support of the online learning setting.

"It's great. It's way better than being in a class for me like even though when you're online it's not other students around you, you can focus better. I think it's better than having a teacher talk to you cuz if you don't understand it's not like you can be like ok I need extra help right now, like one-on-one time. You can't get that. And, I like being able to on the computer by myself and basically just listen to the lectures and stuff like that. It's way easier."

Similar to Casey, Jameel agreed that attempting to learn in traditional high school settings was a more challenging experience for him compared to the online learning environment. He remarked, "… in the regular school know what I'm sayin' it's distractions. If the teacher talkin', sometimes you don't pay attention. I focus here better than at the previous schools that I went to." Once again, the word *focus* surfaced. But, Jameel expanded the conversation from personalization to accessibility. Since the classes were delivered by previously recorded online instructors, WNHS students could continue to complete coursework off campus. Regarding accessibility of online learning, Jameel stated, "I can listen more and then when I'm at home, I can just do it cuz I got a laptop so I just do it at home whenever I got freetime." Jameel's decision to complete coursework at home increased his ability to "pay attention" without the threat of distractions and the restrictions of high school class schedules.

Appreciation for online learning was also expressed by Brian. Recall that I described Brian as the ever-reticent one, very low-key and independent. Online learning was a perfect medium for a student with his more melancholy temperament.

"My experience with online learning…it's been good because I'm the type of person, that I need to choose to do what I'm supposed to do and like I said before, and you know this give me the opportunity cause it allows you to work at your own pace. So you know I gotta bring myself to get up in the morning, get here, and do all that for three hours, maybe more if I want to stay. This is the only thing that I been able to do, to give me the opportunity to do that."

Brian was a strong-willed young man. He respected boundaries, but he needed autonomy. Online learning created room for his independent spirit to flourish. It afforded Brian the opportunity to control his academic fate. Brian indicated his high regard for the ability to steer, to actuate his learning experience without the interference of others in his comment, "you can work at your own pace". And, in a less explicit way, Brian alluded to previous school experiences and what he perceived

176

to be limited learning modalities saying, "This the only thing that I been able, to get me the opportunity to do that." Through online learning, Brian became more engaged in academic instruction. His attendance improved. And, unlike in his previous school experiences, Brian stayed out of trouble.

Beyond Labels

I don't mean to sound like an online learning apologist, but it was/is a learning modality with great utility, especially for students on the margins. Ronsisvalle and Watkins (2005) found that online education is useful for remedial purposes and for addressing the academic needs of students at-risk for dropping out of school. Additionally, Ng and Nicholas (2010) add that students who demonstrate credit deficiency enjoy the privacy of matriculation in online courses. Exactly what "the margins" means is different for every student and every school. Overall and in the context of this book, "the margins" is a reference to a social and educational space apart from the main, a space devoid of access to the benefits and resources of the general school experience.

Interestingly, students don't place themselves in "the margins". They are relegated to this space based on violations of codes of conduct, insufficient performance, personal indiscretions, and other deviations from socially sanctioned youth academic and behavioral performance. Even worse, when marginalized youths attempt to rejoin their peers in the main, those in authority rarely honor their courage because in many cases these youths haven't—to the eye of those in authority—acquired the attributes (e.g. compliance, traditional comportment) and requisite goods (e.g. good grades, unblemished discipline records) required for success in the main.

This situation is reminiscent of the *Divergent* (Lionsgate, 2014) movie franchise. The *Divergent* series imagines a dystopian society that has been divided into five different factions: Erudite, Candor, Amity, Abnegation, and Dauntless. Members of each faction exhibit specific attitudes and behaviors that align with the essence of the faction's appellation. Unfortunately, there are those in society who don't fit anywhere. They are deemed factionless, and they are consigned to the slums and edges. The factionless are shunned. They are scorned. They are the forgotten.

This is the plight of youths on the margins, the adjudicated, the teen mothers, the chronic non-attenders, and so on. They are not AP students. They are not Gifted & Talented. They are not Student Government Association members. They are not athletes. They have nothing of worth that the school (like society in *Divergent*) can benefit from. Well, at least that is the prevailing thought. And, since those with power, prestige, and access to resources (e.g., teachers, administrators, etc.) disregard the value of these factionless youth, their potential goes undiscovered. However, in the movie *Divergent*, there are scenes in which a member of a faction does attempt to help a member of the factionless bunch by giving them food. By the end of the second installment of the *Divergent* movie franchise, *Insurgent* (Lionsgate, 2015), the film's protagonist, Tris, through her own search for identity and liberation, becomes a champion for the factionless. She too is a misfit, but of a different order. Tris possesses attributes of all five factions. She is what they call, divergent. The divergent are perceived to be threats to the political and economic power structure. Tris joins with a few faithful companions and ultimately dismantles the entire social order, thus liberating the factionless and relieving them of their unearned social burden.

178

Clearly, there's tons more details that I omitted. The revelations associated with the movies and the issues of our time are abundant, but in the context of this study, the primary takeaway is that WNHS became a home for "factionless" youths. And, online learning was a resource that they were able to use to their advantage. It was a support that helped them to cast off negative and delimiting appellations and gain their freedom.

Different Perspectives

Other study participants commented on the utility of online learning. Tariq, Za'Nya, Amber, and Dawn all agreed that it helped them to focus and recover academic credits. However, in a bit of a twist of explanation, a few students expressed displeasure or indifference with using online learning. For example, Za'Nya expressed no enthusiasm when she discussed online learning. She stated, "You know I hated sitting behind a computer and doing that work every day. I mean I did it because it had to be done, but I didn't like it all." Za'Nya's sole purpose was to complete high school. Therefore, online learning, as the primary learning modality of WNHS, was the means to do so. In spite of what was clearly an aversion for online learning, Za'Nya did attest to its value and convenience.

> *"I mean even though I didn't like it, it helped me a lot because if I would have went to a regular high school, it would have been more distractions and then I would have had to keep up with eight classes and go to eight classes."*

Akin to Za'Nya, Amber wasn't exactly thrilled with the online learning approach, but she was not as forthcoming with her disinclination. She too recognized that her ultimate goal (high school graduation) was most important and that online learning was simply a technological means to a very important educational end. Amber commented,

> *"Honestly, it worked for me. Umm, I was able to move at my own pace and ask for help when I actually needed. I just really, I don't think it necessarily works for everyone, but I honestly believe it worked for me, especially at the time I was in. At that point in my life, that was perfect for me. I mean you could get online at home, school. I mean it's just really convenient for young people who not only have probably children and other responsibilities at home. Some people take care of their parents, grandparents you know? Then they also on top of that gotta work so they might have to get online at one o'clock in the morning and stay up for a few hours."*

Amber's comments highlighted an aspect of the traditional American educational experience that is sorely lacking — equity. Most citizens would argue that the playing field of success and social mobility is even as long as students have schools to attend. In other words, since all American students *can* attend school, there is equal opportunity to acquire the requisite numeracy and literacy skills needed to become culturally astute and advance in life. Yet, Duncan-Andrade and Morrell (2008) drew a distinction between equal education and equitable education, "An equal education system believes that everyone should get the same education. An equitable education believes that people should receive an education specific to their needs, as defined by their circumstances." (p. 173)

Amber's insight cancels any notion that online learning is an academic panacea, curing all student credit deficiency woes. But again, it levels the playing field and is more inclusive compared to the traditional mode of learning found in many comprehensive high schools. The convenience and accessibility of online learning cannot be questioned. And as the research (Ng & Nicholas, 2010; Ronsisvalle & Watkins, 2005) indicates, online learning is a viable option for students that grapple with complex life-circumstances.

Up until this time, I haven't discussed Everett, the other male study participant. Everett was an industrious young man. He possessed strong communicative and self-advocacy skills. But, most of the time, Everett stayed to himself. He was very focused on completing his coursework. Similar to his peers, Everett envisioned walking across the stage to receive his high school diploma. From time to time, Everett's hunger for graduation compelled him to work feverishly, but not necessarily effectively. He was consumed with quantity rather than quality. When it came to completing classes, Everett was "fast & furious". He'd take a quick "C" over a slow-cooked "A" any day.

Everett was one of numerous WNHS students who maintained a job while attending school. He'd often visit my office to provide me with an update on the happenings at his job. Or, he'd tell about another employment opportunity that he was considering. For sure, Everett viewed himself as an adult even though he was 17 years old at the time. On occasion, Principal Stokes and I would have to chide Everett because he'd speak disrespectfully to female staff members or interact with them in an imperious fashion. Everett was short in stature. Some would argue that he had a bit of a Napoleon complex.

Through the interview process, I gained insight into Everett's history. His background consisted of incarceration, foster care, and bouts with mental illness. Sure enough, Everett was a true criteria student. He was referred to WNHS by officials at the local juvenile detention facility. In retrospect, it is possible that Everett's arrogance and hardheadedness was related to him rarely having control over anything significant in his life. Whether it was punitive or for his well-being, someone else, someone other than a loved one, was frequently making decisions about what was best for Everett. And, it appeared that as he aged Everett decided that he would be the captain of his own ship; the input and desires of others be damned. Even in telling the short story (his version) of his arrival at WNHS, Everett told the story as if he alone was at the helm of the decision-making:

> *"Um, basically it was a choice between WNHS, Cramer, and I think I could've went back to Bailey...I heard about the school through a program. Then, I researched it myself because I was going to come here my freshman school year, but that wasn't going to work because I didn't have enough credits, so I waited til my junior year."*

Everett explained that his motivation for success was fueled by his experiences in juvenile detention. In fact, Everett's experiences influenced his professional life-goal. He explained that being in the foster care system and being evaluated by so many people impelled him to get involved and help. Everett stated that he wanted to become a nurse practitioner in a psychiatric mental health facility.

Unlike the majority of the study participants, Everett saw no difference between online learning and traditional classroom settings. In response to my inquiry about his experience with online learning Everett responded, "It's okay. Some days I don't want to be on the computer and some days I'm happy to. To me it's just like traditional school." Perhaps Everett was so focused on completing high school that the modality offered was irrelevant. He just wanted to finish and move on with his life (Everett graduated in 2013.). Everett proved Amber's point. Everyone viewed and experienced online learning differently.

Dawn provided the final example of a different perspective on online learning. Dawn's transition from the traditional classroom setting into the online learning environment was challenging. She was very transparent in her remarks, *"I'm not gon lie…it was hard at first. Like with the first class I didn't think it was gonna be all of that in just one thing. At first it was hard, but now I'm getting' the hang of it and I'm moving faster like I need to be."* No one else was as candid as Dawn in acknowledging the difficulty that she experienced. It's safe to say that Dawn initially perceived online learning as an easier pathway because of the independence it offered, but she soon realized that online learning also restructured the manner in which course content is packaged and disseminated. The workload surprised her. Thankfully, Dawn gained her bearings and developed a reasonable course completion pace.

Summing Up the WNHS Online Experience

Online learning was a viable vehicle for academic credit recovery for all the students in this study. It was viable because it worked. Online learning enabled students to complete 17-18 week classes in less than half the time. The study participants contended that online learning helped them focus on their work in a way that was nearly impossible in traditional classroom settings. Further, it offered privacy, a premium that is generally unavailable in any public venue. The students highlighted additional benefits of online learning: accessibility, convenience, and self-pacing. Students also commented that the independent approach with online learning afforded them opportunities for one-to-one instructional support. They no longer had to clamor for the teacher's attention amid dozens of classmates, many of whom were more interested in folly than fruitful performance.

In respect to Hope Theory, I concluded that the students' experiences with online learning contributed to their experience with hope because it provided a feasible pathway for attainment of their goal—high school graduation. Online learning seemed to strengthen the students' internal locus of control. As in Everett's case, they had command of their course, their direction. Their academic fate was no longer in the hands of derelict or dismissive authority figures. With online learning, student choice mattered in an unparalleled way. If they worked diligently, they accumulated the credits needed to finish high school. If they were lazy and unengaged, then failure was imminent. The students realized these facts, and they were content. For a few of the students, namely those who'd committed offenses that led to detention or incarceration, autonomy was an unheard of, abstract notion. To some degree, they were conditioned to wait on someone else to give them permission to move forward. Online learning "changed the game". Although they still had teachers who monitored their progress and proffered assistance as needed, the students' learning was on their own terms (Gurn, 2011). And speaking of learning on their own terms, where else or how else could they work on Geometry or Psychology while listening to the latest song by rappers Drake or Lil' Wayne? Indeed, music, headphones, little to no distractions, one-to-one help, and self-pacing combined to create an almost irresistible educational package deal. But, as you'll see in the next section, online learning was just one element of WNHS that influenced the study participants to regard the school as a space of hope. Arguably, the most important element was the WNHS staff.

Figure 8

Students' Experience with Online Learning

Student	Experience
Angel	• *Easier to concentrate.* • *Able to work faster.* • *More efficient with time.*
Maurice	• *Increased concentration.* • *Teacher support.* • *Independence.*
ameel	• *Less distractions.* • *Accessibility.* • *Independence.*
Casey	• *Easier to focus.* • *Extra help/One-to-One support.* • *Able to work faster.*
Brian	• *Self-pacing.*
Tariq	• *Easier to focus.*
Za'Nya	• *Less distractions.* • *Manageable courseload.* • *Increased concentration.*
Amber	• *Increased concentration.* • *Self-pacing.* • *Receive help when needed.* • *Convenient.*
Everett	• *Equivalent to traditional school.*
Dawn	• *Challenging/Rigor.*

(Arrington, 2014)

Chapter 8

EDUCATION THE WOODSON-NEWTON WAY

(Part Two)

D rawing upon the discussion at the start of chapter five related to access, this next section provides insight into student's perception of adult support at WNHS. Remember, *who* youths have access to is a critical determinant to their success. The reverse perspective is crucial as well. *Who* has access to youths, their intentions, philosophies, and objectives can bring either delight or devastation to bear on young minds. The following accounts allow readers to observe the possibilities of strategic relationship building in learning environments.

WNHS Staff

Relationships with WNHS staff made a significant difference in the lives of the students in the research study. The daily interaction with the adults at WNHS helped the students to experience hope. Similar to Brian's elementary teacher, Ms. Summers, members of the WNHS staff were persons of influence who demonstrated care and high regard for their weal. In a couple instances, students discussed the influence of WNHS staff in a general, collective sense. Others offered more specific examples of the influence that staff members had on their lives and how these persons helped them to raise their level of hope.

An Insider's Take

It makes sense that I would exhibit some bias in my writing because I served proudly as a WNHS administrator. Yet, I am able to examine our educational trek with clear eyes. And, what I observed each day was a cadre of adults who genuinely wanted students to succeed. I witnessed numerous acts of sacrifice and generosity. I often watched in awe as some of my colleagues assisted students with personal needs, exceeding the boundaries of teacher contracts and employee handbooks. When it came to meeting students' needs, ours was an environment that often "colored outside the lines". Truthfully, I don't believe education, in these times, is possible without mottled borders. Everything that needs to be done to help children survive and thrive cannot be packed neatly in bureaucratic boxes. No, WNHS at times lived on the edges and flirted with liberating elements that were foreign to traditional education. We took risks, but it was all in the name of love for youths. No one attempted to make a name for him or herself. At the end of the day, we aimed to offer a holistic educational experience that could minister to the wearied souls of youths trying — in most cases aimlessly — to find peace and meaning in life. When I reflect on the hundreds of students that I conversed with over a duration of six years, I can attest to numerous Lazaruses (Lazarus was a man whom Jesus Christ raised from the dead according to the Holy Scriptures; John 11.), students who were academically dead, but raised to new academic and social life through the fusion of online learning, community education, mentorship, personalized programming, and job readiness training and placement. We were a collective that was making things happen in the community. Educators were fulfilled. Many parents were thrilled. And most importantly, students found hope.

The Testimonies

One of the resurrection stories involved Za'Nya. As I shared previously, Za'Nya was languishing at her previous school. I recall her mom telling me how many phone calls she'd get from administrators and teachers. They'd complain about Za'Nya's behavior and poor attitude. When they met with me for in-take, Za'Nya's mom was at her wits end. She didn't know what else to do. Thankfully, Za'Nya found a home at WNHS. As she stated in a quote that I revealed earlier in the book, Za'Nya was "done with school". But, she pointed out that she started to believe in herself and the possibility of school being enjoyable again through her interaction with members of the WNHS staff:

> *"You know everybody believes in me. All the teachers believe in me. You believe in me. Mr. Stokes believes in me so why can't I believe in myself. And so, WNHS gives you hope. It's like whatever you going through, you step in here and you leave it at the door and if you don't leave it at the door ya'll waiting at the door for us, with us, helping us get through it so we can get through the day."*

For Za'Nya, the entire staff was instrumental in her academic and social resurgence ("everybody"; "teachers"; "you"; and "Principal Stokes"). To be clear, the term "everybody" used by Za'Nya was an allusion to administrators, teachers, support staff (e.g., social workers, guidance counselor, school psychologist), and community educators (i.e., individuals from the community that conducted classes that focused on life-skills as well as cultural, political, and social exploration and discovery). When Za'Nya stated, "WNHS gives you hope", I interpreted this remark as her recognition that the staff at WNHS possessed an enabling disposition. Starratt (2004) referred to this as "enabling presence" (p.99). Enabling presence is a relational approach that prioritizes standing with others to help them reach a goal.

Implicit in Za'Nya's remarks is a miniscule contradistinction between WNHS and her previous school(s). She went from being in a setting where she was despondent to matriculating in a school setting where she felt enlivened. And, it all began with belief, belief in the capability of the staff as well as belief in the ability of students. The sense of efficacy among the staff engendered or at least planted seeds of agency within Za'Nya, thus causing her to question, "why can't I believe in myself?" Agentic thought is the third member of the Hope Theory triad. Without agency, students have no inclination to attempt pathways and no reasonable chance of goal attainment. Za'Nya's remarks revealed a perception of WNHS staff as folks who are concerned with the person before being concerned with the student. Shade (2006) pointed out that interactions of this nature contribute to the construction of trust between teachers and students. Trust is an indispensable component of courage, one of Shade's (2006) *habits of hope*. When students know that someone has their back, they are more willing to face their fears and take risks. It's difficult to trust someone who rarely pays attention to you. Apparently, the attentiveness Za'Nya experienced was exactly what she needed based on the circumstances she faced each day.

Maurice nearly echoed Za'Nya's sentiments about WNHS staff. He too revered their others-centeredness and care. Specifically, Maurice commented on the influence of WNHS teachers:

"So, like as in my experience, when I came in here I really didn't have a lot of hope cuz I was comin' off the street, but when you see, you know a lot of positive teachers and a lot of positive things like they just comin' up to you like you...just positive people like that just giving you hope like you know they ask you, "how your day doing?" and everything...You just wanna, even though they teachers and you have something else in mind, you might just be just like them and wanna be a good person you know and have hope for the future cuz when you come inside these doors that's all you see is hope you know."

Positivity was important to Maurice. From his perspective, having hope meant being positive. That's how Maurice defined hope ("having a positive outlook"), and that's the word that he used to describe the sense of hope he encountered each day at WNHS. In particular, Maurice equated the notion of WNHS staff possessing and sharing hope with being positive. His interpretation of the WNHS experience suggested that Maurice perceived that the staff members were consistently positive people. He alluded to the regard for his welfare that the staff members displayed. His comments were similar to Za'Nya. They both intimated that prior to walking through the WNHS doors students may have been carrying personal loads or harboring negativity, but the spirit of the staff and school environment helped them to shift attitudinal gears. Even if it was just for that day, students felt better once they arrived at WNHS. The experience impacted Maurice so powerfully that he wanted what he saw in the WNHS staff. The positivity that they exhibited was desirable in his eyes. And, that good feeling, that sense that everything was going to be okay, made a world of difference.

After considering Za'Nya and Maurice's comments about the influence of WNHS staff, I identified a subtheme that, to my mind, generated a link between the commentaries that explained why the students perceived the staff as an element of WNHS that helped them to experience hope. The subtheme that emerged was "significant care". It's one thing to report what the study participants said during the interviews. It's an entirely different experience when you're actually *in* the interview listening to the manner in which the students share their thoughts. I looked into their eyes when they shared what I seriously believe were sentiments of their hearts. I heard it in their voices. No, the WNHS staff didn't have magic wands that they waved over students' heads to make all their troubles disappear. They didn't offer any incredible elixirs that eliminated students' pain. But, students esteemed these adults. They really believed that WNHS staff cared for them in a way that exceeded the typical regard that teachers may have for students. And, you know what? They were absolutely right.

Tariq attested to the "significant care" that was a common thread in the WNHS experience. Similar to his peers, he equated hope with attentiveness to student needs. When asked if he thought WNHS promoted hope, Tariq had this to say:

> *"It's been promoted by like, I can say mainly the teachers and like ya'll stay here. Like, ya'll really for us. Ya'll really work for us. Like, if I go to another school, they just there for like, they for the*

money or they don't really care about us. They just care about us while we at the school, but ya'll really accept us for outside the school. That's one thing I really love about this school."

Tariq actually used the term *care*. His remarks were the inspiration for the subtheme that I settled upon. Interestingly, Tariq followed a conversational pattern that was broached during the discussions about online learning. In those conversations, several students explained the benefits of online learning at WNHS by describing what they didn't like about previous high schools they'd attended. I found this means of sharing quite fascinating because it revealed that students are much more observant than what most adults, especially school personnel, give them credit for. Students enter schools with memories from former schools. And, although K-12 educators rarely provide opportunities for students to provide feedback (in the classroom), students are constantly evaluating our effectiveness. They're paying attention to what is said, how it's said, and to whom it's said. Students take in everything! That's a fact, and Tariq's comparison between his experience at WNHS and his experience at a traditional high school verified this point.

Further, Tariq poignantly stated that teachers at other schools, that he'd attended, only cared about the benefits they derived from teaching ("They for the money or they don't really care about us".). He really believed that there were teachers that didn't care if students learned or not. Such a telling critique of his previous high school(s) underscored Tariq's gratitude toward WNHS and its staff. His experience adds credence to the notion that teachers who avail themselves to address the urgent needs of marginalized students are concrete examples of hope (Duncan-Andrade, 2010).

Now, the notion that Tariq posited is very interesting because the average citizen knows that people don't enter the field of education to get rich. It's a service industry. The majority of participants willingly sign up because they want to make a difference in the world. They believe that their intellectual imprint is valuable. Moreover, most adults who enter the realm of K-12 education love and want to work with children. With this in mind, it was almost mind-boggling to hear Tariq suggest that there are some folks who are indifferent to student failure.

I'm not naïve. Since I'm a K-12 educator with nearly 18 years of experience, I understand the grind. Life as a K-12 educator, especially in the inner-city, is no cakewalk. You've got to have vision, love, compassion, grit, and a big bag of tricks. There are fleeting mountain-top moments along with many lingering valley experiences. It takes supreme commitment. It requires specialness that cannot be understated. Teachers and administrators are expected to perform miracles with minimum resources. So, I get it. But, it's different when you hear a child reveal that the difficulty of the job (this is my assumption) has worn teachers down to the point that student success is of no consequence. And, if most WNHS students were previously enrolled in schools beset with lots of issues, it's very plausible that Tariq wasn't the only student that observed a different attitude at WNHS.

Caring Goes a Long Way

The late, esteemed Brazilian educator, Paulo Freire (1970), argued for humanization in school settings. In his much celebrated book, *Pedagogy of the Oppressed*, Freire (1970) argued that teachers too often, and perhaps unknowingly, taught in a manner that objectified students. He contended that teachers often viewed students as receptacles that only needed to have teacher-knowledge poured in. In other words, the traditional classroom was a space where knowledge was hierarchically dispensed. It featured a top-down experience that provided no room for reciprocation. Education this way, opined Freire (1970) actually stripped students of their human worth. It chipped away at the edges of their personalities and conscious-ness. It suppressed their voice and in effect dehumanized them. Tariq's comments suggested that WNHS staff members human-ized the students through the care they exhibited. Tariq and his peers weren't mere students; they were people who needed support, love, and encouragement; people with dreams and ambition, people just like the adults. The most telling phrase that Tariq shared was, "They just care about us while we at the school, but ya'll really accept us for outside the school." Tariq perceived that the relationships he developed with the staff members that he worked with went beyond the school thresholds. He believed that WNHS staff members were con-cerned about him and his peers in general. Keep in mind, Tariq had sisters who attended WNHS. So, in his case, Tariq was able to draw upon his experiences as well as the experiences of his siblings. His testimony was infused with bits and pieces of his siblings' stories and examples of support received while attending WNHS.

Angel also discussed the influence of WNHS staff, namely teachers. Her remarks, though stated differently, underscored the students' consistent need for encouragement as well as the consistent supply of encouragement by WNHS staff. Angel commented, "Um, yeah I think they promote hope. Just basi-cally by just talking to some of the teachers you know they really lift my spirit up, and pretty much tell me that I can make it...I can pretty much do anything if I put my mind to it." With respect to the subtheme "significant care", Angel's comment, "by just talking to some of the teachers", shed light on an important aspect of caring—conversation. Angel's explanation complimented Maurice's discussion of positivity. After conversations with WNHS staff members, Angel's psyche and emotions were nourished. She was told that success was in her hands, that winning was an option ("tell me that I can make it"; "I can pretty much do anything if I put my mind to it"). It hearkens back to Everett and the discussion about locus of control. I'm sure for Angel it was good to hear adults remind her that she did have power to affect her future, that her life wasn't limited to someone else's repressive ideas.

Recall that when discussing persons of influence and their experience with hope, several students mentioned the importance of conversations. Dawn, in particular, stands out as one who really gleaned from conversations with her mother and grandmother. Conversations with teachers helped Dawn as well. She stated, "*Um, when you first come here and everything, when you guys talk to us about just stuff and how we need to do what we need to do to get to point A, point B, point C, you just put a lot of hope into us that we can do it and we can make it.*" Dawn's remarks about the talks provided by WNHS staff included a reference to generalities ("just stuff") and directions or a plan for improvement ("how we need to do what we need to do to get to point A, point B, point C"). The latter comment about points A, B, and C is suggestive of pathways to reach specific goals. For example, all WNHS students had teachers who supervised their course activity, and they had homeroom teachers. The homeroom teachers were primarily responsible for providing advisement related to school attendance, behavior, course completion and tips for success at WNHS. Content teachers talked with students about course management and pacing as well. And, if that weren't enough, students had mandated conferences with the Transition Specialist and the Guidance Counselor. The support system at WNHS was well-structured, and it was multi-tiered. These layers of assistance and intervention helped to increase students' potential for success.

Further and to Dawn's point, the support was part of the package that raised student agency. Dawn expressed this aspect in her use of the phrase, "put hope into us that we can do it and we can make it". Ultimately, Dawn perceived that WNHS staff believed that the students were capable of following a plan that could help them reach an expected end. In other words, the staff was confident in the program. Therefore, success was attainable. And, it was. By the time Dawn had enrolled in WNHS, we'd experienced so many amazing comeback stories. We'd seen the process work time and time again. Principal Stokes had a statement that he always quoted, "practice the possibilities". We believed that academic reform was possible, especially when it was guided by an equitable educational plan. Dawn didn't say it in those terms, but as one of the architects of the program's scope, I understood her articulation to mean that we personalized the learning experience. Our goal was to provide a *PEP* (Personalized Education Plan) for all students. So yes, there were relevant conversations about "stuff" that we knew students needed. But, there were also numerous one-to-one talks during which we intentionally examined student's social and academic status. Our focus was candor and clarity. We wanted to provide a clear picture of what students needed to progress. This approach supported student's development of a stronger locus of control. Since we examined what they needed to do and were capable of doing, Dawn and her peers recognized that goal obtainment would be based on what *they* could do, not the teachers.

Jameel added comments related to the care demonstrated by WNHS staff members. His words further clarified students' perception of the influence of WNHS staff. Jameel discussed the impact of a particular teacher:

"Mrs. Picotto, she stay on me about when I got test to take and all that. If you stay on a person, then a person gonna think about it all the time so you ain't got no choice. I like that though cuz most people that do that for em'. So, it's cool."

Jameel appreciated accountability. Rather than view the teacher's monitoring as invasive surveillance or "hawking" (Hawking was a term coined by the students that referred to what they perceived as harassment. Any teacher who stood over students while they worked and gave constant redirection, especially for infractions that students deemed minor, was said to be "hawking".) Jameel regarded the attention he received in a favorable light. He knew that the teacher's persistence would ultimately help him reach his goal(s). Brian's elementary school teacher, Ms. Summers, held him accountable, and he called her the coolest teacher he ever had. He went as far as to say that he loved her like his mother. Clearly, Brian believed that Ms. Summers cared for him. In other words, lack of accountability or negligence is interpreted by some students as a lack of care on the part of teachers.

As I previously stated, bias is one of the limitations of this book. I've got skin in the game, admittedly. That said, I've included a quote from Amber that further attests to "significant care". In full disclosure, I'm mentioned in her remarks. Yet, I don't share her remarks for self-aggrandizement of any kind. I share her remarks because I underestimated the importance of spending time with youth until I read her interview transcript. In reference to the impact of WNHS staff, Amber shared:

"Um, it was this man named Mr. Arrington...okay we sat in the social room. He wrote on this big white board. He made a timeline of my life because I was considering either going straight to school or going through Public Allies. And, I was kinda like well I don't know if I should take a year off of school cuz I was just gettin' my groove back, but I kinda want this experience and I can get money for school...$5000, that's a lot of money, which I'm using. But, to be honest that's still a concept I use to write out my plans. Not only do I write my plans out for a goal that's immediate. I then write down how does that goal fit into my plans for my life, and it's always a mistake and stuff like my baby, but it's still, I'm still able to say what now do I do. I mean I have to change things around. That one day for about 30 minutes made me change the way how I plan out my life and make goals."

Amber's comments underscored the importance of staff-student conversations. More importantly, her experience revealed the value of spending time with students. Spending time with and caring for students fosters hope (Snyder, 2005). Among college students, Snyder (2005) found that academic achievement is strengthened when instructors listen to their students. That 30 minute conversation, the time that I spent listening, helped Amber thoughtfully weigh her goals and the pathways to reach her goals. At the time, I wasn't thinking about Hope Theory and infusing the three components of hope into our conversation. Amber and I had good rapport, and I genuinely wanted to aid her in what I perceived to be a quest for clear direction. In actuality, I relish those moments. Even today, I love hearing youths talk about their goals and interests. I love seeing them smile when they think about their passion(s) or share their dreams. I equally love sharing my experiences with students, especially the lessons that I've learned along my journey. I want to help as much as I can, even if it's only a conversation.

My Own Experience with Teacher Care

I know the power of conversation with caring adults. My life was changed because of a conversation with my high school Physics teacher, Mr. Redmon. Unlike Amber, I didn't get 30 minutes. My conversation with Mr. Redmon lasted about 15 minutes, but that's all I needed. In 15 minutes, Mr. Redmon inspired me to become an educator. Now, those who know me and my family would suggest that I entered the field of education because of my pedigree. My mother is a retired school teacher. My grandmother (her mother) was a school librarian for 35 years. My father has taught at the K-12 level and at the collegiate level. My great-aunt was a pioneer in the local Head Start movement. So, it makes sense that I would become an educator. But, the genetic links to education and service notwithstanding, I became an educator because of the 15 minutes that I spent with Mr. Redmon.

Mr. Redmon, was a young black male teacher. At the time he was a recent college graduate. He attended an HBCU (Historically Black College and University). And, Mr. Redmon taught Science courses. I considered him one of the wonders of the world! First of all, black male teachers were rare. Second of all, Mr. Redmon taught Science classes. Really? That was unheard of! To top it all off, Mr. Redmon was cool! He had great command of the content. He employed solid instructional methods. To my teenage mind, Mr. Redmon was the total package. So, I'd already developed respect for him as a black man. But, our conversation catapulted him to a rarified space.

It was my senior year of high school. I'd already earned enough Science credits to satisfy school and district graduation requirements, but my guidance counselor convinced me (She really made me do it.) to take a fourth year of Science in preparation for college. I obliged and enrolled in Physics during the Fall Semester. The class was interesting. Mr. Redmon made it fun. Then, the second semester rolled around, and "senioritis" started setting in (For those who don't know, I define "senioritis" as a condition common to high school seniors that manifests in a lax attitude towards coursework. Students begin to coast rather than continue to accelerate their learning. Sometimes "senioritis" is marked by decreased classroom productivity and decreased school or class attendance. In its worst form, "senioritis" can lead to depression and/or reckless behavior.). I liked Mr. Redmon, but I did not want to remain in Physics for another semester. After all, I didn't need it. It was superfluous. I could have been doing other things with my time, such as study hall (lol!).

My disinterest grew into frustration, and I began to think about ways that I could get out of this second Physics class. I was exiting class one day and Mr. Redmon noticed my body language and countenance. He inquired about my very disconnected behavior. I told him that I was considering dropping the course. Mr. Redmon looked a bit surprised. Initially, he thought that I may have been concerned about my performance in the class. He checked his gradebook and assured me that I was doing okay based on my scores. I explained that I wasn't concerned about my grade per se; I just wasn't happy with the class. Mr. Redmon looked me in the eyes and told me to meet him in the school library during one of the lunch periods. I agreed.

A short while later, I arrived in the library and thought, "What could Mr. Redmon want to talk to me about?" I wasn't sure. I was a little nervous, but I respected him so I decided to relax. When Mr. Redmon arrived, he sat down, and we chatted about regular "guy things" for a few minutes. Then, the conversation shifted to the topic of endurance. He admonished me to refrain from quitting. He explained that it's a terrible habit to begin. Mr. Redmon also explained that there was great value in a person finishing what they started. He went on to mention that I was on course to earn a "B". While I was listening to Mr. Redmon make the case that I shouldn't drop the course, my mind began to drift. I appreciated what he was saying, but what impressed me more than anything was the fact that Mr. Redmon had spent the better portion of his personal lunch period talking to me. I was undone. I was genuinely stunned because I always thought of teacher lunch time as something sacred. And, I marveled at Mr. Redmon's willingness to take the little free time that he did have and share it with me. I mean, in the grand scheme of things, it didn't matter if I dropped his course, or so I thought. I realized that the conversation wasn't really about Physics. The conversation was about me, and I realized that Mr. Redmon took time out for me. Sure, he loved Physics, but he was interested in me as well.

I told Mr. Redmon that I would finish the course. I thanked him for his time, and we both went our separate ways. I don't know how Mr. Redmon felt after our conversation, but I know that I was inspired. My life was changed forever because in the 15 minutes we spent together I discovered purpose. I knew that I wanted to become an educator. I wanted to inspire other black boys in the same manner that Mr. Redmon inspired me.

From that day forward, I was convinced that making money was great, but making a difference in a person's life was invaluable. Mr. Redmon taught me that day that students have dignity and that the best way to show that you honor their dignity is to conspicuously care for them. I learned that in many cases students will develop trust in adults if their voice is heard. And finally, I learned what Maya Angelou so eloquently stated years ago, "…people will forget what you said, people will forget what you did, but people will never forget how you made them feel." That 15 minutes, in the school library, during his lunch break, Mr. Redmon made me feel special.

Black Males Matter

I would be disingenuous if I suggested that Mr. Redmon's hue didn't matter to me. It did. As a student in a large comprehensive high school, I had a variety of teachers. Some were female. Some were European American. That had been my experience throughout K-12 enrollment. But, to have a black man take time to talk to me about finishing strong was monumental. Amber shared similar thoughts about the importance of African American male educators.

> *"The black men that I was able to see at Woodson-Newton were great influences. The fact that it was black men working in positions that you don't see a lot. And, honestly, I ain't never had a black male teacher in my life. Seriously, I didn't have that many black teachers ever and the fact that I had two teachers and not only the teachers but other examples of black role models in one building was spectacular to see on a daily basis."*

There had to have been something electric about the presence of black men in schools. Amber's entire countenance changed when she shared her thoughts. She seemed to be energized by the remembrance. Amber had more to say about the significance of black males at WNHS:

"Um, their family structure, wife, I mean you just don't see it often...family man, taking care of their family especially where I come from. So, that alone was like inspiration like well, if they got wives, I'm like maybe it's a hope for me after all... It just provided a lot of hope for me that it's going to be a new reign of young men that's gonna be able to provide for the family and not just provide, but take care and love their family, that are in their family homes you know? It's possible that you can find that without people being divorced or broken up or all the other issues that a lot of black families..."

Principal Stokes encouraged all WNHS staff to bring pictures of their families to school and set them in visible places. The rationale was that part of our scholars' success hinged on them feeling a sense of family when they entered the school. It was also a way for students to learn more about their teachers. Obviously, Amber observed these family photos. Since we never asked students what they thought about our family pictures, Amber's comments were very informative. For Amber, the presence of black males and the evidence of these men as family men helped her to imagine what was possible. Amber, like the other study participants, grew up in the inner city where uniparental homes abound. Their neighborhoods are often beset by socio-cultural issues that fatigue the black community such as absentee fathers, high unemployment, and poverty. And in most cases, these homes are headed by single mothers. So, her experience with the black men at WNHS challenged her initial beliefs about the possibilities of whole families existing in urban environments. The fact that these men were, as far as she could tell, attending to the needs of their families ("take care of and love their family") inspired Amber. It compelled her to reconsider her family possibilities and the notion of what a *normal* black family looks like. The influence and presentation of these men helped Amber to imaginatively go beyond what she perceived to be a discouraging situation (Post, 2006).

Deep Impact

In this section on WNHS staff, I hoped to capture the value that students placed on their relationships with and sense of connectedness to their adult leaders. Overall, I discerned a running subtheme that I've called *significant care*. A few students mentioned the term care explicitly. Others used terms and phrases that made it apparent that they perceived that WNHS staff genuinely cared for their well-being. For example, Maurice and Za'Nya both alluded to WNHS staff standing at the main entrance ready to serve, ready to listen, and generally availing themselves for students. Rather than enduring the process of weapons screening that is common in many inner-city schools, the students received greetings and inquiries about their well-being.

All of the remarks shared by the students were insightful, but Za'Nya's commentary was especially compelling and revealed that WNHS staff had deep impact on the students' lives. Her statement, "ya'll waiting at the door for us, with us, helping us get through it so we can get through the day" really conveyed her perception of WNHS staff care and connection.

Particularly, the phrase, "with us" suggested a perception of solidarity; that WNHS staff was traveling or even trudging with Za'Nya along her journey. Similar to Tariq, Za'Nya was convinced that WNHS staff was there to provide support with whatever she was concerned with. However tacit Za'Nya's assumption may have been, her remarks indicated that marginalized youths need educators who will stand with them through suffering and if necessary travel dangerously with them (Duncan-Andrade, 2010) while they pursue their life-goals.

Overwhelmingly, the sentiment among students was that WNHS was not like any other school they'd attended in their past. Sure, there were some programmatic differences. Online learning was novel for most of them. But, to their minds, the people in the building made the difference. Whether it was critical conversations, accountability, or mere presence, the "people in the place" made a difference in the lives of these youths. Student discussions about the influence of WNHS staff corroborated Duncan-Andrade's (2010) claim, that the values, principles, and psycho-emotional condition of educators are fundamental factors in raising hope, especially among marginalized students.

Armed with a very optimistic disposition, WNHS staff members disabused the students from the delimitations they'd previously wallowed in and compelled them to go beyond. Education, this way, shatters the myths of dereliction and incompetence that overshadow public schools. It transmutes ideas of schools as factories to visions of schools as gardens; gardens where students are nurtured and cultivated. And if schools are gardens, then students are flowers in need of significant care. Bridges (2011) argued that this kind of education requires adults who respond to a "calling" to teach:

"The idea of teaching as a calling suggests that teachers who possess an ethic of caring yielding positive socio-emotional outcomes for students of color (heightened self-esteem and feelings of self-efficacy) are motivated by a spiritual connectedness to the students and communities they serve." (p. 329)

Since I do belong to a faith community and I've had some ecclesiastical training, I observe the term "calling" from a religious and spiritual lens. I therefore argue in agreement with Bridges (2011), that there is a spiritual aspect of teaching that produces favorable outcomes for students, families, and communities. In fact, I argue that certain educators are even "called" to serve in certain neighborhoods, in a certain time. I believe that the WNHS staff was exactly what the study participants needed at that time in their lives. I believe that the adults that served them were the right people for them at that time. And, I further believe that the confluence of all the factors that led to the students enrolling in WNHS and the WNHS staff coming together when they did was divinely orchestrated. In other words, the providence of God was at work. In His supreme wisdom, God knew what these youths needed; He knew who they needed. And, in each case, their situations improved. They grew. They became better.

Lessons
I would be remiss if I failed to share the lessons that students learned during their time at WNHS. These takeaways are an extension of the care that students received and in many cases are indicative of revelations that students received while journeying at WNHS. Rather than share all the lessons in detail, I've opted to share two. Angel and Amber shared lessons that,

to my mind, highlight a major point for students and a major point for educators.

Angel's lesson learned was very simple, "I can pretty much do anything if I put my mind to it." For youths on the margins, such a simple statement contains great profundity and power because one of the consequences of being marginalized, of being "othered", is self-marginalization. The experience of being consigned to the borders of a system, a group, or a community begins to weigh on an individual's psyche; so much so that they internalize notions of inferiority and unworthiness. They refrain from even attempting to move forward or be involved. They box themselves in, restrained by the opinion of others, believing that they cannot and should not progress. Hence, Angel's epiphany about her intrinsic power speaks volumes for a young lady who'd essentially given up on herself. It also captures the perspective that all successful WNHS students gained after being welcomed into a learning environment that eschewed failure and any capitulation to defeat.

Amber's lesson was related to conversations. In just a few sentences, Amber expressed what I believe to be the heart's desire of millions of youth. She stated that youth want to be heard and that an important lesson for her was the necessity of listening.

> *"I want to say this because I think this is one of my most important lessons and that is be the ears that is able to listen you know? Be the person that's able to listen. Because a lot of young people are not able to be heard and for many, many, I mean many, many times, the staff was those ears for me...Learn and listening, that's also something I learned through the circle process as well because not only were we able to express how we felt,*

but we were also able to listen to how everyone else felt
around us which is really, really important and I really,
really wish that our society did that more often, which
is listen."

The unfortunate reality is that in some, not all cases, youths commit acts or engage in activities that lead to marginalization because they were unheard. And, the sad reality is that the chances of being heard are further diminished when one lives on the margins. Although she had her own concerns, Amber realized, through listening to her peers, that the opportunity to be heard is critical (Her last remark in which she expressed her wish that society would listen is very telling.). If only we, as a society, would slow down and talk, perhaps we could figure out how to improve the conditions that afflict so many of us... perhaps we would learn the value of authentic human interaction and its healing possibilities.

I can't help but to reflect on Amber's desire to be a teacher as I review the lesson she learned while at WNHS. It's quite possible that understanding the value of listening will prove more helpful than all the theory she will be exposed to in college. Credentials alone don't help you win the hearts of students, but listening to them does.

This chapter revealed that the staff at WNHS won the hearts of the students in this study. And, it wasn't their degrees. It wasn't the content knowledge that they possessed. The leaders at WNHS won the students' hearts because they were fully present to their needs. By listening to the students (Bondy & Ross, 2008; Villegas & Lucas, 2002), by believing in them and articulating that belief, the WNHS staff members demonstrated care that restored student dignity and compelled them to believe in themselves.

Figure 9

Student Experiences with WNHS Staff

Student	Experience
Za'nya	• *Staff believed in her.* • *Socio-emotional support.*
Maurice	• *Staff modeled positivity.* • *Teachers cared.*
Tariq	• *Consistent staff presence.* • *Teachers cared.*
Angel	• *Conversations with staff.* • *Inspirational messages.*
Dawn	• *Goal-setting.* • *Conversations with staff.* • *Staff believed in her/peers.* • *Empowering messages.*
Jameel	• *Teachers were helpful.* • *Teachers were encouraging.* • *Teachers held him accountable.*
Amber	• *Staff willing to listen.* • *Conversations with staff.* • *Staff gave of their time.*
Casey	• *Research project.* • *Discussion about hope.*

(Arrington, 2014)

Figure 10
Lessons Students Learned at WNHS

Student	Lesson(s)
Amber	• *Be willing to listen to others.* • *Listening leads to learning.*
Za'nya	• *Never give up.* • *Never doubt self.*
Tariq	• *Be patient.*
Dawn	• *Move at faster pace.* • *Stay focused.*
Maurice	• *Stay focused.* • *Keep a positive outlook.* • *Be the best you can be.* • *Finish school.* • *Stay motivated.* • *Be yourself.*
Everett	• *Social skills*
Casey	• *Anything is possible.* • *Self-determination above all else; make your own decisions.*
Brian	• *Students need a chance to mature.* • *Effort leads to results.*
Jameel	• *Don't be a statistic.* • *You can make it.*
Angel	• *The power of positive thinking.* • *Perseverance.* • *Change is necessary.*

(Arrington, 2014)

Chapter 9

EVERYBODY'S A LEADER

"A leader is anyone willing to help, anyone who sees something that needs to change and takes the first steps to influence that situation."

-Margaret Wheatley

Hope has to have a home. It has to have a place where it can reside, unfettered, protected from destructive elements that could easily douse its fervor. I liken hope to an ember. It's the spark before the conflagration. In other words, it doesn't take much to generate a fire. But, once a fire builds, it rages and is terribly difficult to extinguish. In this book I've argued in favor of hope. I've supported the notion that although the study of hope may not be acceptable in the halls of "hard science", it is nonetheless worthy of great academic attention. Despite the tremendous amount of research by scholars such as C.R. Snyder, hope itself remains marginalized; skewered in a vice grip of empiricism and pragmatism with almost no chance of being liberated.

While I understand the concerns of irrelevance that are posited by skeptics, I maintain that hope is more than mere wishing as Smith (2005) would have it. Hope requires intellect. Hope requires action. And, hope requires vision that many enrooted in positivist thought fail to acquire. As Post (2006) stated, hope is the ability to see beyond the situation.

When one considers the bevy of tragedies that people are confronted with on a daily basis, there is clearly a need to see more than what is obvious. Think about the new One World Tower in New York City. How could the city of New York rebuild after such the devastating 9/11 occurrence? Somewhere, amid the ashes and the dust, someone or some group of intrepid individuals stood at what we now revere as Ground Zero and became inspired. While thousands mourned their lost loved ones and onlookers stood horrified at the carnage; there were those who'd already decided that the end had not yet come. They determined to rebuild and not only to rebuild, but to do it better than what was completed previously.

The "Soft Stuff"

So, how do citizens rebuild and move forward after natural and social disasters literally obliterate everything they love and deem sacred? Think about the flooding that occurred in Louisiana during the summer of 2016. Think about the ravaging of Hurricane Harvey on the city of Houston and other Gulf Coasts locales in 2017. Think about the pummeling effects of hurricanes that hit the East Coast and Florida panhandle in 2018, or the wildfires that decimated forests and residential area in California. Think about the cruel marksmanship exacted on members of the Parkland, FL community. Or, consider black communities across the United States that march for justice despite the unceasing occurrence of police shootings of unarmed black men. Consider the Latinx families that have been torn apart by the resurgence of Nativist philosophy and cruel immigration policies. How did/do people move on? I'll tell you…it's with the embrace of and demonstration of several constructs that appear "soft" or "fantastical" such as faith, optimism, love, and of course hope.

When I consider the world that millions of youths are born into, I marvel at their ability to succeed, to maintain their sanity and to achieve. Of course, all youths are not forced, through birth, to enter into a life of turmoil and asperity. Many children grow up with amenities and comforts that most adults don't enjoy. But, even in those cases, they are not exempt from being impacted by the evil that generates suffering. So, how do they persist knowing that despite their cushy lived experiences, they have counterparts who never receive a fraction of the privilege that they enjoy? Again, I argue in favor of the "soft stuff", faith, optimism, love, and hope.

The "soft stuff" heals and nurtures the soul. When a person is stricken with grief and jaded by life's whimsicalities, credentials don't necessarily help. If tangible things could heal and nurture the soul, I imagine that the number of suicides would be significantly reduced. At some point, experimentation has its end. At some point, intellect and pure reason lose their utility. But, love, faith, optimism, and hope will always have enduring value. What's more is that an individual can possess all of these virtues along with intellect. In fact, hope actually requires a love of self, faith, optimism, and intellect. It demands foresight and creativity. It needs reasoning ability. Hope is an inclusive construct that derives its life from the contribution of other factors. When the conditions are right, when the proper elements are in place, hope will settle and be at home. When hope is secured, transcendence is inevitable.

Leadership

One of the more exciting facts related to hope is that it doesn't discriminate. Hope embraces people regardless of ability, age, ethnicity, gender, creed, nationality…it doesn't matter. And since anyone can hope (verb) and possess hope (noun), then I argue that anyone can be a leader. Drawing upon the quote that opened this chapter, anyone who cares enough about an issue and is willing to take action, can be a leader (Wheatley, 2010). Isn't that awesome? That means that the invitation to make a difference in our world and to affect change in society is extended to all humans.

Here's a more explicit connection between leadership and hope. Dickman and Stanford-Blair (2002) stated that leadership is a phenomenon that is related to the obtainment of goals (Dickman & Stanford-Blair, 2002). In the context of the research study I conducted, each of the students identified and shared life-goals. They also had a short-term goal of graduating from high school. Enrollment at WNHS was perceived to be a pathway that could help them obtain a high school diploma. The educators who received these students as they were and helped them to devise a plan to complete high school functioned as leaders. Make sense? In other words, the students had an issue or issues (e.g. credit deficient, adjudicated, etc.) that stymied their progression towards high school completion. The WNHS staff members who worked with them and provided guidance relative to their pursuit of high school completion were leaders. The case has been made previously as to the specifics of their leadership (e.g. course completion plans, counseling, affirmation, etc.). The examples and commentary provided by the students in the study revealed that multiple individuals can function as leaders in this context because the objective is simply obtainment of the students' goal.

To some, the explanation above may appear generic or simplistic, but to my mind, that's Wheatley's (2010) point. Leadership doesn't require knowledge of ridiculously difficult algorithms. It has its degree of challenge because people are imperfect and influencing the affective and cognitive domains requires savvy, compassion, and thoughtfulness. But overall, if you care enough, then you can do something to help, you can lead.

In the case with leading marginalized, urban black youths, part of the focus must be prioritizing students' goals within the context of a larger mission. Stated differently, leaders articulate a big picture vision for change or progression on the part of the student, while also helping the student recognize his/her value and contribution. That's how agency is broached and nurtured. That's how dignity is taught and upheld. The leader of students on the margins shows care and honors their dignity by attending to their urgent needs (e.g., conversation, listening, providing material assistance). The same leader spreads dignity by explaining the importance of reciprocating the care and support they've received. He/she explains that the restored youth now has the responsibility of contributing to the enhancement of the human condition within their sphere of influence. In other words, someone thought that they were worthy of investment and support. Others are equally worthy of their investment and support. This is how leadership spreads. This is how hope proliferates.

WNHS staff members believed that youth could assume leadership roles. They endorsed the notion of students being empowered to be agents of change. In fact, the school's vision explicitly stated the phrase "agents of change". Dignity was revered and made plain in the school mission which stated that, WNHS "fosters a compassionate, family-based atmosphere where each person is valued and respected". Student testimonials validated the school mission. Those in the study felt welcomed, wanted, and supported. As a result of such a nurturing environment, students grew socially and personally while they obtained credits for graduation. Granted, personal maturation is supposed to occur in all schools, but the emphasis that school leadership placed on youth cultivation was a bit different as student remarks indicated. Again, all of this occurred while students matriculated through online course offerings and obtained credits toward graduation. Students were encouraged to explore social, cultural, and political issues that affected their lived experiences. They were encouraged to view themselves beyond their present situation(s). They were reminded of their inherent value and encouraged to see themselves as assets and solutions.

Youth Power

In retrospect, I love the notion of youths being our now and our future. That was the viewpoint of WNHS staff. We intentionally attempted to foster a sense of "somebodiness" and inclusion. Students were challenged to opt in to social change rather than wait their turn. In his book, The Fifth Discipline, Peter Senge (2006) posited that youth are often the best group to have at the table of decision when discussing matters of change because they aren't inextricably wed to any specific schools of thought. They rarely have delimiting partisan alignments or philosophical loyalties that could complicate deliberation and/or creative thinking. They observe wrong and are willing to offer solutions. Youths don't need credentials and memberships in fraternal organizations to validate their claims.

In their youthful innocence and uncomplicatedness, they look for what makes sense. And, in many cases, that which makes sense is often simple, not difficult.

Youth voice should definitely be sought after and amplified when issues that directly impact their lives are considered. But, while esteeming youth voice is critical, we must remember that youths benefit from the impartation and guidance of caring adults. See, there is something to be said about life experience, and that often comes with age and exposure. So, in respect to generational gaps, bridges have to be erected that bring youths and adults together. In other words, yes youths are brilliant, compassionate, and creative, but they still need leadership.

Leading Self

The research study that inspired this writing provided insight into the lives of several African American youths on the margins. Each of these youths, in their own way and due to various circumstances, undertook the oft puzzling and frustrating task of leading themselves. They each experienced "turning points", psycho-emotive junctures during which they each appraised their lived experience and made the decision to transcend impediments and pursue specific goals. Seeds of hope—I believe—were planted in their hearts through relationships with individuals whose own stories and triumph over tribulation was interpreted by the youths as evidence of hope. Thus, when the students in the study discussed their experience(s) with hope, they talked about the heroes or heroines of their lived experiences. Consistent throughout each student's account of motivation was the notion of individuals taking control of their situation or being in control of their situations, challenges notwithstanding. Rather than wait for someone else to fix what was wrong in their lives or smooth very jagged circumstances, these folks faced fears and took action. Albeit personal, this is a prime example of leadership, self-edition. The students took these cues and applied them to their lives. Each began a journey to lead themselves out of negativity, out of low expectation, away from excuses and into much more pleasing spaces of productivity and purpose. These influential folks were exemplars. They were leaders without titles. Their lived experiences provoked these youths to embark on the journey toward hope.

Family members planted seeds of hope. Just as Shade (2006) broached habits of hope, I posit that certain behaviors, attitudes, and attributes comprise elements that produce hope. Family members exhibited vision, grit, and buoyancy. Teachers also contributed to elements that engendered hope. Specifically, teachers helped to provide continuous motivation and listening ears. They clarified difficult tasks and talked students through arduous circumstances. Teachers helped students draft plans for completing high school and affirmed their intelligence by requiring them to work and concentrate on their academic targets. Additionally, study participants were able to access places (e.g., church, school, college/universities, community centers, and a non-profit agency) that featured programs, information, and/or opportunities that empowered them to assert their skills and belief and engage in activities that helped them to pursue goals. All of the elements received or experienced through relationships with key people or key places helped the project participants develop or strengthen the core components of hope (goals, pathways, agency). With the emergence of these components and subsequent cultivation, students actually became hopeful. Resultantly, they were able to lead themselves out of academic obscurity into academic relevance. How? They expressed a vision (goal; complete high school). They created a plan (pathway; enroll in WNHS and recover credits). They believed that their plan would work and that they possessed the ability to execute the plan (agency).

Wind-Aided

When I consider the voyage from the margins to the center, I can't help but think about the comeback stories that I've listened to and also witnessed. I think about WNHS students, and I'm compelled to imagine a restored sailboat adrift on a vast sea of opportunity. I think about the sun shining on a beautiful summer afternoon, not a cloud in the sky. I hear gulls screeching in ear-piercing tones. I imagine whales intermittently playing peek-a-boo in this scene, their hefty fins forcefully dashing the crisp blue waters. I see this sailboat, freshly burnished and ready to go. Everything is perfect up to this point. The sailboat has everything it needs. But, it's not going anywhere. Why? No wind.

Just as sailboats need wind support to function and perform at full capacity, students—margins or not—need support. Caring adults are to students what wind is to a sailboat. Put differently, sailboats need the wind. Students need caring adults, especially students on the margins, many of whom hail from historically disadvantaged communities. The impartation of knowledge, love, compassion, and guidance is just what students need to go forward and take advantage of the seas of opportunity that are available to them. Unlike the reality of whimsical winds faced by those who engage in nautical adventures, youths on the margins can't survive with unpredictable support. It's not enough for them to have tools. They need to be shown how to use the tools. Students need folks who can speak words of life and listen when needed. When all is said and done, it's a matter of access. Hope grew in the lives of the study participants because they had access to significant people and places. Similar to a sailboat moving towards its destination, these youths charted new courses towards brighter tomorrows because their winds blew in abundance. Because of its philosophical position and guiding values, WNHS featured adults and programs that were in effect propelling winds, gusts of inspiration that carried refreshed youths forward to their goals. The student testimonials are proof that youths were impacted by the leadership of caring adults and that daily access to these educators gave them a huge advantage.

Incidentally, it's imperative that I point out that I cited no deficiencies with the sailboat itself in my allegory of the sailboat. And, since the sailboat metaphorically represents a youth, I argue the same on behalf of youth. Youths have more that's right with them than not. In other words, the sailboat was primed and ready for the jaunt of a lifetime, but the external conditions weren't quite right. So many times youths are excoriated for their lack of skills or lack of ambition or lack of information. If they fail, it's as if no factor besides their own unaptness is identified as a reason for failure. Rather than point fingers at youths, I prefer to redirect the inquiry and interrogate the adults in their lives. I'd ask them questions such as, "were you fully present to the needs of your youth(s)?" How often did you listen to their concerns? What are their dreams? Do you think your youth(s) felt safe with you? If so, how do you know? These are penetrating questions that indicate a level of expectation and accountability for adults as it pertains to the development of young people. Stated differently, if swathes of youths are failing, then adults aren't doing their job(s). If more and more youths cross the threshold of adulthood devoid of socio-emotional skills, pro-social sensibilities, and critical life skills, then adults are derelict. If youths are not shattering stereotypes and crushing the restrictive rudiments of ageism, then adults have been inattentive and dysfunctional at best in their role as ensamples of productive citizenship and community representatives.

Youths deserve more. Youths deserve to be set free from the curious entanglement of adolescent pressure, social stigma, political and economic conundrums, and media legerdemain. Adults are supposed to be liberators. Adults are given the responsibility of helping youths shed their fears and insecurities and become their beautiful selves. Whether we like it or not, whether we accept it or not, the blood is on our hands as adults if our children don't flourish and engage their destinies. How so? I believe that adults have a divine mandate to bear the torchlight of freedom that will guide youths to dignity and productivity. To care for youths, to lead them, to mentor them is to do God's work. It's a manifestation of ministry to *the least of these*.

Implications for School or Youth Leaders

Since I'm an educator, it's appropriate to speak from that perspective relative to leadership and the notion of introducing and developing hope in the lives of youths. School leaders, administrators in particular, have the unique responsibility of spearheading efforts to create the conditions that are conducive for student success. This includes operational matters, logistical matters, fiscal matters, and so much more that's related to general school business. To my mind one of the more underrated responsibilities is staff recruitment. Well, let me restate that. As a school leader, you can be astute in all matters of school business and operation, but if you don't have the right people for the vision, the conditions will not be optimal for meaningful learning. You've got to have, not just good, skilled people, you've got to have the right people. In this regard, it's not enough to search for folks with impressive credentials and experience. Don't get me wrong. That's all good, but students must be able to connect with individuals who possess and display expertise in care. They need access to what's in educators' brains *and* heart.

Recall that the accounts shared by the students in the research project revealed that they had consistent access to the knowledge and virtues of key individuals. Whether it was family members or educators, the sense of care felt by the students was the same. During the hiring cycle, it's the responsibility of the school leader to be very attentive and discerning when interviewing candidates for any position. It's also the responsibility of the school leader to remind and/or communicate their candidate "wish list" of characteristics to their colleagues who serve on the interview team. This can be done through candid discussions about the school vision and the attributes necessary to bring the vision into manifestation. It can also be communicated through the school leader's example. How he or she models desired virtues and communicative abilities is critical. Of course, there are situations when school leaders receive new employees through a district assignment process that doesn't allow for the school leader's input. There's little that can be done about that initially. However, the wise leader will be intentional about modeling desired behavior and clearly articulating to the assigned individual directly or in group settings, the behaviors and attitudes that are essential to the vision becoming reality.

Sometimes leaders may feel limited in their ability to profoundly convey what they want to see. Or, it could be a matter of timing due to tons of initiatives that they have to manage. When this is the case, thoughtful professional development selection is very important. If you don't have the time or the skill-set to share the way you'd like, or if you want another voice besides yours, it's okay to bring in reinforcements. Again, this must be done thoughtfully. For example, a school leader may have a contingency of staff members who are already displaying the desired skills and attributes that are needed. In this case, *they* can facilitate professional development. This would save money, boost their morale, honor their gifts and experiences, and send the message to the rest of the staff that their school leader pays attention to the work that staff members do. It also suggests to observing staff that the school leader trusts his/her team members.

Another option for professional development could be working with district personnel. For example, in the district where I formerly served there were numerous professionals that loved going to schools and supporting school leaders and their teams. At times they reached out to school leaders to offer their expertise. But overall, school leaders have to be proactive and forward-thinking. They should initiate the contact as part of their plan to cultivate the skills of their school team.

Community partners and vendors are vital to the success of schools. At WNHS we relied heavily on community partners and vendors to educate our scholars in social-emotional skills and life skills. Through their variety of talent, interests, style, and presentation, our company of community educators cultivated life-affirming values and pro-social behavior among WNHS students. Some of the community educators that worked with WNHS had platforms that extended to the national level. A couple of community educators had traveled throughout the United States (they still do) and made connections with renown individuals such as the esteemed professor and author, Cornel West. Our scholars had access to these partners once a week.

One year WNHS scholars met and listened to hip hop activist and former vice presidential candidate Rosa Clemente (Green Party). Other well-respected scholars and community leaders engaged our scholars over the years. I envied WNHS students. They were privy to profound intellectual talks and exposed to stunning creativity on a regular basis. Why? How? WNHS leadership deemed it absolutely necessary to provide access to folks who were serious about emancipatory education and transcendence. Through these essential relationships, life-changing seeds were planted in the hearts and minds of WNHS students.

To reiterate a point made earlier, students on the margins, namely those who reside in historically disadvantaged communities are capable of achievement and success. They need an equitable educational experience that prioritizes identification and procurement of supports that meet urgent needs, context notwithstanding. Administrators are tasked with creating lanes of opportunity for students to access equitable practices, relevant programs, and transcendent individuals. When this occurs, the learning experience is enriched and students are significantly impacted in a transformative manner. Education, carried out in this manner, is a moral imperative. In relation to administrative leaders and the morality of their work, Starratt (2004) pointed out:

> *"For schools to deepen and amplify the way they promote learning as a moral enterprise (one that requires intelligence, to be sure, as well as a planitude of other human virtues), they need leaders—both administrators and teachers—who themselves understand learning as a moral enterprise." (p. 3)*

Starratt (2004) further expounded on the vital role of school leaders:

> *"The leader is responsible to students as human beings, responsible for upholding their inherent dignity as human persons, persons with human as well as civil rights. As young members of the human family, they should be recognized as a work in the making, as vulnerable and fragile, and therefore as requiring a secure and nurturing environment. Their young minds, imaginations, hearts, and characters need both direction and encouragement in their development. Since students' development is the primary work of the institution, their welfare should prevail over all other considerations in school decisions." (p. 52)*

When you genuinely care about those you serve, you see them beyond numbers and names on rosters. Their best interest is valued above all else. Applied to schools, this approach indicates reverence of student dignity that is rooted in an understanding of learning as a moral enterprise. The moral, conscientious school leader will do everything in his or her power to give scholars nothing but the best, be it personnel, resources, or information. For, the moral, conscientious leader believes that regardless of family income levels or records of comportment, all children deserve access to that which is superior, not inferior. Persistence is necessary in this regard. The help of others will need to be enlisted. Patience will need to be exercised. The key is honoring youth ambition, upholding their worthiness, maintaining efficacy, and keeping both a macro and micro perspective.

Implications for teachers

Teachers play a significant role in the introduction and devel-opment of hope in the lives of their students (Duncan-Andrade, 2010; Post, 2006; Snyder, 2005). In sum, the WNHS students in the research project revealed that consistent access to teachers who exhibited optimism and course content expertise inspired students to persist toward goal-attainment. Students alluded to having solid rapport with WNHS staff. They perceived that the adults at WNHS genuinely cared about them. In the words of Freire (1970), the staff members "humanized" the youths. One of the ways the WNHS adults humanized their students was through conversation. As simplistic as it may seem, talking to students can have an enormous impact on students' perception of the teacher and how the adult feels about them. Through conversation with youths, adults have an opportunity to impart life-affirming and life-giving words that ignite a passion for excellence that manifests in improved attendance, reduced dis-ciplinary issues, and increased assessment scores.

Sparks of hope become burning flames when adults become honest about their experiences. Adult transparency and vulner-ability are often viewed as virtues among youth. They want people in their lives who will "keep it real" (At WNHS, we said, "keep it real" and "keep it right".). As the students in this study revealed, there's something powerful that takes place when they hear adult testimony. Seriously, youths sometimes believe that adults don't experience the hardships of life the way that they do. They believe that adults are clueless when it comes to the woes of adolescence. Thus, youths erect social walls to exclude adults when they attempt to talk to them about different issues. This isn't some newfangled phenom-enon. I believe the iconic hip hop duo, Jazzy Jeff & The Fresh

Prince, captured youth sentiment in this regard best when they recorded the smash 1980s hit, *Parents Just Don't Understand*. Sure, that song is nearly 30 years old now, but the perspective that the musicians shared remains the same. That's why honesty is important. Youths in my research project benefited from hearing about the joy and pain that their loved ones experienced. When adults opened up, the students were able to see them beyond their respective titles (e.g., mother, grandmother, aunt, and friend).

Teachers have a similar opportunity to bridge gaps and build relationships. They too, we too, must be willing to be transparent and vulnerable (hooks, 1994). Obviously, wisdom must be exercised, but teachers must be willing to let students into their lives, to the greatest degree appropriate. When this occurs, a notion of togetherness is generated that elevates the educational sojourn from a regular classroom experience to a collective mission for freedom. Teachers can honor student pain and struggle by telling their personal stories of pain and struggle. They can help students find a guiding light by describing their challenges, as well as their paths toward progress and prosperity. This type of interaction must become commonplace in schools, especially those schools that serve marginalized, urban African American youths. When it does, hope will spread to their homes and neighborhoods. The literature has made plain the way to hope (Snyder et al., 2006). We know it can be taught. We know it can be cultivated (Duncan-Andrade, 2010). The key is doing the inner work and starting the critical conversations.

Wheatley (2010) voiced a few insightful thoughts relative to the potency of conversation. First, Wheatley (2010) argued that "conversation wakes us up" (p. 162). Several students in the study spoke of discussions with caring adults that had a jarring effect on their thinking. The WNHS educators that were referenced during the interviews conversed in a way that stirred students to believe in themselves. Affirmation and confirmation of youth intelligence and their inherent value became so commonplace at WNHS that some students expected to receive inspirational messages. Second, Wheatley (2010) argued that "conversation is the practice of freedom" (p. 162). I recall that numerous WNHS students entered our space weighed down by issues (e.g., personal, family, neighborhood). Talks with staff members neutralized the stress and tension that they were experiencing. As the leader who conducted nearly all WNHS in-take meetings, I deliberately inquired about concerns students had or challenges that they faced just so I could tell them that nothing could prevent their success. I can't speak for my colleagues at the time, but I aimed for their hearts. I intended to sow seeds of efficacy. I wanted every youth to know that their prospects for transformation were real.

Third, Wheatley (2010) shared a thought that from my standpoint relates to the crucial nature of listening. She said that, "listening creates relationships" (p. 93). When I reflect on my years of educational service, I wholeheartedly support Wheatley's claim. I like to think of it in terms of deposits and withdrawals. Many of the scholars I served at WNHS had glaring weaknesses and were long overdue for adjustments to their attitude, habits of behavior, and personal vision. Before providing healthy critique (withdrawals), I made sure that I recognized the bright spots, the glows. I made deposits. I affirmed them. I would point out that despite what they'd endured, they were still able to tell their story. They were still alive. My rationale was that they could change if they wanted to. I told them that as African Americans they possessed the blood of overcomers. Their ancestors endured the horrors of the Transatlantic Slave Trade, Reconstruction, and the Jim Crow Era. In spite of the preponderant evil that existed, Africans in the Americas grew stronger and wiser. In the same way, they too could flourish despite the socio-ecological impediments that confronted them on a daily basis.

Conversations Impact Intelligence

Wheatley's (2010) remark about the awakening that is induced through conversation has implications for intelligence. Consider the theory of multiple intelligences. According to Gardner (1983), intelligence has a variety of expressions. It is never static and not necessarily bound to hereditary limitations. For example, some people possess bodily-kinesthetic intelligence which includes body movement, dexterity, and superior hand-eye coordination. Yes, a person can inherit a degree of kinesthetic ability, but it can also be cultivated. Intelligences emphasized in Gardner's (1983) framework include interpersonal intelligence which is the ability to understand and interact with others. People who express this kind of intelligence have the unique ability to discern emotions, motivation, and desires. Verbal-linguistic intelligence is an extension of interpersonal intelligence. This intelligence is recognized in people who have strong command of language when they write or speak. Those who are verbal-linguistically inclined are proficient or advanced in writing stories, reading, and memorization. Additional examples of intelligence within Gardner's (1983) framework include logical-mathematical (e.g., reasoning skills, pattern recognition, able to think conceptually about numbers and associated relationships or patters); naturalistic (e.g., strong interest in caring for environment and other species); intra-personal (e.g., aware of own emotions, feelings, and inclinations, eagerly engage in self-reflection and analysis); visual-spatial (e.g., strong ability to visualize people, places, objects, or concepts; great with maps, charts, pictures, etc.); musical (e.g., strong appreciation for music; can play instruments; understand rhythms, sounds, and patterns); and most recently, existential (e.g., strong interest in spirituality and/or philosophic reasoning about reality, knowledge, life).

Interestingly, at least three of the intelligences advanced by Gardner (1983) were at work in the experiences with hope articulated by the research project participants: interpersonal, verbal-linguistic, and intrapersonal intelligence. How? Through conversation! The students in the study were awakened and stirred by the inspiration, knowledge, and wisdom they gleaned from parents, loved ones, educators, and peers. They learned lessons that assisted them in determining their goals and trajectories. Intrapersonal intelligence was expressed through student reflection on their past and present (Consider Brian and Jameel who discussed their time of reflection while incarcerated.).

Further, academic performance was impacted by blends of interpersonal and intrapersonal intelligence. This combination created a base for the expression of other course specific intelligences. Stated differently, the students were compelled to reflect (intrapersonal) and act based on what was said and demonstrated by WNHS staff (interpersonal). The confidence and efficacy engendered through these daily interactions empowered students to complete courses that were related to other intelligences such as verbal-linguistic (e.g., English), logical-mathematical (e.g., Algebra, Geometry), naturalistic (e.g., Physical Science, Biology), and visual-spatial (e.g., History, Civics, World Studies) intelligences. In a nutshell, social interaction stimulated learning, and it all began with conversations.

With respect to the social nature of intelligence, Dickman and Stanford-Blair (2002) argued that humans rely on information from and interactions with other humans for quality.

The authors further asserted that, "Social interaction creates a flow of energy and information within and between the neural networks of individuals. Such interaction stimulates emotional attention, pattern recognition, cognitive dissonance, and reflective reasoning...it is how you refine your emotional being, resolve your beliefs, and think your best thoughts"(p. 109). Akin to Gardner's (1983) argument, Dickman and Stanford-Blair (2002) posited that intelligence is influenced by and deployed in social and cultural contexts. For instance, the students in the study were influenced by interaction with significant individuals and access to institutions. The students discussed significant associated elements such as conversations, discussions, sermons, visuals, and programs and how the conflation of these elements shaped and molded their sense of being and purpose. Their social experiences enabled them to project a favorable future image of themselves (Dickman & Stanford-Blair, 2002). The individuals that they regarded as important and the key places they discussed provided the emotional nourishment and cognitive charge that the students needed to realize their potential and generate the productivity that would carry them forward to goal attainment.

Dickman and Stanford-Blair (2002) also broached the dispositional dimension of intelligence which involves characteristics or attributes that are related to the way people behave on a daily basis. Plainly stated, social interactions influence dispositions. Scientifically, we know that people inherit characteristics. There are some ways of being that we get honestly from our loved ones. But, there are also characteristics that are grafted into our repertoire of behavior based on contexts. Think about it. The study participants that I introduced were all urban, African American high school students. They lived in tough neighborhoods. Therefore, safety was a common goal and value. In order to be/stay safe, the students had to acquire and/or develop attributes that they didn't necessarily receive genetically such as awareness, discernment, and to some degree fearlessness. An argument can even be made that the students adopted skepticism, whereby they questioned everything and everyone they encountered to preserve themselves and their loved ones.

Beyond the borders of their impoverished and violent neighborhoods, the students developed a different set of behaviors and habits that could help them evade socio-ecological dangers. Their behaviors included attending school daily, completing coursework during non-school hours, and participating in extracurricular activities. Student interpretations about their place in the world were informed by daily observations in the urban setting that they described as "the hood" or "the ghetto; a place with elements that students had to avoid in order to accomplish their goals. Dickman and Stanford-Blair (2002) explained this process of observance of socio-ecological factors and subsequent decision-making,

> *"At any given time, the brain is working to establish a cohesive state of mind among the integrated mental processes that define it. To that end, it is disposed to exercise intelligence in a habitual manner that corresponds to valued patterns of internal and external survival information. The value of dispositional intelligence is assessed by its value to survival...Accordingly, a useful disposition is a means for standardizing automatic responses to stimuli—an alternative to constantly making moment-to-moment decisions about how to respond to the environment." (p. 183)*

To Dickman and Stanford-Blair's (2002) point, the WNHS students that I interviewed developed patterns of behavior based on their need to avert traps and trouble in their surroundings. Despite needing to mature and acquire additional skills for success, I maintain that the students were already *hopers* because of the harsh realities of their environments. They had already identified certain conspicuous impediments. For example, Jameel spoke of growing weary of "seeing the same things". Prior to arriving at WNHS, he and his peers had already decided that they deserved more in life. They opted for an alternative to what was regarded as normal in their lived experiences. Through a process of reflection and perhaps internal confrontation, the students concluded that they had to do things different in order to experience something different. I've referred to this as a "turning point", a psycho-emotional pivot that produced a disposition or inner strength that made hoping logical and doable.

While I give the study participants and other successful WNHS students who were not study participants credit for possessing a measure of hope, I'm certain that their interaction with WNHS staff further cultivated hope. I believe that their sense of agency was enhanced as well as their belief that selected strategies could work and that they could execute the strategies. As Za'Nya's remarks revealed, her conversations with staff provided much needed encouragement and perspective. As Amber suggested, our conversation challenged her to expand her vision and at the same time become more focused. Social interaction with staff was critical to advancing hope and helping these youths continue to pursue their life-goals. Conversations with adults who cared opened lanes for insertion of new ideas and possibilities. The constant prodding by WNHS staff strengthened student resolve to "beat the streets". They were ready for a new song, a paean of victory in lieu of the same requiem so familiar to inner city residents. And with the cadre of WNHS staff and community educators cheering them on, it became evident that they'd found a place of refuge, a home where hope lived.

As I reflect further on my time spent at WNHS, I'm certain that we engendered trust on the part of our students because we honored their voice. We wanted to hear from them, and it was evident. Scholar voice was amplified through Restorative Practices. We conducted community building circles on a weekly basis. Our community educators emphasized scholar voice. They presented topics and lessons that were related to the lived experiences of our students. WNHS staff drew upon the wisdom of our students through "Conscious Reflections". These were exercises of the mind, yes, but we really wanted to learn the perspectives of students on subjects such as identity, race, culture, and economics. Then, of course, each of us had focused conversations with students that were specific to their situations.

Overall, our openness to conversation and the practice of listening was, on the part of WNHS staff, an example of what Gurn (2011) described as meeting students "on their terms" (p. 151). This practice was, in effect, an act of humanization whereby WNHS staff subordinated their prerogatives and objectives in favor of the needs and concerns of our students. And, by humanizing the students in this way, WNHS teachers helped to facilitate growth in the students' lives. Amber even shared that through Restorative Practices she learned the value of listening:

> *"I want to say this because I think this is one of my most important lessons was that there is...be the ears that is like able to listen you know be the person that's able*

236

to listen...Learn and listening, that's also something I learned through the circle process as well because not only were we able to express how we felt, but we were also able to listen to how everyone else felt around us which is really, really important and I really, really wish that our society did that more often, which is listen."

Awakening Consciousness

Amber's remarks helped me understand that youth aren't averse to listening to adults without reason. In fact, they are willing to listen, but they also want to be heard. It has to be an even exchange. Clearly, Amber esteemed the listening skills of WNHS staff. By attending to and giving ear to students' concerns, the teachers further humanized Amber and her peers. They created a pathway to introduce and implement critical pedagogic lessons and experiences. Stated differently, since the teachers showed that they cared for the students, the students reciprocated the care and positioned themselves to receive the instruction that the teachers had prepared. And, with the trust that this dynamic produced, teachers were able to draw upon the experiences and elements of the students' social realities and use them as entry points and springboards to access the general curriculum (Duncan-Andrade 2007; Duncan-Andrade & Morrell, 2008; Hill, 2009; Ladson-Billings, 1994; Sanchez, Araujo, & O'Donnell, 2008; Shade, 2006).

Mayo's (2007) study of the life of critical pedagogue Paulo Freire revealed an element that relates to the crucial nature of educators demonstrating conspicuous care for marginalized youths. Mayo (2007) observed that Freire's (1970) praxis and its eventual goal, "conscientizacao", i.e., "learning to perceive social, political, and economic contradictions and to take action against the oppressive elements of reality" (p.17), were preceded by compassion and regard for the weal of the oppressed. Thus, care was the prelude to the objectives of critical pedagogy. By deciding to dwell among the oppressed and understand their condition, Freire demonstrated care and in effect humanized them. The corollary was a shift in perspective amongst the oppressed. They began to recognize the value, the potential that the "stranger among them" observed. With newfangled perceptions of themselves in their line of sight, the oppressed were empowered to thrust off the undesirable appellation cast upon them by unjust powers. This psycho-emotional shift precipitated a transformation that ultimately culminated in the oppressed rejecting the valorizations set forth by hegemonic forces. Outfitted with improved mental armamentarium through critical pedagogics, the oppressed now had the knowledge and skills to contest social inequality and the ill effects it births.

Akin to Freire, WNHS staff was not faced with the same kind of social challenges. He was born into affluence (Mayo, 2007). Most educators are members of the middle-class (Ferris & Stein, 2012), a strata that could be relatively considered affluent. Yet, the students' accounts revealed that WNHS educators "came down" to share, to be informed; to show support. In doing so, they earned the students' trust. And, together they contended with the harsh realities of the students' lived experiences—albeit conversationally—and relished daily victories while pursuing goal attainment. According to Snyder (2005), the willingness to be available to students beyond the imperatives of teaching and learning is a potent way that teachers can show care as well as generate and raise hope among students. They need teachers who will spend time with them (Snyder, 2005) and who will help them acquire academic literacies (e.g., linguistic, computational, etc.). Their love for students must result in pedagogy that prepares them to negotiate life beyond the classroom (Duncan-Andrade, 2010). This includes being well-prepared for lessons, sound planning, establishment of clear objectives, and energetic instruction (Snyder, 2003).

Listening Precedes Accountability

Almost every adult that is not a millennial grew up believing that accountability to adults was something that was required merely by generational circumstance. In other words, adults are older. They've lived longer and experienced more, therefore youths should automatically listen to what they have to say. If ever we'd muster up the gall to question a command given by a parent, they'd typically retort, "Because I said so!" Or, sometimes they'd bark, "Don't question me!" Both are classic examples of social exchange based on rank and hierarchy. I don't recall ever reading a study that promoted this approach as an effective way to lead children. But, it occurred because in most cases that was what adults knew to do. Furthermore, it's likely that the adults in their lives approached child-adult relationships in this manner.

Contrary to this traditional means of interacting with youth, I argue that accountability is preceded by listening. Youths will allow adults to place demands on them if there is trust. Trust is established through relationship. Relationships begin with conversation. Conversation requires listening. Make sense? Youths will allow us to hold them accountable if they believe that we care about them. I've seen this play out on numerous occasions with numerous students. I've seen the roughest and toughest youngsters humble themselves and respond appropriately to directives because the person that issued the directives had established a critical bond that began with listening.

This is an important factor when considering youth growth and maturation. Furthermore, Jameel mentioned accountability as a form of care and promoting hope. His teacher, Mrs. Picotto closely monitored his online activity and held him accountable for completing assignments. The teacher in this case used humor as a way to "break the ice" with youths. She was consistent. She didn't save jokes for a select few. She smiled. She used endearing terms. She even gave herself a nickname that students would respect because so many of her students had nicknames. This leader met students where they were. But, Mrs. Picotto was only able to do so because she paid attention. She listened to her students, and in this way, she demonstrated care.

Duncan-Andrade and Morrell (2008) discussed the balance between caring for students and holding them accountable:

"Students still need adults with strong content knowledge, adults who understand the demands of secondary and post-secondary education, adults who understand learning theory and adolescent development, and adults who themselves possess academic and critical literacies. Most important, though, these students need adults who are strong motivators and who believe in them and their potential to become transformative intellectuals, adults who understand that they faced difficulties in their lives but who will not give up on the students or allow them to give up on themselves. This means that situations arise when adult as critical educators need to "get on" students, need to get them focused." (p. 103)

Plain and simple, youths need teachers who are unafraid and willing to spend time with them (Snyder, 2005). Love compels individuals to want to spend time with others. Thus, there's a love ethic that should be active when leading any child. Love will demand excellence. Love will allow for sympathy and perhaps empathy, but it won't let sympathy overshadow the importance of skill development. Love understands that students must be equipped to be successful and effective beyond the classroom. In this way, accountability is two-fold. Yes, teachers will hold students accountable. It also means that teachers will hold themselves accountable by being well-prepared to facilitate student learning. Sound planning, establishment of clear objectives, and energetic instruction fosters hope (Snyder, 2003). While forming powerful relational bonds and partnering with students, teachers must target mastery of skills. When this occurs, students will view their teacher as one who understands their needs, respects them for who they are, and is willing to work with them to help them accomplish their goals.

Principal Stokes was a relational leader, and he encouraged WNHS staff to stretch themselves, if necessary, to develop the capacity to facilitate learning through a relational process. In his words, teachers should be folks who understand, "educational paradigms and become pedagogues who possess outstanding psycho-cultural and socio-emotional competencies." He frequently admonished WNHS staff to deliver sound instruction and have the social awareness to help students contest the oppressive realities in their lives and in their communities. Within these critical consciousness refrains, a message of overcoming reverberated throughout the school and permeated the ethos. At the time, no one was promoting the Hope Theory framework as understood and articulated by Snyder (2002), but the essence of setting goals and overcoming obstacles was present. Students were encouraged to observe hope, seize it, and participate with teachers in its development in their lives.

As a member of the staff, I recall feeling a constant need to sharpen my skills as an educator and stay abreast of social, cultural, political, and economic issues that confronted our local community. From my perspective, I had to embrace the notion of being unfinished. And, the only way that I could effectively serve our youngsters was to commit to a self-imposed regiment of learning and growth. I came to believe that to some degree I had to experience what the students were experiencing. This allowed me to engage a phenomenon that Starratt (2004) introduced as "critical presence".

> *"Critical presence is not based on cynicism but rather on compassion and hope for the human condition. It is based on compassion for a humanity that aspires to heroic ideals, yet whose fragility and vulnerability lead to over-estimating possibilities or to shrinking back in fear of the risks involved. It is based on hope for a humanity that has demonstrated time and again a resilience that transforms oppressive situations into opportunities for heroic and courageous transcendence of the human spirit." (p. 98)*

As I was undergoing my own transformation, I could console, guide, and praise students while they engaged their transformation process. Ultimately that's what we were asking the students to do. Enrollment at WNHS wasn't only about academic credits. It was about their lives. Therefore, our approach was holistic. By the end of a student's journey at WNHS, they could attest to not only earning credits, but becoming a better person. The student comments in the research project support this claim. Further, their remarks indicate that through the care that was demonstrated, WNHS staff members were critically present to their urgent needs.

Incidentally, students eventually articulated a desire to express and exhibit the same "critical presence" that they observed. Three students specifically mentioned that one of their life-goals was to give back to their community. They recognized glaring needs and wanted to reciprocate the care that they'd received from family members and others. For example, Za'Nya explained, "you want to be that person they can say, "oh they came out the hood and they did this. You know I could do it to". You know. Not only having hope for you, but creating hope for somebody else". Jameel added, "I mean I wanna to be the person that little kids look up to even though I got a hood image". Amber also made reference to the importance of turning her attention to youth, "young people that's in similar communities like Kingstown that are in poverty, who live in urban communities and who are faced with disparities each and every day. How do we begin to help them help themselves?"

Za'Nya, Jameel, and Amber had become *hopers*. They made it out of "the hood", but they have ambitions to go back and help others get out. Or, in Amber's case, she wants to help youths challenge the issues that afflict them and their communities. The study participant's experience with hope compelled them to take on leadership in their community. What a powerful testament to the possibilities of leadership! My prayer is that more adults will invest in youth. My prayer is that those of us who've attained life-goals will reach back and take the hands of youths, especially those who exist on the margins. They are brilliant. They are creative. They have dreams. What they often lack is support. Sure, money helps, but even more important than money is the wealth found in the heart of one who is determined to serve. Leadership born out of an others-centered perspective produces greatness.

What about you? Will you take the lead? You don't have to have all the answers. Just take the steps necessary to affect change. As I've found, when you begin to take steps along the leadership journey, you'll encounter others of like mind who have what you don't. And together, as a team, you can make a difference. By building relationships, my colleagues and I touched numerous lives and by doing so we motivated students to become equally if not more socially aware and generous.

Chapter 10

ANSWERING HOPE'S CALL

"The high destiny of the individual is to serve rather than to rule."

-Albert Einstein

The research project that I engaged in confirmed the notion that hope helps marginalized youths obtain life-goals in spite of numerous social and ecological challenges. The youths in the study explained that they experienced hope through interpersonal relationships with key adults and access to institutions that offer critical resources related to their life-goal pursuits. The youths in the study proved that they can survive. They proved that they can even thrive amid daunting circumstances and socio-ecological barriers. They are resilient. They are intelligent. They have vision. But, they needed to be led and cared for by compassionate, conscientious adults.

I'd like to circle back to the *Hunger Games* analogy that I previously broached. In reference to the research study that I conducted, the student's accounts of experiencing hope through relationships reminds me of Katniss Everdeen's relationship with Haymitch and her sponsors. When Katniss needed direction, Haymitch shared. When she needed aid, a sponsor supplied a good (the balm) that saved her life. Without Haymitch's influence and the assistance of the sponsor, Katniss probably would have died from the humiliating *Hunger Games* gauntlet. Had she died the potential for liberation for all of the oppressed in the different districts may not have come about. But, because Haymitch took an interest in Katniss and conversed with her, she received counsel and wisdom. Because a sponsor took notice of Katniss' physical need, she lived and was able to generate hope for the forlorn masses in her immediate and broader community.

To President Snow's dismay, Katniss' success spurred uprisings and endangered Panem's trusses of social control. It generated a new narrative, one that suggested that the oppressed can rise, resist, and relieve themselves of the heavy hand of hegemony. In essence, her actions proved to be dangerous to the repressive forces of her day. In the same way, the students in the study prevailed. They surmounted obstacles and transcended negative appellations. Armed with knowledge and a cast of supportive adults, they too have hope. They too are dangerous.

The influence of caring adults in Katniss' situation enabled her to overcome environmental impediments. They helped to give and sustain her life. In turn, Katniss' greatness emerged. The treasure that was already inside of her began to be revealed. The magnanimity of her heart showed forth through her service. As the *Hunger Games* story expands, we learn in the *Hunger Games: Mockingjay Part 1*(Lionsgate, 2014), that Katniss develops into a freedom fighter and humanitarian. She foists a revolution against systemic oppression and galvanizes thousands of oppressed people to fight for the right to live free from the dictates of a totalitarian regime.

Who knew that all of that potential lay inside of her when she was a mere teenage girl hunting in the backwoods of District 12? Who knew that her undying love for her sister would morph into an intransigent commitment to the weal of humanity? That's the point. No one knew that initially. In the same way, we don't know what our youths can do when their best is allowed to manifest. We don't know the impact that our youths can have on their generation. We don't know what solutions they can devise and share with the rest of the world. Therefore, *we* have to liberate our youths from the manacles of racism, classism, sexism, ageism and demonization that constantly beset them. We—adults—have to help them reclaim their innocence and redeem the time of their youth so they can mature, free from bombardments of political maneuvers and economic decisions that ignore what's best for them. Adults have to be voices for "the least of these". We have to make noise and represent youths who too often aren't invited to the tables of discussion in their communities. We have to create safe spaces for youth voice and collaborate with them to ensure that their ideas have support. Our service to them will result in service to countless others. Katniss Everdeen proved it.

Art Guiding Life

Clearly, Katniss Everdeen is a fictional character and Panem doesn't really exist. Or does it? As I articulated earlier in this work, many of our urban centers feature residential sections that are eerily similar to the conditions of the oppressed in the *Hunger Games*. They are surrounded by a miasma of despondency similar to the milieus depicted in the poorer districts of Panem, the exurbs connected to the bustling metropole. It prompts the question that philosophers have wrestled with, "should art imitate life?" Or, should life take its cues from art? In many ways, art does reflect life. Artists and directors as in the case of the *Hunger Games* creators convey messages through storytelling and impactful visuals. Naturally, interpretation of what is seen or heard will always be subjective. But, when certain profound elements of a story are exposed, very meaningful dialogue can commence that encourages reflection.

In many ways, I interpreted the *Hunger Games* as a type of harbinger of what can happen when power goes unchecked and violence is allowed to be or is encouraged as the primary response to dissent. But again, in Katniss' character I see the potential for youth voice and service. To my mind, Starratt (2004) provided a cogent definition for service, "presence". He argued that being present is "being wide awake to what's in front of you" (p. 86). Despite Katniss' will to live and to preserve herself, she couldn't ignore the suffering of others. As much as she may have tried to not see what was really happening in her midst, she couldn't help it. Some call this having a "third eye". Others call it critical consciousness or being critically aware of structural and material inequity and taking steps to confront it.

Inasmuch as Katniss was awake to what was in front of her, Haymitch was also awake to *who* was in front of him. Later in the *Hunger Games* franchise, fans learn that Haymitch was part of a resistance movement. He too was aware of the oppression, and in Katniss he recognized a child with the inner strength, the brazenness, the compassion to make a difference. Through conversation and observation, Haymitch realized that Katniss needed to be mentored, that she needed to at least be presented with an opportunity to become part of something that was so much bigger than what she could have ever imagined. Her initial act of defiance was related to saving her sister. Haymitch eventually elevated her awareness to the possibilities of saving her sister and an entire populace.

Called Upward

Haymitch called Katniss up to a higher plane of human existence. How so? Some of our greatest thinkers have measured greatness by the quantity and quality of one's service. Consider Dr. Martin Luther King, Jr. who uttered these words years ago, "Everybody can be great because everybody can serve...". Or, even more powerful, Jesus taught his disciples that the greatest among them would be their servant (Matthew 20:26-28). You see, the mother of two of Jesus' followers, James and John, wanted her sons to be hierarchically closer to Jesus. She wanted them to have a seat next to him. The other disciples became upset with James and John for trying to secure what they perceived to be the most important place within their circle. Jesus was their leader. Hence, anyone next to Jesus was an esteemed leader and thus great. Jesus explained that servanthood was the pathway to leadership, to greatness. The disciples based their assessment on a self-centered perspective. Jesus countered and corrected their analysis by explaining that being others-centered was most appropriate. He used himself as an example, stating that his mission was to serve and sacrifice himself for the benefit of others.

St. Francis of Assisi answered the call to serve others. He embraced what scholar Peter Holbrook (2008) deemed the "Christological" perspective which espouses that service in its most evident, most tangible expression is rooted in and centered in an abiding faith in the person, work, and ministry of Jesus Christ. St. Francis recognized that Jesus Christ was the paragon of servant leadership and that if his service was to be authentic, if his life was to have the divine dignity that he desired, he'd have to see the face of Christ in himself and those he served.

"Francis listened to Christ's call to rebuild and make anew his house. He listened and heard the words of God, which lead him to minister and care for that which was too bitter for him to acknowledge prior to his conversion. It was through his ministry to and caring for the marginalized of his time, the lepers, the poor, and the sick, that he saw the face of Christ." (Holbrook, 2008, p.21)

In other words, service in the Franciscan leadership tradition honors Christ and brings glory to God. It is through a Christological perspective that one develops the depth of love and quality of service that truly affects change and engenders hope necessary to war against the "structures of oppression" (McLaren, 1997) that hinder the formation and continuity of true community. Boff and Pixley (1989) argued that a life that is "Christocentric" (p.115) produces a yearning for justice and community. The authors further argued that faith in Christ "has the capacity of assimilating, purifying, and deepening genuine natural and secular aspirations" (pp.115-116).

You may be wondering what Jesus and St. Francis have to do with the *Hunger Games* or the staff at WNHS. Well, if we zoom out for a moment, we can extract a couple simple nuggets of wisdom. First, in each case, others-centeredness was prominent. The WNHS staff centered the concerns of the students they served. Several gave up positions in comprehensive high school settings to do work that to their minds had more meaning. Katniss could have easily focused on saving herself and those closest to her. Instead she broadened her vision and shouldered the burdens of many. Second, sacrifice was the cost in each man's case. Jesus, of course, died on an old, rugged, Roman cross. St. Francis left affluence to dwell among lepers.

Several WNHS staff members left more comfortable positions where they were working with some of the "better behaved", more overtly skilled students in favor of assisting juvenile delinquents. Katniss sacrificed comfort, basic needs, and in many instances placed herself in dangerous situations to save others. But, whether one embraces the Christian tradition of service or not, the premise is that service begins with a response to a beckoning, divine or otherwise, to rebuild, replenish, and/ or restore community (Holbrook, 2008; Palmer, 2000).

Hence, our greatness starts to bloom when we opt for others. It emerges when we deny ourselves and turn our face and heart towards those outside our fortified walls and guarded zones of comfort. In both our national and global context, service in this regard is an option for the poor (Boff and Pixley, 1989). As St. Francis experienced, solidarity with and service to the poor, to the marginalized, the "least of these" (Matthew 25:31-46), began with a revelation of the love of God through Jesus Christ and the courage to bear one's own cross as did Christ. He was first transformed; then he influenced transformation in his environment and among others (Palmer, 2000).

The findings from my research study indicated that the transformation of the participants occurred because of the service of caring adults. It began with the adults being present to the needs of students judged as "the least" and enabled them to fathom life apart from the struggle they'd become accustomed to. Or, the adults began to speak to and call upon their potential so that even amid complex circumstances the students were developing agency. They were becoming fire proof. Rather than being consumed by their troubles, the students began to stand and keep moving forward in spite of swelteringly heated situations.

The service delivered by the adults included talking with students; listening; engaging in thought-provoking dialogue; guiding students through exploration of important socio-political and cultural issues; and facilitating online courses. It's important to note that service in its purest expression isn't defined or at least should not be defined by the provider. No, the petitioner should determine the manner of service. It can be very tempting to determine what is important or urgent when serving marginalized populations. Freire (1970) highlighted this caveat in his discussion of "banking education". He suggested that schools have been guilty of doing education *to* students rather than *with* them; that teachers treat students like receptacles that can only receive deposits of knowledge that they later regurgitate on tests. Freire (1970) regarded this type of experience as delimiting and in effect dehumanizing. In lieu of this mode of teaching, Freire (1970) espoused an approach to teaching that elevates students to a position of partnership with teachers. He called for "problem-based education" that honors the voice of students and consults with them to address issues of inequity. In other words, adults don't have all the answers and true learning doesn't occur if students are relegated to passivity. Invitation to discourse, through relationships, through conversations, expands the borders of social exchange and increases possibilities of learning experiences. Within these illuminating settings, students (petitioners) are able to articulate their needs. And, the providers (educators) can properly serve.

With respect to the students in the research study and at WNHS, imposition was viewed negatively (Snyder, 2005). We did our best to serve in response to what students emphasized as a need upon their enrollment at the school. Service wasn't thrust upon them. Granted, delivery of services and service-related resources was pre-planned due to the school's criteria and programmatic focus. At the same time, students had options. They could select the sequence of courses that they'd enroll in. When needed, they could ask for guidance with personal matters. They could request additional help. More often than not, conversation as a form of service was consensual. There were students who rarely came to me for counsel. Then there were those who visited my office daily. Again, our aim was to lead, educate, and serve on the terms of the students (Gurn, 2011).

Hundreds of students prospered in our midst at WNHS because we were a home for hope. All of the ingredients were present. We emphasized goals. We discussed strategies. We constantly reminded our students of their intelligence and strength. We believed that they could succeed.

WNHS staff established goals for enrollment. We established goals for discipline and course completion. When we realized that some students needed more face-to-face instruction, we set a goal to insert regular classroom instruction into the student's week. The physical layout of the school wasn't exactly optimal for the adjustment, but we figured out a way to make it happen. Our staff meetings were times of strategic thinking and collaboration. We engaged in problem-solving and devised ways to address concerns. Our leader, Principal Stokes, constantly reminded us of our responsibility to our students as well as our ability to actually make a difference in their lives. I was always stirred to act after listening to his exhortations. Although I didn't conduct the research to verify this claim, I assumed that hope was working in our lives, at least in the educational domain. And, if this was true, then it made sense that we could help students who'd already made room for hope in their hearts.

Make Room in Your Heart

This brings me to my final thought as it pertains to service and raising hope among urban African American youths on the margins. Those hurting, those in need have to have access to persons who can help meet their needs. WNHS staff were accessible. Our physical location was important because it was easily accessible. We were located along two major transit lines. Students could get to WNHS from any part of the city. In addition, once students entered our space they learned about other community resources that could help them. We learned that it's not just about being available. It's also important to become knowledgeable about resources that can address specific needs. That's part of developing the component of agency. In other words, teach youths how to fish.

Surely the task of helping youths accomplish life-goals is not easily achieved in isolation. When attempting to go-it-alone, supporting youths can be frustrating, bewildering, and disappointing. Adults can expand their capacity for empowering youths by establishing relationships with individuals and/or institutions that feature expertise and provide information that youths can draw from. Parents and caregivers can partner with schools, community centers, agencies, and places of worship to receive information about useful programs and services. Institutions can consult youths and their families to gain a more accurate understanding of their urgent needs, and then customize programs and services accordingly.

There are myriad ways for individuals and institutions to become positioned as a support to youths. But, the first step isn't one that is publicly noted. The first step involves introspection, during which one examines his/her priorities, ambitions, and concerns; determining what is most important in their life (Groups and organization can work through this process too.).

The next step is identification of potential obstacles and any associated elements. This step also includes appraisal of one's willingness and ability to confront and successfully overcome any identified obstacle(s). Step three requires the individual to think about strategies to actually achieve what is deemed most important; whether or not they possess what it takes to implement the strategies; and whether or not the strategies can lead to success. The final step is affirming the selected strategies and one's ability through positive self-talk and then taking action.

No one can reasonably expect to support youths particularly those on the margins, unless they too become *hopers*. This is a point that has been explicated in a variety of ways throughout this text. So, am I attempting to prod adults toward hoping? Of course! How else can an adult realistically exhort youths and compel them to persevere? You can't give what you don't have.

Loeb (1999) shared a definition of hope that further clarifies the importance of becoming a hoper. He maintained that hope is, "a way of viewing the world, which can be strengthened and refined through experience, helping us persevere despite all obstacles" (p. 334). We all are living during a time when we really don't know what's going to happen. Vagaries seem to be abundant. For instance, the 2016 Presidential election left many stunned. Nearly half of U.S. voters didn't participate. The majority of blacks didn't vote. A portion of the Latino community voted for a candidate whose campaign rhetoric was often flagrant and acerbic. Some women preferred the candidate who purported to be anti-Washington over gender loyalties. There were twists and turns galore. Truthfully, I don't think most people took President-elect Trump (at the initial time of this writing) seriously. The average adult didn't think he'd stand a chance against Hilary Clinton. I know I didn't. But, the election results told a much different story. With their votes, people in red states essentially demanded a new tune be played and a new song be sung by political figures. Their vote revealed that promises of change and hope aren't enough. It's time for results.

While Trump supporters initially reveled in victory and rejoiced at the prospect of the United States returning to a "more glorious version of itself", there are many—citizens and otherwise—who were horrified. Immigrants feared and continue to fear being deported. Differently-abled citizens and their loved ones viewed the next leader of the "free world" as one who was ignorant of their needs and even derisive towards them. Muslims were and still are concerned that they will become targets for broods of hate crime opportunists. Some blacks wonder if the nation will legally regress to the strictures and tenuousness of the Jim Crow era. Whether or not the concerns I've mentioned are valid is really a secondary or even tertiary point. The running thread is the fear of the unknown. A man with tons of business experience, but no political resume to speak of is the chief leader of the United States. People have been afraid. They've been flummoxed because they haven't really known what to expect over the duration of his term besides outlandish remarks, overt bigotry, political chicanery, and socio-cultural retrogression.

Ironically, it's within this moment that Loeb's (1999) words are critical. There's no guarantee that the 2020 presidential election will result in the installation of a new regime that will take significant steps towards helping the American populace secure the blessings of true liberty. To have hope from Loeb's (1999) standpoint is to maintain a certain impenetrable disposition, one that defies pessimism and sneers at excuses. To have hope, as Loeb (1999) asserted is to see opportunity where others see an impasse; it's to see possibilities when others are loathe to use their imagination; it's to believe that situations are at the mercy and disposal of the viewer, not the other way around. To have hope is to have vision and a sense of purpose when the world around you seems to be rudderless.

The fact is that change is an immutable feature of the human experience. Nothing is certain. You win some. You lose some. There is joy. There is pain. There are things that don't make sense. There is unfairness. There is stupidity. There is love and hate. There is good and evil.

Life is complex. It's a phenomenon that is oxymoronic in a weird, productive way. Suffering can teach us lessons that luxury cannot. Pleasure, particularly in excess, can cause pain. Simplicity often leads to profound revelations. Success, growth, or prosperity, however one interprets it, blooms from dirt and dung issues and scenarios. If we can't endure the foul, we cannot take hold of our future. This is why hope is relevant. In the midst of our consternation and frustration, dendrites are firing and synapses are being activated. Our understanding expands. Our knowledge is deepened. Our skills are refined. Our goals are eventually apprehended.

Sure, I can imagine that there are outliers who are able to amble through hardships and landmine-like conditions with no external support. But, most people need a mentor, a sponsor, a coach, someone who has been, "strengthened and refined through experience" and who is therefore hopeful. That's what the world needs. That's who the world needs in these uncertain and perhaps downbeat times...citizens who care. The world needs citizens who reject despondency; citizens who will hope. If we can grow hope and wed that hope with an embrace of servant leadership, then we will have a powerful contingency of citizens with the capacity to contribute to the overall well-being of society.

The study participants proved that personal narratives with maculate beginnings can become beautiful tales of victory. The adults who cared for these youths proved that those on the margins are worthy of investment. Adult availability and impartation was crucial to the youths garnering the wherewithal and audacity to believe, powerfully wielding their disposition as a weapon against despair. Together the youths and the adults proved that what begins as an aggravating cacophony can end with soul-stirring melody and soothing harmony. Despite care-fraught childhoods, capricious adult support, derelict teachers, and personal strivings, the study participants overcame and advanced. How? They made room for hope.

What would happen if more people took the time to listen, to give, to serve? How great could the United States be if every person sensed a call to greatness, a call to go beyond? I know what would happen. Hope would proliferate. Cold nights of darkness and disappointment would give way to ever-expanding dawns of justice. Magnanimity would abound and the promises of democracy, the essence of the American ideal would come into view. Now is our time. There's too much on the line. We owe it to our children. It costs us nothing to hope, but it will cost us everything if we don't.

REFERENCES

Abu-Jamal, M. & Hill, M.L. (2013). The classroom and the cell: Conversations on black life in America. Chicago: Third World Press.

Adams, D. W., (1995). *Education for extinction: American Indians and the boarding school experience, 1875-1928.* Lawrence, KS: University Press of Kansas.

Allen, I. E. & Seaman, J. (2011). *Going the distance: Online education in the United States, 2011.* The Sloan Consortium. Retrieved from http://sloanconsortium.org/publications/survey/pdf/learningondemand.pdf

Anderson, C. (1999). Code of the streets. Decency, violence, and the moral life of the inner city. New York: W. W. Norton & Company.

Ankara Papers. (2004). Racism, multiculturalism, culture and identity. *Ankara Papers, 14(1),* 13-23. Retrieved from http://0-web.ebscohost.com.topcat.switchinc.org/ehost/detail?vid=6&sid=c7afdeae-a676-4681-8376

Anyon, J. (1997). Ghetto schooling: A political economy of urban educational reform (1st Ed.). New York: Teachers College Press.

Arrington, M.L. (2014). Never giving up: A phenomenological study of hope in African American students in a small urban public high school. (Doctoral Dissertation). Available from Proquest Dissertations and Theses database. (Cardinal Stritch University____)

Asante, M. K. (2003). *Afrocentricity: The theory of social change*. Chicago: African American Images.

Asante, M. K. (2008). *It's bigger than hip hop: The rise of the post-hip hop generation*. New York: St. Martin's Press.

Bailey, T. C., Eng, W., Frisch, M. B., & Snyder, C. R. (2007). Hope and optimism as related to life satisfaction. *The Journal of Positive Psychology, 2(3),* 168-175. doi: 10.1080/17439760701409546

Batman v. Superman. Warner Brothers Pictures. (2016)

Boff, C. & Pixley, G.V., (1989). The bible, the church, and the poor. Maryknoll, NY: Orbis Books.

Briedis, M. (2009). Phenomenology of freedom and responsibility in Sartre's existentialist

ethics. *Filosofija, 17(3),* 71-82. doi: 10.3846/1822-430X

Bridges, T. (2011). Towards a pedagogy of hip hop in urban teacher education. *The Journal of Negro Education, 80(3),* 325-338. Retrieved from http://0-web.ebscohost. com.topcat.switchinc.org/ehost/detail?vid=14&sid=-c7afdeae-a676-4681-8376-87f7bde053f5%40session-mgr13&hid=23&bdata

Brown, D.F. (2004). Urban teachers' professed classroom management strategies: Reflections of culturally responsive teaching. *Urban Education, 39(3)*, 266-289. DOI: 10.1177/0042085904263258

Cesaire, A. (2000). *Discourse on colonialism*. New York: Monthly Review Press.

Chang, E. C., & Banks, K. H. (2007). The color and texture of hope: Some preliminary findings and implications for hope theory and counseling among diverse racial/ethnic groups. *Cultural Diversity and Ethnic Minority Psychology, 13(2)*, 94-103. doi: 10.1037/1099-9809.132.94

Christenson, C. M., Horn, M. B., & Johnson, C. W. (2008). *Disrupting class: How disruptive innovation will change the way the world learns*. New York: McGraw-Hill.

Coates, T. (2015). *Between the world and me*. New York: Random House.

Cone, J. H. (1997). *Black theology and black power*. Maryknoll, NY: Orbis Books.

Creswell, J. W. (2010). *Qualitative research & research design: Choosing among the five approaches*. Thousand Oaks, CA: Sage Publications. .

Cress-Welsing, F. (1990). *The isis papers: The keys to the colors*. Chicago: Third World Press.

Davidson, C. L., Wingate, L. R., Slish, M. L., & Rasmussen, K. A. (2010). The great black hope: Hope and its relation to suicide risk among African Americans. *Suicide and Life-Threatening Behavior, 40(2)*, 170-180. Retrieved from http://0-web.ebscohost.com.topcat.switchinc.org/ehost/results?sid=c7afdeae-a676-4681-8376-87f7bde053f5%-40sessionmgr13&vid=18&hid=23

Delpit, L. & White-Bradley, P. (2003). Educating or imprisoning the spirit: Lessons from ancient Egypt. *Theory into Practice, 42(4),* 283-288.

Dickman, M. H., & Stanford-Blair, N. (2002). *Connecting leadership to the brain.* Thousand Oaks, CA: Corwin Press.

Dryfoos, J. (1998). Safe passage: Making it through adolescence in a risky society. New York: Oxford University Press.

Duncan-Andrade, J. (2010). Note to educators: Hope required when growing roses in concrete. *Harvard Educational Review, 79*(2), 181-194. Retrieved from http://edreview. org/harvard09/2009/su09/s09dunca.htm.

Duncan-Andrade, J. (2010, May). *Effective educators of urban students: The gangsta, wanksta, rida paradigm.* Paper presented at Transition High School, Milwaukee, WI.

Duncan-Andrade, J., & Morrell, E. (2008). *The art of critical pedagogy: Possibilities for moving from theory to practice in urban schools.* New York: Peter Lang Publishing, Inc.

Dyson, M. E. (2001). *Holler if you hear me: Searching for Tupac Shakur.* New York: Basic Civitas Books.

Dyson, M.E. (2016). The black presidency: Barak Obama and the politics of race in America. New York: Houghton Mifflin Harcourt.

Fanon, F. (1952). Black skins, white masks. New York: Grove Press.

Feige, K. (Producer), & Coogler, R. (Director). (2018). Black panther [Motion Picture]. United States. Walt Disney Studios Motion Pictures.

Feldman, D. B., Rand, K. L., & Kahle-Wrobleski, K. (2009). Hope and goal attainment: Testing a basic prediction of hope theory. Journal of Social and Clinical Psychology, 28(4), 479-497. Retrieved from http://0-web.ebscohost.com.topcat.switchinc.org/ehost/results?sid=c7afdeae-a676-4681-8376-*87f7bde053f5*%40sessionmgr13&vid=20&hid=23&bquery

Ferris, K., & Stein, J. (2011). The real world: An introduction to sociology (3rd Ed.). New York: W.W. Norton & Company.

Folkman, S. (2010). Stress, coping, and hope. Psycho-Oncology, 19, 901-908. doi: 10.1002/pon.1836

Freire, P. (1970). *Pedagogy of the oppressed*. New York: The Continuum Publishing Company.

Gardner, H. (1983). *Frames of mind: The theory of multiple intelligences*. New York: Basic Books.

Gardner, H. (2011). *Frames of mind: The theory of multiple intelligences* (3rd Ed.). New York: Basic Books.

Giroux, H. A. (2009). *Youth in a suspect society: Democracy or disposability?* New York: Palgrave Macmillan.

Gladwell, M. (2008). *Outliers: The story of success*. New York: Little, Brown, and Company.

Glaude, E.S. (2016). *Democracy in black: How race still enslaves the American soul*. New York: Crown Publishers.

Gordon, G.L. (1999). Teacher talent and urban schools. *Phi Delta Kappan, 81(4),* 304-307.

Grewal, P. K., & Porter, J. E. (2007). Hope theory: A framework for understanding suicidal action. *Death Studies, 31(1)*, 131-154. doi: 10.1080/07481180601100491

Grimes, E. K. & Carter, U. B. (2008). *Why our children hate us: How black adults betray black children*. Philadelphia, PA: Grimes & Carter, LLC.

Gurn, A. M. (2011). Critical pedagogy in the classroom and the community. *Curriculum Inquiry, 41,(1)*, 143-152. doi: 10.1111/j.1467-873X.2010.00536.x

Hahn, D. (Producer), & Allers, R., Minkoff, R. (Directors). (1994). The lion king [Motion Picture]. United States. Buena Vista Pictures.

Hilfiker, D. (2002). *Urban injustice: How ghettos happen*. Seven Stories Press.

Hill, C. E., Thompson, B. J., & Williams, E. N. (1997). A guide to conducting consensual qualitative research. *The Counseling Psychologist, 25(4)*, 517-572.

Hilton-Pitre, T. (2009). Counseling African American girls in a white school setting: The empowerment groups for academic success model. In Abul Pitre, Esrom Pitre, Ruth Ray, Twana Hilton-Pitre (Eds.), *Educating African American students: Foundations, curriculum, and experiences* (pp. 153-172). Lanham, MD: Rowman & Littlefield Publishers.

Hoffman, G., Koules, O., Burg, M. (Producers), & Wan, J. (Director). (2004). Saw [Motion Pictures]. United States. Lionsgate.

hooks, b. (1994). Engaged pedagogy. *Teaching to transgress,* (pp. 13-22). New York: Routledge.

Howard, P., Butcher, J., & Egan, L. (2010). Transformative education: Pathways to identity, independence and hope. *Gateways: International Journal of Community Research and Engagement, 3,* 88-103. UTSePress.

Howard, T.C. (2001). Telling their side of the story: African American students' perceptions of culturally relevant teaching. *Urban Review, 33(2),* 131-149.

Irby, D. (2012). Hustlin' Conscientiousness. Paper presented at Milwaukee Area Technical College, Milwaukee, WI.

Irvine, J. J. (1990). Black students and school failure: Policies, practices, and prescriptions. Westport, CT: Praeger.

Jacobson, N. (Producer), & Ross, G. (Director). (2012). *Hunger games* [Motion Picture]. United States. Lionsgate.

Jenmorri, K. (2006). Of rainbows and tears: Exploring hope and despair in trauma therapy. *Child & Youth Care Forum, 35(1),* 41-55. doi: 10.1007/s10566-005-9002-7.

Johnson, J. W., Washington, B., Dubois, W.E.B. (1999). Three negro classics. New York: Avon Books.

Kandil, R. M. (2011). The Egyptian education system & public participation. *Social Policy, 41(2),* 58-64. Retrieved from http://0-web.ebscohost.com.topcat.switchinc.org/ehost/detail/vid=9&hid=119&sid=3df7ff

Kafele, B. (2004). *The handbook for teaching African American students.* Jersey City, NJ: Baruti Publishing.

Kafele, B. (2010). Teaching black male students. *Principal Leadership, 10(7),* 76-79.

Kane, N. (2007). Frantz Fanon's theory of racialization: Implications for globalization. *Journal of the Sociology of Self-Knowledge, 5(3)*, 353-362. Retrieved from http://scholarworks.umb.edu/humanarchitecture/vol5/iss3/32/

Karenga, M. (2002). *Introduction to black studies.* (3rd Ed.), Los Angeles: University of Sankore Press.

Kunjufu, J. (1988). To be popular or smart: The black peer group. Chicago: African American Images.

Kunjufu, J. (2001). *State emergency. We must save African American males.* Chicago: African American Images.

Kunjufu, J. (2002). *Black students: Middle class teachers.* Chicago: African American Images.

Kunjufu, J. (2004). *Countering the conspiracy to destroy black boys.* Chicago: African American Images.

Kunjufu, J. (2005). *Keeping black boys out of special education.* Chicago: African American Images.

Ladson-Billings, G. (1994). *The dreamkeepers: Successful teachers of African American children.* San Francisco: Jossey-Bass.

Laverty, S. M. (2003). Hermeneutic phenomenology and phenomenology: A comparison of historical and methodological considerations. *International Journal of Qualitative Methods, 2(3)*, 1-29.

Loeb, P. R. (1999). *Soul of a citizen: Living with conviction in a cynical time.* New York: St. Martin's Griffin.

Luce, R. (2005). Battlecry for a generation: The fight to save America's youth. Colorado Springs, CO: Cook Communications Ministries.

Lynn, M. (2004). Inserting the 'race' into critical pedagogy: An analylis of 'race-based epistemologies'. *Educational Philosophy and Theory, 36(2),* 153-165. doi: 10.1111/j.1469-5812.2004.00058.x.

Mayo, P. (2007). Critical approaches to education in the work of Lorenzo Milani and Paulo Freire. *Study of Philosophy of Education, 26,* 525-544. doi: 10.1007/s11217-007-9064-0

McClaren, P. (1997). *Revolutionary multi-culturalism: Pedagogies of dissent for the new millennium.* Boulder, CO: Westview Press.

Merriam-Webster. (1998). *Collegiate Dictionary* (10ᵗʰ ed.). Springfield, MA: Merriam Webster.

Meisenhelder, T. (1982). Hope: A phenomenological prelude to critical social theory. *Human Studies, 5,* 195-212. Retrieved from http://0-web.ebscohost.com. topcat.switchinc.org/ehost/pdfviewer/pdfviewer?sid=-c7afdeae-a676-4681-8376-87f7bde053f5%40session-mgr13&vid=55&hid=23

Memmi, A. (2006). *Decolonization and the decolonized.* Minneapolis, MN.: University of Minnesota Press.

Milwaukee Public Schools. (2007). Futures First Initiative: Proposal. Milwaukee, WI: Author.

Milwaukee Board of School Directors. (August 2010). Regular board meeting: Student expulsion statistics. Milwaukee, WI: Author.

Moulden, H. M., & Marshall, W.L. (2005). Hope in the treatment of sexual offenders: The potential application of hope theory. *Psychology, Crime & Law, 11(3)*, 329-342. doi: 10.1080/10683160512331316361

Moustakas, C. (1994). *Phenomenological research methods.* Thousand Oaks, CA: Sage Publications.

Myers, J. (2009). *How to hear from God: Learn to know his voice and make right decisions.* New York: Faith Words.

Ng, W., & Nicholas, H. (2010). A progressive pedagogy for online learning with high-ability secondary school students: A case study. *The Gifted Child Quarterly, 54(3)*, 239-251. Retrieved from, http://0-search.proquest.com.topcat.swithinc.org/education/docprintview/274707610/.

Pajares, F., Britner, S. L., & Valiante, G. (2000). Relationship between goals and self-beliefs of middle school students in writing and science. *Contemporary Educational Psychology 25(4)*, 406-422. doi: 10.1006/ceps.1999.1027

Palmer, P. (2000). *Let your life speak: Listening for the voice of vocation.* San Fransico: Jossey-Bass.

Parker, L., & Stovall, D.O. (2004). Actions following words: Critical race theory connects to critical pedagogy. *Educational Philosophy and Theory, 36(2)*, 167-182. doi: 10.1111/j.1469-5812.2004.00059.x.

Peckham, I. (2003). Freirean codifications: Changing walls into windows. *Pedagogy Critical Pedagogy Approaches to Teaching Literature, Language, Composition, and Culture, 3(2)*, 227-244. Retrieved from http://0-web.ebscohost.com.topcat.switchinc.org/ehost/pdfviewer/

pdfviewer?sid=c7afdeae-a676-4681-8376-87f7b-de053f5%40sessionmgr13&vid=63&hid=23

Perkins, U. E. (1995). *Harvesting generations: The positive development of black youth.* Chicago: 3ʳᵈ World Press.

Pitre, A., Ray, R., Stubblefield, L. (2009).The challenge of implementing black history: Student narratives of a black history program. In Pitre, A., Pitre, E., Ray, R., and Hilton-Pitre, T. (Eds.), *Educating African American students: Foundations, curriculum, and experiences.* (pp. 125-138). Lanham, MD: Rowman & Littlefield Publishers.

Pitt, B. (Producer), & Vaughn, M. (Director). (2010). *Kick-ass* [Motion Picture]. United States. Universal Pictures.

Post, D. (2006). A hope for hope: The role of hope in education. *Philosophy of Education*, 271-279. Retrieved from http://www.academia.edu/1094361/A_Hope_for_Hope_The_Role_of_Hope_in_Educatin

Public Allies. (2013). Retrieved August 2, 2013, from http://www.publicallies.org/site/c.liKUL3PNLvF/b.2775807/k.C8B5/About_Us.htm

Rivera, R. (March, 2009). *Good life pre sentation.* Paper presented at the Transition High School R.O.C. Institute, Milwaukee, WI.

Rogers, D. D. (April, 2010). *The penta-cultural youth.* Lecture presented at the Transition High School R.O.C. Institute, Milwaukee, WI.

Ronsisvalle, T., & Watkins, R. (2005). Student success in online K-12 education. *Quarterly Review of Distance*

Education, *6(2)*, *pp.117-124,184*. Retrieved January 20, 2012 from, http://0-search.proquest.com.topcat.swithinc. org/education/docprintview/231079782/

Roven, C., Snyder, D. (Producers) & Snyder, Z. (Director) (2016). Batman v. superman: Dawn of justice [Motion Picture]. Warner Bros. Pictures.

Sanchez, R. M., Araujo, B. E., & O'Donnell, J. (2008). Mediation, resistance, and resolve: Critical pedagogy and multicultural education in a cross-cultural context. *Multicultural Perspectives, 10(3)*, 133-141. doi: 10.1080/15210960802197615

Schott Foundation for Public Education.(2013). Opportunity to Learn. Retrieved from http://www.otlstatereport.org/national/summary/state-comparisons. Author.

Senge, P. M. (2006). *The fifth discipline: The art and practice of the learning organization*. New York: Doubleday.

Shade, P. (2006). Educating hopes. *Studies in Philosophy and Education, 25*, 191-225. doi: 10.1007/s11217-005-1251-2

Shakur, T. (1999). *The rose that grew from concrete*. New York: Pocket Books.

Smith, N. H. (2005). Hope and critical theory. *Critical Horizons, 6(1)*, 45-61. Retrieved from http://www.academia.edu/1284885/Hope_and_Critical_Theory

Snyder, C. R. (2002). Hope theory: Rainbow in the mind. *Psychology Inquiry, 13*, 249-275. Retrieved from http://www.jstor.org/discover/10.2307/1448867?uid=37395

52&uid=2129&uid=2&uid=70&uid=4&uid=3739256 &sid=21102722379463

Snyder, C. R., Feldman, D. B., Shorey, H. S., & Rand, K. L. (2002). Hopeful choices: A school counselor's guide to hope theory. *Professional School Counseling*, 5(5), Retrieved from http://0-web.ebscohost.com.topcat.switchinc.org/ ehost/detail/vid=4&hid=119&sid=3df7ff

Snyder, C. R., Lopez, S. J., Shorey, H. S., Rand, K. L., & Feldman, D. B. (2003). Hope theory, measurements, and applications to school psychology. *School Psychology Quarterly, 18(2)*, 122-139. Retrieved from http://0-web. ebscohost.com.topcat.switchinc.org/ehost/pdfviewer/ pdfviewer?vid=22&sid=d395fafd-7869-4bf6-8b66-a3e35 9035f94%40sessionmgr4&hid=23

Snyder, C. R. (2005). Teaching: The lessons of hope. *Journal of Social and Clinical Psychology*, 24(1), 72-84. doi: 10.1521/ jscp.24.1.72.59169

Snyder, C. R., Lehman, K. A., Kluck, B., & Monsson, Y. (2006). Hope for rehabilitation and vice versa. Rehabilitation Psychology, 51(2), 89-112. doi: 10.1037/0090-5550.51.2.89

Starratt, R. J. (2004). *Ethical leadership*. San Francisco: Jossey-Bass.

Stoller, S. (2009). Phenomenology and the poststruc-tural critique of experience. *International Journal of Philosophical Studies, 17(5), pp.707-737*. DOI: 10.1080/09672550903301762.

Taylor, S. J., & Bogdan, R. (1998). *Introduction to qualitative research methods: A guidebook and resource* (3rd Ed.). New York: Wiley.

te Reile, K. (2010). Philosophy of hope: concepts and applications for working with marginalized youth. *Journal of Youth Studies, 13(1),* 35-46. doi: 10.1080/13676260903173496

Transition High School. (2008). Retrieved June 14, 2011, from http://www.transitionhs.com

Ward. D. B., & Wampler, K. S. (2010). Moving up the continuum of hope: Developing a theory of hope and understanding its influence in couples therapy. *Journal of Marital & Family Therapy. 36(2),* 212-228. doi: 10.1111/j.1752-0606.2009.00173.x

Watkins, W. (2001). *The white architects of black education: Ideology and power in America. 1865-1954.* New York: Teachers College Press.

Watson, C., & Smitherman, G. (1996). *Educating African American males: Detroit's Malcolm X academy solution.* Chicago: Third World Press.

West, C. (2008). *Hope on a tightrope: Words & wisdom.* New York: Smiley Books.

Wheatley, M. J. (2010). *Leadership and the new science: Discovering order in a chaotic world.* San Francisco: Berrett-Koehler.

Williams, C. (1987). *The destruction of black civilization.* Chicago: Third World Press.

Wilmore, G. S. (1998). Black religion and black radicalism: An interpretation of the religious history of African Americans. Maryknoll, NY: Orbis Books.

Wilson, A. (1991). *Understanding black adolescent male violence: It's remediation and prevention.* New York: Afrikan World Infosystems.

Wilson, A. (1993). *The falsification of Afrikan consciousness: Eurocentric history, psychiatry, and the politics of white supremacy.* New York: Afrikan World Infosystems.

Woodson, C. G. (1933). *The miseducation of the negro.* Washington, DC: The Associated Publishers.

Womack, Y.L. (2010). Post black: How a new generation is redefining African American identity. Chicago: Chicago Review Press.

Wright, B. E. (1984). *The psychopathic racial personality and other essays.* Chicago: Third World Press.

Yohani, S. C. (2008). Creating an ecology of hope: Arts-based interventions with refugee children, *Child Adolescence Social Work, 25,* 309-323. doi: 10.1007/s10560-008-0129-x

Young, J. C. (2006). *From roots to wings.* Chicago: African American Images.

Zacharias, R. (1996). Deliver us from evil: Restoring the soul in a disintegrating culture. Dallas: Word Publishing.

APPENDIX A

Conscious Reflection Rubric: Characteristics of High-Hope Individuals

High-Hope Characteristics	Present	Absent	Unclear
Enjoys goal pursuits			
Confident in selected pathway			
Decisive			
Affirmative self-talk			
Resilient			
Flexible			
Positive Emotions			
Zealous			
Active			
Embrace challenges			
Confront stressors			
Strong sense of social support			
Perform better in school athletics			
Social capital			
Cope w/pain, illness, stress			

APPENDIX B

Summary of Dominant Themes and Subthemes Related to the Characteristics of Students Who Experience Hope.

Dominant Theme	Subthemes	Elements Associated with Themes	Examples of Elements
Disposition of Students with Hope	*Facing Fears*	• *Risk-taking* • *Confronting challenges* • *Overcoming Obstacles* • *Learning from failure* • *Using criticism as motivation*	• *Traditional school* • *Online learning* • *Self* • *Incarceration* • *Motherhood* • *Credit Recovery*
	Unwavering Optimism	• *Endless possibilities* • *Looking at the good/bright side in situations* • *Thinking bigger* • *Embracing opportunities* • *Focusing on the future* • *Positive outlook*	• *Previous academic failure* • *Deviant behavior* • *Chronic truancy* • *Expulsion*
	Refusal to Quit	• *Keep going* • *Never give up* • *Always strive for the best* • *Stick to it* • *Generate plans of action* • *Focus on the end* • *Never doubt self* • *Don't accept "no"* • *Just believe*	• *Past mistakes* • *Opinion of others* • *Overage* • *Pregnancy* • *Credit status*
People and Places Matter	*Significant Relationships (Interpersonal)*	• *Parents* • *Extended family members* • *Educator* • *Peer*	• *Conversations* • *Being heard* • *Stories* • *Lifestyle* • *Successes*

	Significant Relationships (Institutional)	• *Church* • *College* • *Universities* • *Community Centers* • *Non-profit Organization*	• *Programs* • *Partnerships* • *Service opportunities* • *Recreation* • *Links to careers* • *Safety*
	Avoiding Negativity	• *The Ghetto* • *People*	• *Poverty* • *Crime* • *Drugs* • *Destructive retail (liquor stores)* • *Bad influences*
The Power of Reflection	*Faith*	• *Family members* • *Church*	• *Prayer* • *Sermons* • *Relevant discussions* • *Testimonies*
	Discovering self	• *Family members* • *Jail* • *School* • *Respected individuals*	• *Critical conversations* • *Restrictions* • *Poor grades*

(Arrington, 2014)

APPENDIX C

Summary of the Aspects of WNHS that Students Attributed to their Experience with Hope

Dominant Theme	Subtheme	Elements Associated with the Subtheme	Example of the Elements
Elements of WNHS	*Online Expediency*	• *Increased concentration* • *Accessibility*	• *Work faster* • *Less distractions* • *Complete more work* • *Convenience* • *Better for non-traditional students*
	WNHS Staff	• *Significant care* • *Lessons*	• *Academic support* • *Critical conversations* • *Accountability* • *Consistent attendance* • *Listening* • *"Never give up"* • *"You can make it"*

(Arrington, 2014)

APPENDIX D

Final Themes Related to WNHS Students and their Experience with Hope

Theme	Subthemes	Commentary
Disposition of Students with Hope	• *Facing fears* • *Unwavering optimism* • *Refusal to quit*	*Students were resolute in their decision to pursue goals, impediments notwithstanding.*
People and Places Matter	• *Significant relationships* • *Avoiding negativity*	*Each student linked their view of hope to a human or community resource.*
The Power of Reflection	• *Faith* • *Discovering self*	*These two were crucial as it related to turning points in students' lives.*
Elements of WNHS	• *Online expediency* • *WNHS Staff*	*Each student saw a connection between their current view of hope and their experience with these two aspects.*

(Arrington, 2014)

APPENDIX E

Elements Related to Hope

(Arrington, 2014)

CPSIA information can be obtained
at www.ICGtesting.com
Printed in the USA
LVHW021713100220
646429LV00003B/147

9 781545 678817